Spark!

A journalist and former nurse, Norah Casey is now a publishing entrepreneur and well-known radio and television personality. She was a Dragon in the popular television series *Dragons' Den*. She presents the RTÉ 2 series *The Takeover*, transforming businesses through staff mentorship. She has taken that role into a new area in her most recent television work, a series in which she mentors young Traveller women in business skills. In the recent past, following a stint co-anchoring Newstalk's daily *Newstalk Breakfast* programme, she presented a weekly radio show on the station, *MindFeed*.

Having run many successful publishing companies in London, Norah bought her own business, Harmonia, in 2004, with a strong portfolio of brands and events. Harmonia is Ireland's largest magazine publishing company: it publishes the top three best-selling women's magazines in Ireland—*Irish Tatler*, *U Magazine* and *Woman's Way* – along with a range of lifestyle and consumer titles.

Norah has been Ireland's Publisher of the Year no fewer than four times. She has served on numerous boards, and is currently a member of the Press Council of Ireland, the London-based Women's Irish Network and the International Women's Forum. She is also a former Veuve Clicquot Business Woman of the Year.

Twitter: @norahcasey
Facebook: Norah Casey
www.harmonia.ie
www.norahcasey.com

Spark!

*How to reignite your passion
for life – and become the person you
always dreamed of being*

NORAH CASEY

PENGUIN
IRELAND

PENGUIN IRELAND

Published by the Penguin Group
Penguin Ireland, 25 St Stephen's Green, Dublin 2, Ireland
(a division of Penguin Books Ltd)
Penguin Books Ltd, 80 Strand, London WC2R ORL, England
Penguin Group (USA) Inc., 375 Hudson Street, New York, New York 10014, USA
Penguin Group (Australia), 707 Collins Street, Melbourne, Victoria 3008, Australia
(a division of Pearson Australia Group Pty Ltd)
Penguin Group (Canada), 90 Eglinton Avenue East, Suite 700, Toronto, Ontario, Canada M4P 2Y3
(a division of Pearson Penguin Canada Inc.)
Penguin Books India Pvt Ltd, 11 Community Centre, Panchsheel Park, New Delhi – 110 017, India
Penguin Group (NZ), 67 Apollo Drive, Rosedale, Auckland 0632, New Zealand
(a division of Pearson New Zealand Ltd)
Penguin Books (South Africa) (Pty) Ltd, Block D, Rosebank Office Park,
181 Jan Smuts Avenue, Parktown North, Gauteng 2193, South Africa

Penguin Books Ltd, Registered Offices: 80 Strand, London WC2R ORL, England

www.penguin.com

First published 2014
001

Copyright © Norah Casey, 2014

The moral right of the author has been asserted

Set in 13.5/16 pt Garamond MT Std
Typeset by Jouve (UK), Milton Keynes
Printed in Great Britain by Clays Ltd, St Ives plc

A CIP catalogue record for this book is available from the British Library

ISBN: 978-0-241-97007-2

www.greenpenguin.co.uk

MIX
Paper from
responsible sources
FSC
www.fsc.org FSC™ C018179

Penguin Books is committed to a sustainable
future for our business, our readers and our planet.
This book is made from Forest Stewardship
Council™ certified paper.

To Dara – the Spark in my Life

Contents

CONTENTS

Introduction: The Power of You

When I was younger and more idealistic about life, I read an extraordinary essay that changed my whole view of the world. Until about two years ago I had forgotten it and the amazing insights it contained. I found it in the basement, among the boxes of research for my as-yet-unfinished PhD. It is really only a matter of luck that I came across it at all. The box was worn and the bottom finally crumbled under the weight of all those long-unopened binders and papers. I was searching at the time for a new challenge in my life and among the many possibilities on my list was the option of revisiting that doctorate and the early work that had begun in London more than a decade previously. But there, among the papers that tumbled from the now bottomless box, was the essay that had once captivated me. As I sat down on the stairs to the basement and read those long-forgotten pages, I could feel the stirrings of something new inside me – a new way of thinking, if you will, that has remained a constant companion since then: sometimes it's like an annoying tune that gets tangled up in your brain in an endless loop; at others it's the little spark that lit a fuse that kept me going through some tough times. I promise to share with you the incredible essay that lit a tiny light inside me if you will allow me to explain why I wrote this book.

It's not easy to lay yourself bare. One of the hardest parts of living through the moments, hours and days since my husband, Richard, died has been the isolation. It is part of our journey through life that we experience catastrophic events, and none is more devastating than the loss of the person you love. I am an honest person at heart. By that I don't mean that I'm a slave to the truth at all costs. I am, however, true to myself, and in my personal and business life I have a reputation for telling it how it is. Bluff, bluster, semantics – I have no time for them. So, it was hard for me to keep up the banal responses when people asked how I was doing in the aftermath of Richard's death. I found myself saying the things people often say to ensure the moment is not too awkward for either party to the conversation. 'Time is a great healer' was always my favourite, and we would nod at each other and move on to the order of business, whether it was buying the groceries or doing a deal.

Some time after his death I decided to do a radio interview with a woman I admire, Marian Finucane. She has had her own dealings with personal tragedy so I agreed to talk about me and my life, but I knew, even if I didn't admit it fully to myself, I would be talking mostly about the terrible tragedy that had happened. I don't remember thinking too much about it. I went into the studio and chatted comfortably about my magazine-publishing business, my boy, Dara, and the trajectory of my life from childhood, growing up in the Phoenix Park, to becoming a nurse, a journalist, a boss and a business owner. Inevitably, the conversation turned to Richard's diagnosis with cancer and the months we endured while it progressed relentlessly through his body until his death.

I wanted to be honest. I didn't want to whitewash the emotions I'd experienced and pretend they weren't real and devastating. I managed to remain somewhat composed until I reached Richard's final moments. I began to cry – in the studio – full-blown tears. I was embarrassed. Marian, ever the professional, filled the silence and went to a break. I drove away shattered, but also lightened – just a little – by speaking honestly about something that happens to all of us. Since then I have spoken many times about grief, about those emotions we are often embarrassed to share, even with those close to us.

Recently I was on my way into Newstalk to do my weekly radio show and a woman stopped me in Drury Street. I was late and thinking only of getting to the studio on time. She grabbed my arm and said, 'I know you're probably in a hurry but I just wanted to tell you that you could have been speaking for me because that is exactly how I felt and I could never tell anyone.' We hugged. I have had thousands of letters and talked to many people about their loss, strangers like the woman on Drury Street, who felt a connection. I stopped opening the letters because they were difficult emotional accounts of loss and sadness.

Being honest and brave enough to admit my vulnerability and the cataclysmic impact of Richard's death wasn't the easiest of things to do. For one thing, people knew me as a 'Dragon' from *Dragons' Den*. I had built up a persona in the public eye as a formidable business woman (tremendously helpful if you're negotiating, by the way). But sometimes when you take a courageous step, life rewards you in other ways. That is why I wanted to write this book and share with you my own extraordinary journey from there to here.

Spark! seemed an apt title. It was from that little flicker on the basement stairs, rereading that essay, that I reignited my life and learned how to live again. This book is about my experience. Put aside any pre-conceived notions of 'self-help' – *Spark!* is as far as you can get from that. There are no blinding flashes of brilliance. I'm a graduate of the University of Life, and where there is evidence, I try to share. What I offer you is my own story and how I found a different way of thinking about who I am and how I could be better at being me.

The more I know about life, the more amazed I am that we achieve what we achieve. My life was far from mundane up to that pivotal turning-point, but I was driven to succeed without truly thinking about the value of what I was achieving.

I gave myself permission to choose life. I like the simplicity of that idea. Most of us don't get to make the decision about how we live our lives. For the most part, that is not because we are denied the right to do so: many on our planet have no choice, but most of you reading this do. You have probably never thought, *really* thought, about what a privilege that is. Conscious living is the most important lesson I have learned.

Mostly we go through life on autopilot. We live carelessly, as though life is disposable: if this one doesn't work, another will be along soon – not in a flippant way: we just don't think too hard about the passage of time or the imprint we want to leave behind. Then something unexpected happens. It could be the loss of a parent, a sibling, a loved one, which is often the first time we face our own mortality and the fleeting period of time we have on Earth. It could also be the loss of a dream, a shattering blow to our ambitions or the devastation of physical or mental impairment. It may paralyse us, rather than being a catalyst to action. We get lost in the emotional aftermath.

I don't meditate. I'm not a fan of contemplation. I have always worked through difficult emotions: it seems healthier to accept and move beyond the debilitation they cause.

What makes us uniquely human is the ability to learn from our experiences, to work through them and move on. We live this extraordinary life and are the only species to understand fully how miraculous that is. Yet it is often our emotions that cripple us and make us incapable of being the best we can be. I have faced loss before – my dad and my sister – but nothing prepared me for losing the other half of me. I constantly find myself saying, 'I am no different from anyone else,' because I'm not. But I found a compelling reason to live life even more fully than I had lived it before.

To start with, I lived in a sort of frenzy – as though time would run out when I had only half finished what I set out to do. At times I adopted a more leisurely pace, as I took stock of where I had got to. And now? Well, now I strive for just beyond the level I feel I can attain because to strive for what I know I can achieve would be no challenge at all.

Let me tell you about that extraordinary essay. Back in 1948 a man who studied economics at Yale University in Connecticut, and in London, was working for the forestry service in Pennsylvania. He had the perfect credentials to write a story that put me, you and the whole of humanity into context. Many have tried to retell it or put their own twist on it, but he was the genius who painted this vivid picture in my mind. He called it: '"But a Watch in the Night": a scientific fable'. His name was James C. Rettie. In it he talked of a fictional planet, Copernicus, created five billion or so years before the birth of the Earth. On that planet there was an intelligent species who learned the art of film-making. From their unique vantage-point, using time-lapsed cameras and super-powered telescopes, they made a film about the history of the Earth's 757 million years.

A team from Copernicus arrive on Earth and show the

movie at midnight on New Year's Eve. It plays continuously until midnight on 31 December a year later. It plays at twenty-four days a second, 1,440 years per minute, 86,400 years per hour, two million years per day. What unfolds is an extraordinary account of the history of time, from the pre-Cambrian period and the advent of a living organism up to the present day. It describes the desolate months of January, February and March, with raging torrents, mountains melting and new ones thrusting upwards in seconds. With the onset of April, the first single-cell living organisms appear in warmer waters. By the end of May the first vertebrates are swimming in the oceans, and by June, oil and gas deposits are forming. July sees the first land plants fighting against constant erosion to gain a foothold – paving the way for land animals. Early August sees multitudes of fish appear in the seas, and by September, crude lizards appear – the first amphibians. A few weeks later the dinosaurs arrive – lasting 140 million years. Feathered creatures take to the air in October and animals who have babies that look like smaller versions of themselves emerge – the first mammals. Flowers, trees, insects arrive in November, and a little later mammals have taken control of animal life. December arrives: rivers are formed and mountains that we know today have risen out of the seas.

By now the humans in the audience are beginning to wonder if the Copernicans have forgotten to include them: up to Christmas Day and beyond, they have not been mentioned. Then on 31 December, about twelve noon, a 'stooped massive creature of man-like proportions' is seen – Java Ape Man. He uses wooden clubs and crude stones for tools. Massive ice sheets cover most of Europe, Asia and America. Woolly mammoths and caribou fight for survival in the cold, inhospitable climate. It's time for dinner on 31 December and still no sign of man. At 11 p.m. Neanderthal man arrives, and at 11.30 Cro-Magnon man is living in caves and drawing crude animals on the walls. A quarter to midnight sees Neolithic man with stone tools. At five or six minutes to midnight civilization dawns, and in the final fourth, third and second minute before the clock chimes midnight, the Egyptians, the Babylonians, the Greeks and Romans make an appearance. At one minute and seventeen seconds to midnight the Christian era begins, Columbus discovers the New World at twenty seconds and in those final moments, humans 'swarm' the planet.

There is an important insight before the end of the essay, but I would encourage you to read it for yourself and make your own judgement (http://wedelenglish.com/wp-content/uploads/2011/02/But-a-Watch-in-the-Night.pdf). The author signs off: 'We have just arrived upon this earth – how long will we stay?'

Squeezing the history of the world into this timescale makes me consider how precious and precarious life is. How unbelievably fortunate we are to live here, now, at this time. I looked back on what I had done and how I had come to be me, and made a conscious decision to live differently. I encourage you to do the same. I want to be a speck in the next time-lapsed motion picture of Earth because I can be. For all the Richards who didn't get to fulfil their potential and all the people who, through illness, disability or disadvantage, don't get a choice to be who they want to be, I must take the precious gift of health and life while I have it and use it in the best way I can.

1. Losing Your Spark: So Here's What Happened to Me . . .

I had the idea for this book one day when I was contemplating the enormous seismic shift in my life over the previous three years. I have been fortunate and unfortunate. That makes me no different from anyone else on this planet, of course, but that seismic shift unseated me, pushed me out of my comfort zone and robbed me of the future I had anticipated. All of that led to a great deal of thinking, reassessing and adapting. I felt a strong urge to sit down, write the book and put it out. I'm sure many people will ask, 'Why? Why should Norah tell us about life and living?' I'm not claiming to have special knowledge on life, but I can give an insider's view on grief, its effects, its aftermath, and its twin powers of destruction and creation. And as for why I should tell it, well, I'm a huge believer in honesty. I think honest, upfront communication is the best way to confront life, death and everything in between. If we don't talk about these things, we'll never get to grips with them, and the sad fact is that we must because death comes to all of us.

This, then, is my story, and that's all it is: a personal account of one life. In order to tell it, I have to go right back to the beginning of me, and me and Richard, and my hopes for the future we would share. I need to do this to show you the journey I had been living during those three years: to show you how my life was decimated and how it was rebuilt. I'm going to retrace those steps so that the things I'm discussing throughout the book are made real in the example of my own life.

One of the key things about my personality is that I'm a stickler for strategy – it's the philosophy I live by. In my professional life I don't obsess over the past or wallow in the present, I'm always trying to picture the future, the possible and impossible, the maybe and the definite wants – that's where my head naturally spends its time, dreaming up new goals and working to make them happen. I was no different when it came to my private life – much to Richard's amusement, I was constantly envisaging and planning our wonderful future, all that we would do and see together. And we all know what they say about the best-laid plans.

Life with Richard

I met Richard Hannaford in May 1991 and my first impression was of a man who was handsome, funny and charming. We had been seeing each other for a year when he got down on bended knee, in the muddy grasslands of the Phoenix Park, among the deer, and asked me to marry him. Of course we both knew what my answer would be because we had already declared our love for each other. I couldn't imagine a future without him.

Before we met, Richard and I had both left difficult relationships, so we spent many months getting to know one another before we even held hands, let alone kissed. And maybe because of that – because we connected on a deeper level, before physical intimacy – we were as one. I have been challenged many times in interviews and discussions on whether it is possible for humans to pair for life – do 'soul-mates' exist? I am not certain that a word or phrase can describe a strong partnership built on trust, loyalty and commitment. And I struggle to find words to describe the person who completely 'gets' you – who understands why you are who you are, who doesn't judge, who makes you laugh, holds you when you cry, shares your dreams and passions. It's impossible to describe that sense of togetherness unless you have experienced it. Richard and I were the real thing. We were the other half of each other. We thought the same way, laughed at the same things, and it was a struggle, on occasion, to allow others to share our space. Whatever the word is for it, Richard and I were bonded in the best possible way.

Although we were both living in London, we got married on New Year's Eve in 1996 at the University Church in Dublin's St Stephen's Green and had our reception at the Shelbourne Hotel. It snowed. It was one of the best days of my life. It wasn't just the trappings of the wedding, it was the deep commitment we made to each other on that day.

I don't think I really understood what marriage meant until the moment when we began to recite our vows. Ever the strategist, I had got caught up in the planning, the organizing, the guest list, dress, flowers and food, all of the event's trappings. And, as I'm being honest about everything else, I may as well 'fess up to the fact that I wanted to get married in a church because it added to the magic, rather than because it was a house of God. None of that mattered on the day: we could have been on a windswept cliff in the West of Ireland, or in the bustle of London's Oxford Circus at the moment when we tied ourselves together for life. It was more important than anything I had ever done in my life until then and yet it wasn't until we made those promises – practised so often they'd lost meaning – that I got it. The chill on my neck, the hammering of my heart, the sweat on my palms, my eyes locked on his – I can remember every second of the dawning realization that I wanted to be connected, bonded and attached to someone who meant everything to me. My life would have been a shadow without Richard, and it frightens me sometimes to think that I might never have understood that. Now I am beyond grateful that I lived that life – not for as long as we both wanted but we still experienced something many people will never understand. Thankfully.

The day didn't go unfailingly to plan, though. Great weddings – especially Irish ones – are made even greater by the mishaps. As you might imagine, with my eye for the minute detail, I thought I had anticipated every eventuality and weeded out anything that could tarnish the memories. I had been managing the whole thing from London with military precision – well, the army I relied on, my family, felt that way.

I like to think that it was only those things outside my control that let us down on the day. My brother, Leo, had organized a vintage Rolls-Royce to take me and my dad to the church. We lived in a lodge in the Phoenix Park, and when the Rolls arrived, it backfired and died. Everyone else had already left for the church so we were stranded. Wet snow was falling and my father, Harry, was not known for his handyman skills. While he and the driver stared dismally into the engine, hoping for divine intervention, I watched helplessly from the porch. It was New Year's Eve in the 1990s in Dublin, and even the buses couldn't be relied upon. After many dire warnings from the cleric at the church, I knew that the bride being fashionably late was not an option. There is no delaying at the University Church or you are in danger of butting into another wedding and missing your slot – the thought alone was enough to make my head spin.

Leo had stayed behind to film his angelic sister gliding off in the vintage Rolls. Sadly, the first footage he took was of me swearing profusely into the camcorder – nothing angelic or ladylike about that, other than the lovely white dress and veil. Sometimes only the F-word will suffice to vent your frustration. Eventually, the Rolls was persuaded to start. It creaked as the combined weight of my father and I settled into the narrow confines of the back seat (were people really that small in the olden days?).

After a shaky start, the driver – not used to the neighbourhood – decided to take a detour through some rundown housing estates nearby. After the first hundred yards we had acquired a few small passengers, who were hanging off the back and balanced precariously on the bumper – until it broke and began scraping along the ground. The driver was keen to stop to investigate but, after a few snowballs with stones embedded in them hit the window, he decided to drive on.

We pulled up at the entrance to the University Church – the bumper dragging noisily along the ground and the engine smoking. During the journey, something else unexpected had happened. Perhaps it was because of all the ranting and raging, the storming up and down the hall, but my hold-up stockings had fallen to my ankles. I hadn't tested them in advance – my mistake – so I didn't know that the elastic bit at the top was not as effective after you had applied copious amounts of body lotion to your legs. Now, I was distracted by the uncomfortable sensation of wanting to hike up my stockings and not being able to do so. The dress had an enormous bustle and I feared not just my father but also the driver might be treated to an eyeful if I tried to deal with my stockings. I hatched a plan to get them back where they belonged, which hinged on finding a quiet space in the vestibule of the church before I had to walk down the aisle. Given the delay, however, we were now two minutes over our arrival time and the priest was waiting outside on the pavement as we drew up, anxiously checking his watch. He hustled us straight into the vestibule and signalled for the music to start. Not only were my stockings now sagging around my ankles, they were also soggy and black, having trailed from the car to the church. I couldn't even lift the hem of my dress in case the assembled onlookers saw the state of them. The elastic rim was now draped over my beautiful white silk shoes as I shuffled up the aisle, trying to look dignified and swan-like.

Worse was to come. My father handed me over to Richard as we reached the altar, then took his seat. With that, the priest motioned for us to kneel. There was nothing I could do. I hesitated for a fraction of a second, then plunged to my knees. The only saving grace was that the first few rows were the only people who could see the tragedy of my wet, dirty stockings wrapped around my ankles and shoes. To this day I am comforted by the thought that most of them wouldn't have realized what they were looking at – perhaps a new fashion trend in footwear? On that most precious of days, I spent an inordinate amount of time thinking of the cold wet mess at my feet and how many people could see the travesty. Richard kept nudging me, with a sixth sense about my distraction.

Finally, we were invited to go into the sacristy to sign the register. I got my sister, Carissa, and my nieces to shield me as I shuffled to the corner to remove the damn stockings – even on a freezing day in December, bare legs were preferable to malfunctioning nylons. And darling Leo caught the second camcorder moment of the day: me huddled in the corner, flanked by the bridesmaids, fiddling with my undergarments and finally handing over the grubby stockings to my sister. Lovely.

Later, as Richard and I were sipping champagne at a window on the first floor of the Shelbourne, watching our guests – in evening dress – winding their way through Stephen's Green, with a light dusting of snow falling as the dusk settled, we wondered at the perfection of the moment. We were only an hour married. We laughed like crazy about the Rolls and the stockings, to the point of embarrassment for the Shelbourne staff, who kept smiling politely trying to understand the joke. And now we were in each other's arms, eyes moist from the beauty of that scene – where everyone we loved was on their way to be with us on the day we had made the supreme commitment to a life together.

We were, of course, the last to leave our wedding party – we couldn't miss a moment of it. As we changed for the evening, which we would spend with even more friends, Richard took a photo of the wedding dress. The lovely silk bow that was carefully attached to the back had come undone and someone had spilled a large glass of red wine on the train. It was exactly how a wedding dress should look after a great wedding. I bundled it into the Selfridges box it had come in, and I have never opened it since.

That day was a good demonstration of how different Richard and I were and of how that difference had brought us together. I planned and strategized, tried to anticipate things before they happened, while Richard took each minute as it came and laughed when things went 'wrong'. I'd never have thought I'd end up with someone who approached life so differently from me, but it's the old classic of opposites attracting and contrasts blending. Richard tempered my need to control, showed me how to bend with the unexpected; I taught him how it could be beneficial to be a little more organized when it came to planning a future we wanted to share. In the early days of our relationship, Richard used to tease me constantly about my need to look ahead in our lives, to imagine our future and work towards it. The phrase 'what will be will be' couldn't have been further from my thinking. He, on the other hand, was more relaxed about us and where we would end up: he had a quiet confidence that we would get married, have lots of beautiful babies and live a long and happy life. On more than one dreamy evening in the early stages of courtship, he would paint a beautiful picture of our life. He always said that radio made better pictures than television, and maybe it was because of his long years in radio broadcasting that he had an incredible ability to use words magically. While I relied on logic and science, he always had an unwavering faith in us.

It wasn't that I obsessed about pushing strategic thinking into my personal life, but it's an inevitable consequence of buying into that way of thinking that you end up with no demarcation between personal and business. It's just how your brain is wired. And the then business environment was conducive to strategy. It was possible, in fact, to determine the future and predict certain patterns. I had discovered this new-found theoretical base to my life shortly after I'd met Richard. He would visit me at Ashridge College of Management (on Sundays only), where I was studying strategic management, and marvel at the alien world of business that I lived in. He was a BBC correspondent and, while he worked incredibly hard, he didn't have an in-tray. It was one of the first differences we saw in each other. My evenings were spent worrying about the items on the list I hadn't got through – weekends meant the car boot was loaded with files I had to digest before Monday. Richard lived in the moment: he broke news stories, did interviews, wrote commentary and comfortably worked between radio and television, but when the day was done, it was done. His motto would have been 'Be the best you can be in that moment.' There was no sense in worrying afterwards if you'd got the right news snippet or chased the best lead: what was done was done and the following day would bring new challenges. Richard was practising mindfulness – the mental art of living wholly in the moment – before it became a buzzword. In us, the strategist and the mindful met. It produced interesting results and gave us a different perspective – not just in the early days, but also in the final days. It is only now, with the perspective of time, that I can see how differently we coped with the adversity we were forced to face.

Losing Richard

Richard and I were out one Saturday night in early May. We were with some good friends, Margaret (Mags) Nelson, who runs the radio station FM104, and her husband, Joe Nally, whom I had known for years in London. In the months that followed I came to look on that evening as the last time we were both truly happy. Afterwards life changed utterly. It was one of those wonderful dinners, filled with the laughter and chat that only come when you can truly relax. Among Irish people, such evenings always involve some singing.

When I first met him, singing was not Richard's strong point. Unfortunately for him, I had grown up in a musical house – my father was a great piano player, his brother played the accordion, my older brother the concert flute, younger brother the guitar, and we all sang, outdoing each other most of the time. So when poor Richard came to visit me at home, he would be cajoled into singing when his turn came – in fact, the Casey siblings were only being polite and never expected too much by way of a tune from my Englishman. And Richard didn't disappoint. I had forewarned him about the necessity to have a party piece if he was to survive the first weekend at my family home, and having lived in Lincolnshire, he had learned a version of 'The Lincolnshire Poacher'. If you know the song, you will understand that he only made it as far as the first few lines before my fellow Caseys barrelled in with, ''Tis my delight on a Friday night . . .' We were all spared the ordeal of his singing.

I'm telling you all this because Richard underwent a transformation during our first few years living in Ireland. He took singing lessons, learned a few solid crowd-pleasing songs and became the most sought-after performer at dinner parties. So on the night in question – lubricated by a few glasses of wine – he sang his personal favourite, 'The Taxman' (a.k.a. 'Sunny Afternoon' by the Kinks), followed by the Beatles' 'Back In The USSR', then Otis Redding's '(Sittin' On) The Dock Of The Bay' and Sting's 'An Englishman In New York'. He was the toast of the restaurant that night.

The following day we were in the kitchen cooking lunch for my mum, Mags, and my sister, Catherine. Richard had started the day with a fuzzy head, and he was now complaining about a bad pain in his back. With not a jot of sympathy for his self-inflicted state, I continued to rib him about the old liver having to put up with one or two glasses too many the night before. But he began to look very pale, and as the pain worsened, he went up to lie on the bed. I checked on him every now and then that afternoon and evening, but the pain wasn't getting any better. By the following morning, I knew it was something serious: he had bright red blood in his urine and the pain was very severe. We called his doctor and he was admitted to hospital.

There followed a series of tests and procedures. On his birthday, 17 May, Dara and I visited him in the hospital with a cake and presents. The Queen had landed in Ireland for her first state visit and for Richard, in particular (being British), this was hugely significant. We had been involved with the British Embassy in arranging one of the key events planned for her visit, and enjoyed reviewing her first day in Ireland. Richard had been in hospital for a week, and although they were doing tests daily, there was nothing conclusive in the results. Yes, his kidney was enlarged, but the medics felt he might have a virus or some lingering kidney-stone problem. The day before they had used a scope to take a look inside it to try to find out what was happening.

We dissected every nuance of Her Majesty's first day, and Dara and I were happily sitting next to him, eating his birthday cake and encouraging him to open his presents. The doctor came in with a nurse and asked if Dara could leave for a bit. Dara wasn't happy because he wanted to be with his dad, but I asked him to go to the car to fetch something. Richard and I both knew that we were about to be told something very bad. We squeezed hands and held our breath as the doctor told us that Richard had a tumour in his kidney. He said it was a bladder cancer in the wet lining of the kidney and that we had two options: to undergo a course of chemotherapy and then have surgery to remove the kidney, or to do it the other way round. On balance, he felt chemotherapy first would be the best course of action.

We were devastated. Before we could even assimilate the news, Dara was back in the room and the doctor and nurse were leaving, saying they would talk to us further the following day. We kept our composure in front of Dara and tried to reassure him that it was only about further tests. We couldn't tell him his dad had cancer when we had only just found out ourselves. Later I had to leave Richard alone in that bed with lots of hand squeezing and hugs to signal my distress and worry.

As soon as Dara was asleep that night I called Richard. We talked in circles, speculated about what each word and inflection in the doctor's voice could have meant, and wept. It was utterly terrifying.

Like most twelve-year-olds, Dara was intuitive: he knew that something was wrong and was worried we were keeping it from him. The following day we went to visit Richard, and together Richard and I explained to him about the cancer – we drew diagrams of the kidney and where the tumour was located. We got books for him about living with a parent who has cancer and what side-effects to expect from chemotherapy. Dara was very frightened. He had lost one of his closest friends to cancer when he was nine years old.

Thomas and Dara had known each other since they were very little. Thomas was diagnosed with neuroblastoma when they were at primary school and had endured unbelievably tough treatment regimens and long spells in St John's Ward in Crumlin Hospital for Sick Children. Having been in remission for a while, his cancer returned when he was nine and there was nothing more they could do to prevent its spread. It was a traumatic time, devastating for Thomas's mum and his dad – he was an only child. Most of us who were close to them did the best we could to offer comfort and support. Dara was with Thomas during his final months, playing games with him when he was able, or quietly lying on the bed with him to watch a movie or read a book. Words can't describe the sorrow we all felt when Thomas died – such a lovely, courageous young boy.

His parents, Marie and Plamen, shadows of what they had once been, tried to come to terms with their little boy lying dead in their living room as they prepared for the final parting. Dara came early to see him, to say his own private goodbye. There is nothing in this world like the pain of a child whose heart is broken at such a young age. He cried and grabbed hold of his friend, trying to wake him up, begging him to come back. It was a catastrophic moment in his life and it changed him. His grief for Thomas was heart-wrenching and impacted on every aspect of Dara's life.

It had a huge impact on my relationship with Dara, too, because it bred mistrust. Thomas's mum and I had discussed whether Dara should know that Thomas was terminally ill during the months leading up to his death. Thomas didn't know he was dying, and I felt it would have been too big a burden for Dara to know such a terrible truth about his friend and have to try to hide it. So we decided that he was better off not knowing. Although it was painful to hear the two boys talking animatedly about what they were going to do when Thomas was better, it was good to hear them laugh and joke about football training, new movies or birthday plans – normal boys' stuff.

As Thomas's illness progressed and his weight dropped, I assumed that Dara would notice that his friend was now very sick. In the final days, as Thomas mostly slept and wasn't able to talk for long, I thought that, deep down, Dara knew he was dying. The day before Thomas passed away, I talked to Dara. I knew it was only a matter of time now and I wanted to prepare him. But I was totally unprepared for what happened next. As I was quietly explaining that Thomas was not going to get better, Dara started to laugh. 'You're joking, right, Mum? Thomas and I were just playing together last week. There's no way he's dying – this is just a joke, right?' As I continued to explain, Dara flipped. He began screaming and running round the house, shouting, 'You're lying! You're lying! Thomas is not going to die!' And I knew that Dara had not seen his friend's fragility, that he was totally unprepared for his death and, despite lots of people telling me that 'children just know', he didn't know.

After Thomas died, Dara continually questioned why we hadn't told him. He felt it was a betrayal – not those words, but the words of a nine-year-old boy who feels his mum and dad kept a huge secret from him.

That was the backdrop to our conversation with Dara about Richard's cancer. He quizzed us endlessly about whether it was the same type of cancer that Thomas had had. Would his dad die? When we reassured him, he reminded us that we hadn't told him about Thomas's cancer. Over those first few days, we told Dara several times that his dad's cancer was different, that his was the kind you could treat. We explained about the operation and the chemotherapy, and how Richard could survive with one kidney. We were in the dark ourselves, of course. We just didn't know it then.

Sometimes, even though you know that the most important thing in the world to you is your family and their health, you can't turn off the ticking clock that keeps urging you to keep moving, keep working. The demands of business – particularly when you are the owner – are relentless. At least, that was what I felt that first week after Richard received his diagnosis. We were privately trying to come to terms with his illness and weighing up the treatment options. We weren't ready to share the news with anyone. It was odd and stressful trying to maintain our outward composure, especially as all of our friends and work colleagues knew that Richard was undergoing tests. But we agreed that we would keep it to ourselves until we had come to terms with it. The stock answer to questions was, 'No news yet – still waiting for test results.'

Magazine publishing is not for the faint-hearted. In 2011 we were in the grip of the recession and fighting for every ad page, so keeping close to clients was a priority. It was enormously difficult to be me during that period. By that I mean I was expected to bounce into meetings, brimming with ideas, plans and energy – that's my style and has always defined me. I'm not sure I pulled it off completely, but I know that while there was a battle raging inside my head, I remained outwardly composed. Also the sheer number of pages and relentless deadlines for print mean you have to carry on. And then there was the enormous project I had taken on a few months previously: working closely with the British Embassy on the Queen's visit to Ireland. I was organizing a series of fashion shows at the Convention Centre in Dublin, where we showcased the best of British and Irish designers. She was to attend a fashion show prior to a special concert being organized by Harry Crosbie. So much planning had gone into the event and such a large team was involved that I felt I could not absent myself. Typically, I had made myself pretty much indispensable to the whole show. Richard and I agreed that I would throw myself into it and we would continue as best we could, while not discussing his diagnosis with any-one else.

It's funny thinking about that period now, because it ended up being one of the most memorable occasions for Richard.

The British ambassador, Julian King, had suggested that I select a small group of key people to introduce to the Queen at the end of the show. I asked that Richard be one of them. It created a great deal of banter between us – he was irked at the idea that his Irish wife was going to introduce him to the Queen, he being a British citizen. I thought it was hilarious and ribbed him endlessly about it. Of course, that was before we received the news of his cancer. The ribbing became shallow in the final days, but it helped us keep up appearances. Richard was released from hospital, pending an appointment for chemotherapy.

I was choreographing the final fashion show, with the Queen in attendance, and had just a few minutes to dump my radio mike and race to the side of the stage, where ten people were waiting for me to introduce them to HM and the Duke of Edinburgh. Richard was first in the line-up, looking handsome as always in a beautiful suit. The anxiety of the past few days was etched on his face and the two of us locked eyes and squeezed each other's hands in the seconds before the Queen arrived. The ambassador had introduced me to her earlier (my first time to meet her also) so I introduced her to Richard. She shook his hand and spoke to him for a few moments, and we moved on to the designers Paul Costelloe and Louise Kennedy, the hairdresser Dylan Bradshaw and the rest of the team. As the Queen left us to take her seat for the concert, I turned to Richard and there were tears in his eyes. We hugged and held each other – we knew but didn't say that he might never have another encounter like that. He told me he hadn't expected to feel so emotional about meeting her: the symbolism of her presence and the significance of her being in Dublin were more momentous than actually meeting her. Richard was not the kind of person to be bowled over by royalty or celebrity – during his BBC days he had rubbed shoulders with state leaders and many members of the royal family – but this was different: he was facing his own mortality against the backdrop of a key historic moment. It meant something very personal to him. Later, as the illness took hold, he referred back to that moment many times and said how glad he was that he got to shake the Queen's hand that day. An event that had felt like a tremendous burden just after he was diagnosed became important to him in the context of the final months of his life.

I always look back on the weeks that followed as the most tumultuous of my life. Within a few days of his initial diagnosis, we took the decision to move Richard's treatment to St James's Hospital, one of the regional centres for cancer. It was the right decision because the bad news was only just beginning. In less than a week, a further scan revealed three tumours in Richard's liver and that the cancer had invaded all of his lymph nodes. While we were still reeling from that bombshell, the medical team arranged for him to have a PET scan. It revealed a tumour on his spine. It seemed incredible that only ten days previously we had been laughing and singing with friends. It was so hard to absorb the enormity of what we were facing that we found we couldn't talk about it – we couldn't put it into words.

We listened as the doctor told us that surgery was no longer possible: the options open to us were now limited. Other words – frightening words – peppered the conversations. There was no longer a sense of fighting to beat the cancer, the language was more about containment, remission, buying time. There was no question any longer that Richard would survive. The realization that, whatever happened, he had only a limited amount of time left – whether that was a year or five years, we didn't know and didn't ask – seeped into us.

We were awkward with each other. There were just no words that would work for us. It was the first thought I woke up to every day and I knew it was the same for Richard, but not once in those early weeks did we admit it to one another. I could hardly bear to admit to myself what was happening, and to say it out loud would have been to accept that it was real. When you spend much of your life being in control, it is the scariest thing imaginable to have it ripped away from you in such a brutal manner. I would try, in a ham-fisted way, to reassure him, to say it would all be okay – a farcical mantra that I kept up on the journey to and from the hospital each day. I knew there were times when he gritted his teeth and tried hard not to shout at me. If the situation had been reversed, I am fairly certain I would have been shrieking like a lunatic. But Richard was not me, and the only tell-tale sign of the strain and anger was occasional heavy breathing.

There was a plan of defence, however. As the tumour in his spine was close to the spinal cord, the team at St James's decided it would be best for Richard to have radiotherapy first, at St Luke's Hospital in Rathgar. This would hopefully contain and, if we were fortunate, reduce the tumour. There was no question of eradicating it. Although Richard had some pain in his spine, it was manageable, and we settled into regular radiotherapy sessions and long waits at St Luke's. Fortune wasn't smiling on us: at the halfway mark, after a few treatments, Richard had a scan to see how the tumour was responding. Hard to imagine that the news could get worse but, unbelievably, the radiation had caused the tumour to shift between the vertebrae and the pressure had cracked his spine. The medical team referred him to the spinal injury unit at the Mater Hospital, but we had already been fore-warned that spinal surgery would mean the chemotherapy had to be delayed and, given the aggressive nature of the cancer, that wasn't a good plan. We opted to head straight into chemotherapy and put off the surgery, but we spent a few long days in the outpatient clinic at the Mater Hospital to maintain contact with the surgeon so that Richard could have the operation when the chemotherapy was finished. At any rate, that was the plan.

And so began the endless trips to St James's oncology unit, followed by St Luke's, followed by St Vincent's, until finally we arrived at Blackrock Hospice – only five short months after diagnosis.

On the Monday of the week Richard died, I spent the day with him at the hospice. On Sunday, the doctor, an amazing palliative-care specialist, Dr Paul Gregan, had asked to talk to Dara, to allow him to speak about his dad and any worries he had. He asked Richard if he wanted to join in the discussion, but Richard declined. Dara and I held hands while Dr Gregan explained to him all about Richard's cancer. He drew a picture of his body and marked out all the parts where there was cancer. It would be hard to find any organs that it had not invaded.

Dara watched carefully and scrutinized the diagram. When he had finished, Dr Gregan asked if he had any questions. Dara took a deep breath and said, 'Is my dad dying?' To which the answer was 'Yes.' Then he took a further courageous step and asked, 'When is he going to die?' I could never have asked that question. I didn't even know if I wanted the answer. But my brave twelve-year-old boy was taking the lead for all of us.

Dr Gregan told us it would be a matter of days. And that was how I found out how close to death Richard was. I had no idea it would be that soon. He had pneumonia, but he was being treated with strong intravenous antibiotics. He was in the hospice, but only for respite care and until his pain-relief medication settled down. He was sleepy – but wasn't that as a result of the morphine and the infection? I was a nurse and I admonished myself that I hadn't seen the signs, but the fact is, I hadn't. Richard was having a course of chemotherapy with Professor John Crown at St Vincent's – he had received his last dose only the week before. We had both hoped that this would buy us some time. But the signs were there. I had just chosen to ignore them.

A few days previously, when a nurse in the hospice had met me on the way out of the ward, I mentioned that Richard was sleeping a lot and didn't have much of an appetite. She looked me in the eye and said, 'You know your husband is very sick?' Of course I knew he was sick – he had cancer in most of his major organs. But I had missed the cue, what her tone was telling me. Revisiting that conversation afterwards, I realized she had been saying he was close to the end. Maybe your mind blocks these things out.

Now, in a small room off the ward, the bald, uncompromising truth of Richard's life and death was given to Dara and me. There was no blocking it out, no escaping it. As I held on to Dara and he cried inconsolably, I kept repeating that phrase over and over in my mind. 'A matter of days'. That was all we had left.

Dr Gregan stood and told us that he was now going to talk to Richard about the conversation because he was obliged to do so – it was the correct thing to do. He went into the room alone. When he emerged, about thirty minutes later, he told me that Richard had wanted to know only one thing: had Dara asked the hard question? Dr Gregan told him Dara had. And Richard said, 'So what was the answer?'

To which Dr Gregan replied, 'I told him you were dying, and it would be a matter of days.'

So now we all knew the truth. Dara and I went in to see Richard. It was awkward. I don't know why. We had spent so long avoiding the truth, maybe. But there was no need any more. We clung to each other, the three of us, cried and comforted one another. Richard told Dara how much he loved him and how much he would miss him. He spoke about all the important things that Dara would face in his life and how he would be there for him in spirit. He shared all his hopes for his boy. It was a searingly honest conversation, but it was also the first and only time that we could say all the things we wanted to say to each other. I will always be grateful to Dara for asking that hard question. Without it, he would never have had the chance to hug his dad and hear him say how much he loved him, how much he wished he could be with him as he ventured into the world, but how he had such hopes for him – his brave boy. And I would never have had the chance to tell him how much I loved him and how I wished with all my heart he was not going to leave us, but that I would be with him all the way to his final breath. That he wouldn't be alone. I pledged to work hard to make sure that all his hopes and dreams for his son came true.

When, eventually, the words ran dry and we had cried ourselves out, we stopped discussing it. He accepted that he was going to die, but he didn't want to talk about it any more. The conversation took a different course – Dara and Richard began chatting about school work and rugby. We never spoke of it again.

Richard's mother and brother were in Dublin to visit Richard that weekend and, before long, they arrived, as did my mother, sisters and brothers. It was almost a party atmosphere. Dara was lying in the bed, snuggled up to his dad. Richard's mum, Adria, had brought over an album of old photos of Richard growing up and there was lots of laughter and banter with his brother, Simon. That afternoon was a gift. A special time that healed the rawness of what we had just shared together.

That evening we had some quiet time. Richard used to read to Dara every night as he drifted off to sleep. Now Dara had taken to reading to Richard and there was something tremendously poignant about that. The beauty of my boy reversing roles and reading to his dad. There was a stillness about Richard that night. He was calm.

I left him late that evening, sleeping soundly. When I returned early the next day he was still sleeping. He drifted in and out of sleep that day and I stayed by his side, quietly reading. Dara left early with my sister – he was exhausted and worried about this change, this calm. That evening, Richard's intravenous line was blocked and a young doctor was called to put a new one in. It was for his antibiotics – the only fight back we had against the pneumonia. The doctor was struggling to find a vein. It was uncomfortable for Richard and he was fully awake, holding my hand tightly. What remained unspoken was that if she couldn't find a vein, the IV antibiotics would stop and the fight would truly be over. We already knew that the pneumonia wasn't responding to the medication. We knew that his death was inevitable, but there was still an undercurrent between us of refusal to give up. As the doctor continued to do her best with the needle, Richard looked up at me with what I imagined at the time was a twinkle in his eye. Yes, I know that sounds extraordinary, given the circumstances, but he had a wicked sense of humour and he was searching for a distraction. The doctor kept glancing at us, wondering had we lost all our faculties because this was how the conversation went.

Richard said, 'When I get out of here, you and I are going to go on the biggest blow-out holiday ever – we deserve it.'

'Okay so – anywhere in particular?'

'Mm, let me think. Maybe Paris? No, I fancy Rome – I always loved it there. No, hang on, I know where we should go. Venice – the perfect spot. And we'll stay in the best hotel. After what I've been through, we deserve the best. Let's stay at that place, the Gritti Palace, or, better still, the Danieli. And I'll want the best suite in the place, a balcony overlooking the Grand Canal, with a view of St Mark's and all the islands in the distance. And we'll have a special dinner – everything we would ever want. Let's sip some Bellinis while we wait for the menu. So, come on, what are you going to have for starters?'

'I think I would like beef carpaccio with the finest olive oil and maybe some truffle shaved on top.'

'Okay, that's good. I'm going to have the best smoked salmon with capers and brown bread – I might make them fly it in from Frank Hederman in Cork. So main course – what are you having?'

'Definitely lobster Thermidor and, as I can have anything, the thinnest chips ever.'

'You're so predictable. I'm going to have ostrich steaks.'

'Where on earth are they going to find ostrich in Venice?'

'Well, they'd better figure that out, or I'm not going to give them the business – after everything I've been through, you'd think they'd make an effort!'

'Okay, okay. We'll get the ostrich steaks ordered in advance. What's for dessert?'

'I have a few ideas on this one, but I'm going to settle for a classic crème brûlée, and for you, madam?'

'Something retro – Baked Alaska maybe . . .'

Somewhere around the main course, the young doctor said she might give up looking for a vein and try again in the morning. She asked how Richard would feel about that. We both knew there would be no vein found in the morning. He smiled at her and said that was fine and he was anxious to get back to his meal. She left quietly and he continued with this magical meal, ordering the best wines, until finally he was sipping a rare Middleton whiskey on the terrace while looking over the lights of Venice. He was drifting back to sleep, holding my hand, with that lovely vista in his mind. He never woke up. I texted close friends and family that night and told them that Richard and I had shared an amazing dinner that evening – our last.

The following morning he received the Sacrament of the Sick, the Last Rites, from a wonderful priest, Father Paddy. He was unconscious, but very distressed. I was, too. It was the worst part of the end of his life for me and I struggle still to get it out of my head. Father Paddy told me that the young fight death until the end. It's not natural for them to go so soon, and they resist it. It felt exactly like that. It was a final rage against the injustice of it and I held on to him throughout whatever torments he was suffering. He eventually settled into a deep sleep, his features once again composed, and he looked more like my Richard.

While he didn't want to see many people in his final days, I knew his close friends would want to say goodbye to him – that it would mean a lot to them to see him one last time. I also knew that Dara, our family and I needed that support: we needed to feel friends around us. I hoped that if Richard was still there, still able to hear, he would be comforted by the sounds of all those who were dear to him. So on his final day, all of his friends came to say goodbye. One by one they sat at his side and whispered goodbye, told stories, brought back memories – there were tears and laughter. Some prayed, others read poems. They were good friends and helped carry us through the worst of all possible times. They went and got food from a kind chef nearby and shared a final supper at the hospice, until eventually it was time for them to leave.

Dara was minded by my sister, Carissa, throughout all of these dark days. She and my other sister, Catherine, took him home then. He had thought long and hard about whether he wanted to be there when his dad died, and decided that he had said his goodbye. He was exhausted and frightened. My brother, Leo, stayed at the hospice with me and settled down into one of the relatives' rooms upstairs.

I sat with Richard and held his hand. The hours drifted by and I worried that I might fall asleep and he would die without me there. The lighting was low in the room and his breathing was deep and regular. It was hypnotic. I kept up a steady stream of stories that would keep him company, but I was struggling to maintain my composure. The last thing I wanted was for Richard to hear distress in my voice in his final hours. I was holding his left hand and gently stroking his face and hair. I hoped this would be comforting. After a while the nurse manager, Tracy, joined me and she held his other hand. She started chatting to me about my time in nursing and how I had met Richard. We were murmuring softly, and at times laughing quietly at something funny I recounted about my early courtship with Richard, when his breathing changed, then stopped. I took him in my arms and he was gone. There was no drama. There was no need. Just silence. He left this life quietly and with dignity, to the sound of us murmuring and the comfort of my arms around him.

I stayed with him on my own for a while, just thinking about our life together. I held his hand and continued stroking his hair. Maybe that was more to comfort me than him at that stage. I cherished that time alone with him.

After a while I woke my brother, and we agreed to leave it until the morning to tell the family. There was only one person I wanted to be with right then, and that was Dara. But he needed his sleep for what lay ahead. So Leo called my brother, Ciaran, and my mum, and we went home to see Dara, who was sleeping on the couch between my two sisters. I woke him and told him the news. He hugged me and obsessed about finding a pen. He wrote a card and stuck it on the fridge door, where it remained for over a year. It said: 'The greatest dad in the world died at 4.30 a.m. on 12 October 2011.'

Life without Richard

I have often thought, then and since, how the Catholic Church comes into its own at a time of loss. The ritual of seeing Richard laid out that day – still in his hospice bed – cold to the touch, but still looking like himself. The calm that descends from the chanting of the decades of the rosary. We prayed and prayed over him. There was nothing else to be said. It helps that together we pray, say the same words, respond to each other, and the years fall away until you're back at school, repeating those familiar sentences. It's a comfort.

The journey towards separation was beginning. The following day we faced Richard in a coffin with the lid off. He didn't look like himself and it was alien to see my handsome, vibrant husband in a casket. Dara was upset, but also a little scared of the change in his dad. He kept asking what they had done to him. He was distressed when they closed the lid – as was I. But I knew that he had to be prepared for the final moment the following day. My nieces took over the house and fed everyone that night. The brothers and sisters made sure everyone's glasses were filled. I had spent the day searching for some of Richard's BBC tapes so I could listen to his voice again, and I played some of them. It was magical and strange to listen to his beautiful mellow tones coming from the radio. I was tremendously comforted by hearing his voice. We played some during the final moment at the crematorium – it was amazing to hear him, so beautiful and vibrant. I felt he was there with us.

Sometimes you meet someone you feel you have known for ever and you wonder why your paths have never crossed before. And so it was that Father Alan Hilliard came into our lives on the day after Richard died. I can't imagine a more perfect man to celebrate Richard's life. He has become such an important part of our lives now that I can't believe we only met him then and in those circumstances. He took the trouble to spend a long time with Dara, my family and me until he felt he understood Richard and would do him justice. He made the funeral service the best possible goodbye. And that was so important to us. Saying goodbye properly and acquitting ourselves well. I feel we did that.

I had said goodbye to my father, a sister and some close friends, but nothing could have prepared me for the enormity of losing Richard. I comfort myself with the knowledge that it was better to have had one true love than never to have loved at all. I tell myself over and over how lucky I was that I met and married my soul-mate. I know many people settle for less, endure marriages and relationships, often because they fear the unknown or the prospect of a lonely life. So I know I am fortunate. But because he was the love of my life, because we were inseparable, because he was the other half of me, when he left me, the pain was almost unendurable.

We'd had the next chapter of our life worked out – a plan forged over glasses of wine, late-night promises and a great deal of negotiation. Richard wanted to own land – to live next to the sea – and he wanted to plant trees, lots of them, just for the sake of it, because he loved the beauty of trees. When we were driving, he would often stop the car suddenly and make Dara and me traipse through fields because he had spotted an amazing oak tree, an unusual grouping or a stunning evergreen. He could stare for hours at a magnificent poplar – he had an old leather-bound book of trees with black-and-white etchings that he used to analyse the leaves and figure out the species. Dara and I endured many long detours. Over time, we even got quite good at naming the trees – and even better at distracting him if we spotted a tall oak on the side of the road.

So trees, land and the sound of the ocean were at the top of Richard's wish list and, of course, he wanted to return to his beloved broadcasting. He had been with the BBC for eighteen years when he left to come to Ireland with me when I took over Harmonia. In the early years he still made and presented programmes for RTÉ and the BBC, but as the business got busier and we realized that our future was bound up in making it a success, he joined me at Harmonia as the editorial director. Although print was not his first love, he took to it with gusto and surprising ease for a 'radio-man'. He learned to love the discipline of words – painting pictures with no sounds or visuals. He had a degree in English literature, so it wasn't surprising that he excelled at the use of language. And he presided over the best part of the business – the creative talent.

When people describe Richard they almost always say, 'He was a gentleman', and he was. He was incredibly nice – the staff learned quickly that it was far better to approach Richard than me with any problem.

His next chapter always included a new business division for Harmonia, in which television and radio production would run side by side with the magazines. A happier future he could not imagine. Back to his radio and television days – the chance to develop and shape future programming. It was a wonderful vision for the next phase in our life.

As for me, I longed for a chapter that included some downtime. I had been working since I was seventeen, with only twelve short weeks off when Dara was born. Don't get me wrong: I loved the manic rollercoaster of publishing, the deadlines and the deals. In 2004 I did a management buy-out of two of the companies I was running in Dublin, and Harmonia was born. A wonderful few years followed. I had bought the business and where there had once been a team of directors, there was now only myself and a financial controller. So I was running most of the divisions – a good thing in terms of staying close to the business, but not conducive to downtime. I worked through the first few years, taking time off only in January (a dead month for magazine publishing). But Dara was growing up fast so for me the next chapter included time off for us as a family and a chance to enjoy the fruits of all that hard work.

So I know this may sound strange, but the hardest part of learning to live without Richard was the loss of that chapter we had both signed up to – his absence engulfed the present and the future. Good friends would often tell me that they could feel Richard's presence – they meant it as a comfort to me, I know that now. At the time I wanted to scream and yell about how insanely stupid it was to talk about his presence when he had left this huge gaping hole in my life – when every moment of every day was about trying to work out how to live with it. Worse, I was plagued by the idea that other people could feel him and I couldn't – what was wrong with me? I was stuck in a moment and couldn't move on – not a natural state for me.

Grief can have a paralysing effect, and for some time, that was how it was for me. I was locked into the moment of loss, unable to move forwards or think beyond it because all that I had been focusing on as 'our life, our future' was gone. Entirely. It had disappeared with the man I loved and there was no way for me to get it back. In those days and months after Richard's death, I felt that stasis would go on for ever, that I would live in a half-state of suspended animation. But if there is one truth in life, it's that time changes everything. No one can prevent it. So for me and, more importantly, for Dara, I knew there would have to come a time when things changed. It was just that then, in that moment, I couldn't see how that change could possibly come about.

2. Living with Adversity

Everyone faces adversity during their life. It's part of being human. And there is no rating scale for adversity: mine isn't any bigger than yours because I lost someone I loved. Sometimes it's not one big incident but a string of events that leads to a lack of warmth in your life, a sense that you're battling ceaselessly and senselessly. I had 'one big incident', but that wasn't, in fact, the true moment of adversity. I had to learn that the constant pain of living without Richard was just as bad, if not worse, than the moment of loss. As each month passed after his death, pain piled on top of pain, until I was stratified with grief, anxiety and fear.

I've always thought it odd that adversity should make you stronger – you'd be inclined to think it would break you into unrecognizable pieces – but that has been my experience. The German philosopher Friedrich Nietzsche coined the phrase 'What does not destroy me, makes me stronger', and perhaps he was right. There is a scientific basis to this assumption (more on that below), and then there is life experience. I know that I have been transformed by what happened to me. In a positive way? For the most part, yes, but it came at a very high price. I have spent enough time playing the 'What if?' game to know that it is pointless and debilitating. I can't change what happened, but I can make sure that I don't waste a second of the time I have left. Richard wouldn't begrudge me a single breath and I feel honour-bound to live a full life to make up for his early passing.

The truth was, I believed I was living my life to the full. I am no different from anyone else in this – when we live day to day in the minutiae of our lives, the bigger stuff can go unnoticed. The triumphs and highs are measured in comparison to the lows and disappointments so that we drift in and out of contentment rather than true happiness. In my own experience, it is a truism that you only really understand what happiness is if you have experienced real sadness. Similarly, you only appreciate wealth if you have been poor, wellness if you have been sick. Experiencing the extremes at either end of the spectrum makes you fully appreciate the polar opposite. The same is true of life itself. It was only when life was taken away that I understood how inert I had become. And when I say life – it was Richard's life that was taken, but it felt like mine, too. I no longer had my life partner. I no longer had the future we had planned. In the dark times, I felt as if my life was over.

It wasn't, of course. I would have preferred it otherwise but, with or without my consent, a new phase had already begun. Even as I was facing Richard's death and living with grief, my new life was taking shape. I would have drifted on in my old life, content and comfortable, had it not been for Richard's death. It changed me fundamentally, forced me to take stock of who I was and what I wanted to achieve. It made me wonder why I had never thought before about the bigger picture and my own contribution to it. That big adventure that I had set out on all of those years ago – to achieve certain ambitions – had got lost in the everyday challenges of making my way in the world. And time just passes, of course. Without any conscious thought, we arrive at a point in our lives and wonder what happened. I remember my brother speaking at his fiftieth birthday party: 'Lots of people ask me, "How on earth did you get to be fifty?" And I reply, "I just woke up this morning and I was fifty."'

When you are living in grief, time becomes almost a physical presence – you talk of having to 'fill it'. There is a daily battle with the clock as you try to readjust to this altered state of being. There is a word – which I always saw as cold, without energy or emotion – that remained constant in my mind. That word was: endure. When you are enduring, you are existing and getting by rather than fighting or overcoming. It is the word that best describes the eight months after Richard died. I endured. It is not a state of mind that allows for happiness or laughter. Equally, it does not allow for wallowing or self-pity. You face the world stoically and get through it minute by minute, hour by hour, day by day. If people, as they constantly did, shared their memories of Richard or passed on their thoughts and sorrow at his passing, I learned how not to listen, how to have some appropriate stock phrase at the ready so I didn't have to think about the emotions behind the words.

'You're very good, thank you. It's only time that will help, but Dara and I are keeping busy.'

How many times did I utter those banal words? Countless. It was a defence and it gave the well-meaning friend or colleague the chance to move the conversation on. I know how difficult it is to approach the subject with the recently bereaved and often the only way people can do it is by telling you about their own loss – a father, sibling, friend. It's an attempt to share the experience, but it is one of the most difficult parts of condolence conversations. So many times, when people offered me a word of comfort, they lost themselves in their own grief to the point at which I would find myself patting their hands or giving them a hug. Thankfully, for the most part, politeness allows us to use stock phrases that get us through awkward moments of having to refer to our innermost emotions.

Each person will develop his or her own coping mechanisms, and mine was to get busy and stay busy. It came naturally to me to take that route and I didn't question it. When I look back at that time, I am astonished that I did what I did. How did I fit in all of those speaking engagements, strategy sessions, interviews, business breakfasts, client lunches, after-dinner talks? There was hardly a blank space in the diary. Richard died in the early hours of Wednesday, 12 October 2011. His removal was the following day and he was buried on Friday, 14 October. Dara and I spent the weekend with family, but one week to the day of his death, Dara went back to school and I returned to the office. The following day, 20 October, just eight days after Richard had died, I was on a conference platform speaking with my fellow 'Dragons' for a *Sunday Business Post* event at the Royal Dublin Society. I remember Gavin Duffy making a lovely speech about Richard and me, and how amazing it was that I had agreed to continue with the speaking engagement. This was greeted with warm applause from the audience and all the while I was thinking how strange it was to mention it because of course I would keep the engagement – what else would I do? I felt disassociated from what was happening and I didn't see that I had a choice. During those first few weeks I did things that I wonder about now.

In November I compèred the Women of the Year Awards for Irish *Tatler*. It's a glamorous black-tie event and compèring meant two long stints at the podium, before and after dinner. But it was my ninth year doing it. How hard could it be? As it turned out, it was incredibly difficult: a tiny chink in the façade, and the first time I allowed myself to contemplate his absence. Richard had been by my side through all of these high-profile events – he held my hand in the final moments when nerves threatened to get the better of me. It was his voice at the microphone who introduced me to the stage, and while I was presenting he was always right in front of me – in my eye-line – in case I needed anything. He sat next to me during dinner, taking the heavy load of the conversation because I'm always quiet and distracted when I have to make a big speech.

At the end of those big nights, when I fretted about how well the evening had gone, Richard had a phrase he always used. Over the last glass of wine before bedtime he would sum up the evening with 'We acquitted ourselves well.' It was perfect, not proud or boastful, but reassuring: we had passed off a difficult task with honour; we had lived up to the moment. I remember talking about that phrase at his funeral because it was such an important aspiration for him: to acquit yourself well in all that you do. That evening, when I faced the podium without Richard, I was struck by how apt was that choice of words. I missed him so much that night. I missed all of the little things he did that no one else would even notice. I missed his voice when I shakily climbed the steps to the stage, his eyes watching me, his hug at the end of the night. But most of all I missed his calm reassurance that we had acquitted ourselves well. It struck me that no one would ever be by my side and say those words to still the voices that dented my self-belief.

That night was a rare slip for me. For the rest of the time, I felt I kept the wall in place, holding memories and emotions at bay. I was heading up a busy, fast-moving publishing company with a plethora of other investments. I didn't have the option of slinking quietly into meetings hoping no one would notice. I was the focal point of everything I did at a time when I wanted to hide away from the world. I had always been a high-energy, ideas person. I loved fuelling discussions, sparking debates and pushing people's thinking. I was never happier than when I was walking the floors of Harmonia, chatting to teams, sitting next to whoever was up against a deadline or working on a big project. I hate being behind a desk. To my mind, the only way to lead your staff, to enthuse your teams, is to walk the floor and get close to them in their own work space. It was fun and energizing. It helped create a culture of openness and togetherness at Harmonia – it made the place special.

Now, though, everything I used to love about being the boss became everything I loathed. I wanted to walk up the stairs into my office and close the door. My worst days involved meetings where I was expected to lead and inspire. I didn't want to be the pivotal person in any group or encounter. I mumbled my way through perfunctory agendas, resenting the fact that people expected me to energize them when I had no energy myself. I didn't want to be the nucleus of the business. I wanted silence and space. But I had no choice. I was the boss and business doesn't stand still. For the first time in my life, I hated my job. I dreaded going into work, and the tiny reserves that kept me going were being depleted by the effort it took to get through those days. As a result, my personal life ground to a halt. I didn't want to cook for myself, I couldn't read books, I couldn't enjoy music. I just wanted to curl up on the sofa and watch trashy television, think nothing and feel nothing. Endure.

All of this begs the question: how did I endure? This huge curveball came out of nowhere and shattered my future. It took away a part of me along with Richard and it stole the next chapter, the one we had planned together. So why didn't I drop out of life, give up, become a shadow? Two reasons: Dara, and the fact that Richard's death shoved me on to another track. It gave me no choice but to envisage a different future. I had to do that for Dara, and in the end I realized I had to do it for me. The truth was that when the initial rawness had abated, my tremendous loss inspired me to look at my life differently and to ask myself, 'Is this the best I can be?' Out of endurance came a persistent challenge to myself. 'Is this it – are you done?'

There is, as I mentioned above, a scientific aspect to what I was feeling and experiencing throughout this time. There's even a specific phrase for it: psychological survival instinct. In other words, what doesn't kill you makes you stronger. Research into the psychology of surviving adversity tells us that humans are resilient in the face of difficulty – up to a point. In 2010 an interesting study was published in the *Journal of Personality and Social Psychology*. It looked at three groups of people (2,398 participants in total). One group had faced no adverse events in their lives, the second had confronted a few, and the final group had met frequent adversity. It found that the middle group had better mental health and well-being than those who had a history of no adversity or those who had suffered multiple such episodes.

This study is part of a much bigger research project that began in 2001 to look at resilience and how people cope with stressful or traumatic events. While the ability to cope with adversity varies from person to person, certain experiences are more devastating than others. The loss of a grandparent might be very traumatic for one person who has deep emotional ties with that grandparent, while another, who doesn't have that bond, may only experience a fleeting sense of loss. What we do know from multiple studies is that humans do not cope well in general with certain severe adverse events: assault, either physical or sexual, natural disasters, disability following trauma or disease and the loss of a loved one appear on the list of significant life-changing events that impact on our well-being. But this study was attempting to discover whether there were potential benefits in experiencing some adversity as opposed to none. The findings show that experiencing some challenges makes us stronger. We cope better with the tough times if we have had some experience of such: we build up psychological survival instinct.

I was gratified to learn that: in business I often talk about failure being a route to success. I have always learned a lot from the things I didn't get right – if everything went smoothly, we would never learn anything. I talk to aspiring leaders regularly on the subject and hear a common response: failure is one of the hardest things they have to learn to cope with, but it is not something to be feared. Losing Richard was not about my failure, but it did teach me a great deal about myself. Why did losing my father and my sister not create the same impetus? I ask myself that question all the time, and I think the answer is, I had Richard by my side so I could cope with the pain of losing them without the catastrophic consequences of his death. It was only when I was stripped bare – back to being a single human being, wending my way alone through the world – that I was forced to take stock and determine a different plan. Adversity is an unlikely route to making that gear change.

That said, I understand that the idea of adversity being helpful may anger some people. When you lose someone or face any kind of challenge, you may experience the desire to shut down. The temptation to follow the loved one is strong. I have good friends who suffered loss and grief and who now live a 'shadow life'. They go through the motions of daily living, but their hearts are not in it. The joy and the meaning are absent. I was lucky in that I had Dara, which meant crawling under the bedclothes was not an option for me. It wasn't about me being super-strong, it was about me as a mother with a responsibility to my twelve-year-old son, who was grieving the loss of his father. I couldn't be a shadow because Dara desperately needed a solid person in his life to lean on. But I do understand how the shadows can engulf a person, how it can take more strength than you have to fight them off.

Ask yourself: am I living a shadow life? Perhaps you bought this book because you are and you wish to change. I want you to know that it's possible to emerge from adversity transformed and stronger, and that it's worth the fight. First, forgive yourself for the bad days and the bad thoughts. You're only human, and when you're in pain, it's easy to bow beneath its weight. Forgive yourself and let it go. Next, accept that you have to plan a new future, one that incorporates the loss, the adversity, whatever it is. Be honest about that: whatever happened, it is now part of your life and you must live with and beyond it.

Honesty – that's a very important word. Honesty can knock down walls and build bridges, so use it to your advantage. Have an honest conversation with yourself about how you feel and how you would like to feel, then give yourself the freedom, the permission to move on. Find your resilience and make the changes you need to make. See your lowest point as the downward curve of the springboard: once it reaches the lowest point, it must return upwards.

I didn't feel resilient in those first raw months of unend-
ing grief, but alongside the pain there was a new feeling, and
it was out of this that my future would eventually grow. It
was the inescapable feeling that I had a moral imperative to
live life to the full. There are so many people on our planet
who will never fulfil their potential. There are mothers who,
out of necessity, reserve all of their energy for finding
enough food and clean drinking water for their child. There
are others, so many, who don't have a lifetime to achieve
great things because their days are numbered through disease and early death. Once you acknowledge that huge
numbers of people are deprived of the ability to live fully,
you must also acknowledge that those of us who are given
the chance to do so should give our all to achieve as much as
possible. Richard had been robbed of life and I had been
robbed of my envisaged life with him, but I still had my life.
It was that sense of needing to be fully alive that kept me
going in the dark hours and, eventually, led me out into the
light.

3. Moving Beyond Endurance: The Moment of Reignition

We have looked at adversity and I have been honest about how hard it is to live through loss than with it. I didn't want to gloss over any of that because confrontation is important, healthy and helpful. I hope anyone who has suffered a similar loss understands me and also finds, perhaps, some comfort in that shared understanding.

In this chapter, I want to share with you the journey I took towards the realization that I could live a more vital life, could be a better person than I was. I also want to give you some insight into how far I had drifted from feeling that I was the best version of myself I could be. I didn't wake up one morning with a eureka moment: it was a gradual process of realization.

After the paralysis, the time came for movement. Wherever you are on the arc of adversity, take heart from the knowledge that movement always follows stasis. Time will change things – for worse, for better. It will not always be about endurance. There will be a time when you move beyond that, begin to reassess life and, hopefully, make new plans. In the following pages I hope you will gain some understanding of what worked for me, in the hope that it will work for you, too.

Stopping and thinking

After Richard's death, the crippling grief and the debilitating sense of enduring, I needed some time away from business and people, and so did Dara. About eight months after Richard died, in June, I rented a beautiful house in Wicklow among the trees. Dara and I moved there, with a view to staying for eight weeks. We left all of the pressures and deadlines of school, work and socializing behind and took long walks together, enjoying the peace and tranquillity of the woodlands and river. Sometimes, when it is hard to process the complexities of loss and the new landscape of your life, your mind needs respite. For me, tramping through the damp, mossy undergrowth with rain as a constant companion became a joy in itself. I didn't need to think beyond the beauty of the trees and the sounds you can hear when you find the space and silence to listen. I woke each morning to the music of the woods – a melody of birdsong and the gurgling of the river. Conversations turned to the more mundane things in life. When you live close to nature and spend time outdoors, you become obsessed with the weather and, in particular, rain. Most importantly, the kind of rain. Soft, gentle rain is best for long hikes. The discomfort of a walk in a rain-lashed forest is not to be underestimated, the large plopping drops that hit you at irregular intervals, and the sheets of a downpour that feels like it will never end. What's wonderful about weather conversations? They require almost no brain power – it's almost a subconscious conversation, without thought. I used to joke to Dara during those days that all we talked about was the rain – when it would start or stop and the type it was. In fact, it was a blessed relief from the heavyweight conversations of the boardroom.

Taking time to stop and think things through is really beneficial. If you don't, life trundles along in a state of endurance and time passes, but you aren't getting anywhere.

It's good to acknowledge that you need to get off the merry-go-round for a while and live a bit differently. Everything *is* different, so embrace that and go with the flow, rather than pushing against it.

Confronting fear and going with gut

We were immersed in our gentle Wicklow sojourn when I was asked if I would stand in for well-known TV3 presenter Vincent Browne during his holiday. I said yes, without giving it much thought. I had the time to do it, and I had enjoyed presenting television programmes in my early journalistic life. I had spent the intervening years on the other side of the table from Vincent and others like him, as a commentator on current affairs and various issues, and it was some time since I had sat in the hot seat as the interviewer. Friends and family gently reminded me that I was supposed to be taking some time out, the unspoken comment being that I was 'running away' from time with myself. I genuinely didn't think that was the case. I was just doing a favour for a colleague and revisiting something I used to enjoy doing.

A week later I pulled up outside the TV3 studios. As I parked and looked up at the building, it struck me, suddenly and forcefully, that I had truly lost my mind. What was I thinking of, going on national television to present Vincent Browne's show? It was years since I had even read an autocue. The panel included a government minister, and while I'm a current-affairs geek, the agenda was wide-ranging and daunting with lots of information to retain and use when the time was right. I was sick to my stomach with fear. The stupidity of thinking I could just sail back into a role I barely remembered and do it while the nation watched almost unhinged me. How I didn't put the car into reverse and drive back through those gates, I will never know.

I headed for Reception, smiled, said who I was, signed in and went straight to the bathroom, where I lost the sandwich and tea I'd had before leaving the house in Wicklow. I washed and recovered, and told myself all sorts of inane things to bolster my self-confidence. In the end it was an inherent trait that made me walk out of that bathroom and meet the producer with a confident handshake. I always confront fear, even if the consequences aren't that good for me. As a nursing student, that was what drove me to study burns, even though that was my biggest fear. And even though I'm terrified of heights, I have been to the top of the Eiffel Tower, the Twin Towers, when they were there, and even the Petronas Towers in Kuala Lumpur. Another thing about me: I can't bring myself to let someone down. And, thankfully, I didn't because, although I had no way of knowing it at the time, that night changed the course of my life.

I went into a quiet room, reread my research notes, memorized the key points, worked out the questions I would ask and the follow-ups, then read through the script. A few more trips to the bathroom later, and I was being miked up. I had been in that studio many times as a guest, but never as a presenter. As I settled into the chair, my stomach was fluttering, my heart was beating too fast and my hands were shaking. My mouth was bone dry and I found it difficult to keep up the smiling *über*-confident persona I was projecting to the guests and crew. Plus things were speeding up: before I could calm myself, a voice in my earpiece was saying, 'One minute to go,' and the floor manager was counting down. The familiar music started and I turned to the autocue. I can't say that my nerves suddenly departed, but as I began to speak and consciously use inflection and facial expressions to add emphasis, I could feel the butterflies starting to settle and my hands had stopped gripping each other. My breathing started to even out and my heart stopped trying to jump out of my ribcage. My brain was fired up, interested and ready for the discussion, and my body was catching up fast. This was something I enjoyed doing. All sorts of memories must have been travelling back from the archives to the brain, telling it that this was a pleasurable activity, that I was comfortable doing it and there was no need for panic.

The rest of the programme is not important – it was a robust debate, I loved every minute of it, and was surprised and regretful when the producer gave me the final-minute warning. The credits were rolling, I chatted for a minute or two to the guests and the team, with the promise that I would be back with them the following day. It was late: I wanted to get back to my hideaway in Wicklow, and to Dara.

I was driving out of the gate and towards the motorway on autopilot as I mentally reanalysed the programme. It's a habit of mine and a good discipline. I retrace questions and interruptions, reflect on how much listening I did when others were talking (I always try to do this, rather than think-ing about the next question). I weighed up the balance of the programme, the key moments that would become a talking-point around the country. I was so wrapped up in this solo post-production meeting that I almost forgot the turn-ing for Enniskerry. The realization brought me back to the present, and then it struck me: I couldn't remember the last time I had felt more alive and more engrossed in something other than the overwhelming sadness and loss that had taken me over in the previous months. In fact, I couldn't remem-ber the last time when I had felt more afraid. I'm used to public speaking and being in the media, and while a small amount of nerves is good for you, this had been way beyond that. Now I felt good and couldn't wait for the following day, so I could feel that good again. It was the most amazing respite ever from the torment of constantly thinking about something I couldn't change and couldn't control.

That, then, was the start of a new journey for me. I did the programme the following night and again was on a high afterwards. I called my mother, who was used to having heavy conversations with me that relied more on her counselling skills than anything else. She had watched both programmes, but even she was unprepared for the excited babbling daughter on the phone. I was caught up in the world of current affairs again. I felt at that time that I was really happy to be standing on my own two feet, relying on my own abilities once more. I had spent so long working with teams and helping others to push themselves, I had forgotten that I need to be pushed too. I had been outside my own safety zone of competence and had faced the possibility, a very real one, that I would fail – and fail spectacularly, in the public eye. But I'd still gone on and done it. And even though in my earlier life I had stood up to fear and challenged it, this was so unexpected that I couldn't ever have predicted it. Why was that? It was a question that led me to another important part in my journey back, but not before I had had my fill of the high I had experienced over the previous two days.

Undertake the unexpected

Another phone call, another challenge. The following week I stood in as holiday cover on Newstalk *Breakfast* with Chris Donoghue. Ivan Yates had left some time previously and

Shane Coleman was temporarily standing in until a replacement was appointed. I am not daunted by early rising, so
didn't think it would be a problem getting into the studio for
5.15 a.m. I was still in Wicklow, so I set the alarm for 4 a.m.,
Monday to Friday, for two weeks. People close to me continued to question the wisdom of filling my therapeutic
break from the business with 'stuff'. While I felt it might be
true to some extent that I was running away, I knew it was
also true that spending a lot of time thinking about something I couldn't change wasn't remotely therapeutic. I wasn't
ready to accept what had happened and my mind needed
respite from the constant 'what if?' and 'why us?'.

The first morning at Newstalk wasn't quite as nerve-racking
as my first night on TV3, but it challenged me in a totally different way. While I knew Chris, I didn't know the rest of the
team, and although I had done one stint with Shane on that
programme, I had only been reviewing the newspapers and
doing some of the links. When a team is very focused and on
deadline – as the hard-working Newstalk *Breakfast* team always
is – it's difficult to find the time to induct a newbie. Everyone
was helpful, but also busy getting ready for 7 a.m. when we
were on air. I had presented shows on LBC and Liberty
Radio in London, but again it was some time ago and they
were both weekly magazine-format programmes – nothing
like the duration and pace of a three-hour current-affairs
show. Rapidly changing stories require fast reading and the
ability to get to grips immediately with the main issues.
Changes to the morning schedule are commonplace, and
even if you have spent the previous evening researching an
interview or story, chances are it might not make it on air if
something else breaks in the meantime.

That first morning was difficult in all sorts of ways – fitting into a team, understanding the metre of the show (what always happened and when), even simple things, like allowing for a regular jingle or knowing that one item always follows another. Chris was a great support, and over the first few days I got to know the team, and relied on them hugely. It was a totally new experience and all-consuming. When 10 a.m. came and we were in post-production, I felt the morning had flown by. (I was yet to experience those mornings that go on for ever!) It challenged my brain in a way that it hadn't been tested for some time. And I started to do things I had not done for more than a year: I was chatting to friends and family about politics, news and interesting guests. It was something different to talk about – not the loss of Richard or the pain or how well Dara and I were coping. I was meeting people for coffee, engaging with new people and talking to Dara about something other than his dad. I was interested in life again. While my personal circumstances hadn't changed, my work life had – dramatically. It felt far better than sitting comfortably in my office ensconced in well-navigated, familiar territories. This was new, challenging and risky.

I know my circumstances are particular to me – let's face it, not everyone is lucky enough to get phone calls that set up challenges and allow you to achieve something. Nonetheless, I know from family and friends that everyone is given opportunities: there are knocks on the door in one shape or another, even if it's just an invite to a party. The thing is, it means you get to decide to leave the door shut or open it. My advice would be to fling that door open and let the newness in. I honestly don't believe you will regret it.

Seeing the future

When the two weeks on Newstalk *Breakfast* were up, I enjoyed some time out. Even after only two weeks of 4 a.m. starts it was blissful to lie in until 7 a.m. the following Monday. But I had time for reflection, too, and this time my thoughts were more about the future and less about the past. I started to wonder about myself. The phrase that kept repeating in my head was 'Are you done yet?' I questioned myself over and over about what I wanted to do next. Would I go back into the business and continue to drive Harmonia forward? There was little excitement bubbling inside me at the prospect. How about finishing that PhD on the power of the written word in terms of memory retention and recall? I'd loved spending two years on it, so maybe it was time to pick it up again and finally complete it. But I hadn't too much interest in doing that either. How about packing up with Dara and living somewhere else for a while?

On the strength of this thought I took a couple of days in London to visit our house there. It had been rented, and when the tenants left, I asked the agent to leave it vacant so I could make a decision. I asked a friend, who is also a great painter, decorator and all-round handyman, to meet me at the house so I could get it ready for us to move back in. But I'd spent only a few minutes alone in it before I realized that I could never live there again. It was where Richard and I had begun our life together. Every room held memories of previous times. It was overwhelming. I handed back the keys to the agent and returned to Ireland, certain I didn't want to live anywhere but Dublin, where friends, family and familiar spaces would mind us in the years ahead.

All of this meant I couldn't silence the nagging voice in my head, which kept demanding, 'Are you done yet?'

One morning I was walking among the trees and my mind turned to a more productive way of reaching some decision about the future. The team at Harmonia had been supportive and patient throughout Richard's illness and in the long aftermath, but I had a deadline by which I had to give them my decision regarding the business. That deadline was now a matter of days away. I was sorely tempted to sell the business because it was a constant reminder of Richard, and so much of what we had planned to do was bound up in Harmonia. I needed an answer, but how was I to find it? The plan I came up with was to search for the answer to my future in my past.

Reviewing and questioning

In the next chapter I will share with you my own process of self-analysis (maybe that's too big a word), but it started with me simply going back to my childhood and remembering what I wanted to be when I grew up. Perhaps the business side of my head wanted to work through a problem in a more scientific way by checking each step in life to this point – whatever the impetus, it worked for me. I found it really useful to take a more detached look at my younger self.

The best analogy I can give you is that I felt as if I was looking back at my browsing history and clearing out the cache, so that unhelpful memories or perceptions that were embedded in my mind from historical events would not influence the purity of thought I needed to make plans for the future. Life has a way of carrying you along without too much thought, so this was the first time I had questioned why I had taken certain decisions: to be a nurse, to move to journalism, to be the boss. I reviewed the learning I had gleaned (formal and informal) along the way, and the milestone of buying the business. I looked at my work and personal lives and saw how the two intertwined. I noticed that there were times when work was fulfilling while personal life was hard, and then those lovely years after I had met Richard and my professional life took a back seat while our relationship blossomed.

I didn't make notes or fill in a chart as I did this. For me, it was important just to think it through. I knew that when I came to more momentous recollections, they would stand out in my mind – I didn't need to write them down. This was a new way for me to work things out – usually I expend no end of Excel spreadsheets and words in coming to an answer to anything. Instead, this was the simple process of recall during walks, time in the gym, upon drifting off to sleep, in the early moments after waking. I began to set aside time each day just to contemplate the past. I couldn't stray into the last year of my life at that point, but the exclusion of that period helped me exorcize the negatives and celebrate the achievements.

It was through this self-analysis that I recalled how ener-gized and happy I had been when I was writing, broadcasting and presenting in my twenties. What I found compelling about any achievement – even if it was only a great profile interview – was that I had done it myself. One of my proud-est moments was getting my first feature article published. I loved working between radio and television. There was no in-tray. No long list of things that hadn't been achieved, no worry about the following day or the constant feeling of never being on top of the mountain. It wasn't about sitting at emails all day, waiting to clear other people's in-trays. Nei-ther was it about motivating others to deliver – there was no selling of a vision, or developing strategies, or creating a cul-ture in which people thrived. Don't get me wrong: I loved doing all of those things. But I knew instinctively that that was not what I wanted to do next. I wanted to stand on my own two feet and see what I still had inside me. I wanted to pursue a career back at the coalface of the media, where I wasn't the boss and I had responsibilities for no one but myself.

One thing that struck me was the fear that had gripped me at TV3 just a few weeks earlier. When I thought about it, I realized I had stayed in the slow lane for too long. I enjoyed being competent at and rewarded for doing things I knew I did well. As a result, it was some time since I had pushed myself to do something unknown. And although I had presented in the past, that night at TV3 had been a leap into the unknown. I wanted to do it again, feel the excitement and energy of being afraid and overcome the fear by pushing myself to succeed.

Through all of this – the days of reflection and self-analysis – I was moving towards a different scenario about the future. Instead of it being filled with loss, the absence of Richard and the life we had planned together, it began to fill with all of the things I still had to do. Not a panic reaction to my mortality – which happens to all of us when we lose someone close – but a much more subtle shift in thoughts and ambitions. Richard had never fulfilled all his potential and for me to waste my life now would be immoral. I suppose, in the end, it was the will to live.

Making decisions

I took some key decisions after that quiet period of reflection and analysis. I decided that I needed to take a year away from business and that I would pursue my first love of working at the more creative end of the media – back on the front line. I also decided that I wanted to be busy. It had worked for me over that summer and I still saw time as something that needed to be filled. Newstalk had asked me to take on the role of co-presenter of *Breakfast* for a longer period. I considered their offer carefully, and I said yes. RTÉ had asked if I would co-present their new afternoon show, *Today*, which would be broadcast from Cork every Friday with Bláthnaid Ní Chofaigh. I said yes. I had done a pilot programme for RTÉ 2 called *The Takeover*, which had achieved high ratings, and the production company asked if I would present a six-part series over the winter. I said yes. Clearly, I was finding ways to fill the space. I put some temporary arrangements in place at Harmonia and my two stalwarts at the time – finance director Michael Fitzpatrick and commercial director Rachel Supple – took on the dual role of managing the company for the year. I agreed to do a day a week with the business.

So, that autumn my life changed dramatically. Although I was getting up at 4 a.m., that worked for me and Dara: each evening I would do the teleconference with the team at Newstalk to discuss the following morning's programme, then spend the rest of the evening doing my homework alongside Dara. We were both in bed before ten. Even when I was travelling round the country filming *The Takeover*, I always came home each night to Dara. My 4 a.m. alarm call gave me time to have his lunch and schoolbag packed and his uniform ready for him before I went into Newstalk for 5.30 a.m.

The Friday routine was different. After *Breakfast* I went straight to Cork, usually arriving at 1 p.m., in time for hair, make-up and rehearsals. RTÉ Cork was the best fun and the best antidote to a week of heavy news items and politics.

Bláthnaid was a great co-host and the team made me laugh from the moment I arrived. It was an uplifting end to the week, and although when the season ended I knew it wasn't right for me long-term, I am so glad I got the opportunity to do it. The journey home with Bláthnaid was the highlight of the week. We laughed, cried and put the world to rights, and when we finally hit my house, around 9.30 p.m., we always had a glass or two of wine while waiting for her husband to pick her up. It was the best therapy imaginable.

It's often said that you shouldn't make snap decisions in the wake of a loss or life-changing event, and I would second that advice. I think you need time to live the new life, to weigh up your new reality. I was stumbling through these things, but with hindsight I can see it was a good idea to take time out in Wicklow, to give myself time to think before I made those big decisions about the future. I would recommend anyone facing adversity to do the same: give yourself a breathing space, some dedicated thinking time and perhaps even a deadline by which to make certain decisions. This will help you to be objective and focused, so that you make the right choices for your life.

4. The Three Chapters of Life

I have shared my personal journey with you in detail now, through death, grief, then into living a new life and shaping a new future. It took time, plenty of tears, wrong turns and anxiety, but I did get there in the end. The key to this book, of course, is, why did I do all of that? The quick answer is: to become the best version of myself I could be. I wanted to live all of my life, even the bad bits, even the hard bits, and that is what I'm still trying to do every day. If I have a philosophy, it's this: don't let life's events derail you. Find the track you want to be on and stay true to it, work at it and celebrate your achievements. When adversity arrives, as it most certainly will, face it with honesty and courage. This is the nub of *Spark!*: that it is possible to be truly alive for all of your life. You have the power to assign meaning to every single thing that happens to you, and that's a pretty staggering power, when you think about it.

This chapter is the start of the hard work – for you. We are leading up to the self-analysis that you need to do to figure out where you are in life and where you'd like to be. Before that, though, I want to set up a framework for that discussion by looking at the three key phases of life and what they mean for us. When I was contemplating my own past, I found myself thinking of my life as a story. I often refer to my own life and, in particular, the next phase as a 'chapter' – one I hope I can write for myself. I thought that perhaps the book of life is not a bad analogy. I found it easier to look back when I divided my life into three parts, or chapters. I began my life stages at twelve years of age, so I examined: 12–38, 38–58 and the final chapter, 58+.

In particular, I wanted to reflect on what generally happens in each chapter and what happened to me. It led me to think differently about the part of my life that remained, the final chapter. My own belief is that the final chapter, 58+ years, is the phase of our lives when we can finally fulfil all our ambitions and be a better version of ourselves. But in order to do that, we need to understand what happened in the first two chapters and why we need to plot the course of the final one much earlier in our lives.

By dividing life into three chapters, I have made a number of assumptions. One is that average life expectancy is eighty-one years (although I have left the final chapter open-ended) and that the first twelve years of our lives are excluded. These are approximate ages when various events happen to most of us, albeit there will be exceptions. I have subdivided the three chapters into three sub-chapters, to reflect some of the changes and diverse experiences that happen in our lives during the first, second and third phases.

The shape of things to come

This book began with me sharing my journey towards making some dramatic changes in my life. I had come to a moment when everything had changed irrevocably, but after a careful review of my life, I concluded that the next part could be even more fulfilling and exciting than the first. To get to that future anticipation, I had to travel back in time to my younger self. When reflecting on the past, not in a judgemental or remorseful way but in exploring the decisions and key phases in my life, I came to a very obvious conclusion. So obvious, in fact, that I couldn't believe I hadn't thought of it before. While I was drifting into my forties, believing that the time for renewal and active growth was slowing down and would eventually decline, I was consciously not looking forward. The same is true for most of us: the early part of our lives is all about what we want to be; the second half is about how we (in most cases) never became what we'd imagined.

Being self-critical about the past is a waste of good brain-time – it serves no purpose. So I tried to look at it objectively, then move on, without emotional reactions to what had gone before. What amazed me was the discovery of how much I still had to do – how I could be a better student, or achieve the goal I had forgotten about, how many places I still needed to see and people I still wanted to be.

I began to realize that we are trapped in a life plan determined by our predecessors, our parents and grandparents mainly, many of whom had no choice but to accept that a final chapter of life meant vulnerability, illness and a diminishing of faculties. All of that has changed, and there is no reason why we collectively shouldn't live life to the full in every chapter.

My thoughts on the first two chapters of my own life led me to the understanding that, for the most part, we design our own futures. We face inevitable decline and death partly because we are not proactive in preparing for the final chapter: we often do little to ensure that we stay healthy, active and challenged for as long as we have life to live. We almost predetermine our own downfall as we age.

What happens is usually along the following lines.

In the first chapter, we cram everything in with a huge

appetite for life. After the age of twelve we face many new challenges: these are our primary learning years. We sit exams for the first time, make new relationships, deal with separation from our parents, explore new places and wrestle with some of the biggest life choices, all in the first thirty-three years of life. It is an uphill drive to develop and grow as a human being – not necessarily to reach the pinnacle of our potential, but a strong drive towards it. It's a constant roller-coaster of new challenges and experiences, and we feel alive and energized.

The second chapter begins in our thirties, and while the momentum is still going for the early part of those years, we gradually lose it as we head towards our forties. I call these our 'settled years' and it's the part of the book of life when nothing much happens. It's the time when we want to put down roots, to meet and commit to a partner, to have children, take on a mortgage and settle into a career. We don't think too much about what we still want to be because we believe we're already there and living it. We rarely pull back from our lives and challenge ourselves to do something different.

We often settle into a routine – going to the same places, a particular restaurant once a week, a regular shop for groceries. I have friends who cook and eat the same dinner on set days of the week. During these years, there is comfort in stability and sameness. We like to go back to familiar places on holiday and we have a circle of friends that rarely changes. Life ticks over . . . until, before you know it, the big four-oh looms, and all the negative perceptions we have built up over time about what that might mean are suddenly rearing up, demanding attention. The even larger five-oh hurtles towards you and life appears to have passed you by without you ever consciously recognizing or accepting the inevitability of ageing.

The third chapter usually follows a period of denial – possibly for the whole of your life up to that point. There are echoes of 'It will never happen to me' from your past amid the realization that it has happened to you. Just like everyone else, you are ageing. It's time to put away childish notions of dying in a blaze of glory before old age because, when it comes down to it, most of us choose life. We want to live a long life, but we don't want to be dependent, vulnerable, impoverished or ill. Yet we do very little to prevent that happening, even though the science is there to prove that, with early intervention from ourselves, we can continue to live in good health and drive ourselves onwards to fulfil our ambitions and dreams. There is no reason to stop growing in terms of your abilities, intellect and skills, but there is every reason to act early and plan for it.

Look at the diagram on page 60 and think about it in terms of your own life.

The A trajectory is what most of us believe the three chapters of our life will be like, with key phases marked out in the three sub-chapters. (These are explained further in the following pages.) Its 'normal life path' shows significant growth in the first chapter, a small growth and eventually a plateauing of development in the second chapter, followed by a slow decline in the third. That's the traditional view of ageing.

What if your life could look more like the B trajectory? The first chapter is the same, but you begin slowly to kick-start your growing again in the second chapter, and in the third chapter, that growth gains momentum as you set about achieving your new or yet to be completed goals. It's not

The Three Chapters of Life

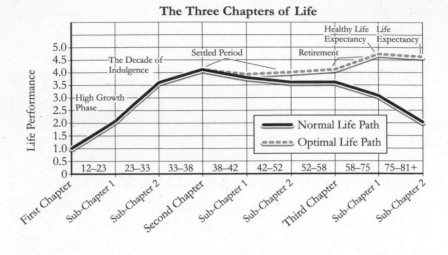

about slowing down or plateauing or giving up. Instead, the 'optimal life path' is about always living, regardless of age.

Not all of us have the same experiences at the same time, so what happens and when in our lives is only relevant in the context of how we feel now about those events and how they occurred. If we are satisfied with the key stages in our life to date, we are more likely to set new challenges for the future. However, if we missed out on an experience or were side-tracked from a key ambition, we may want to make it part of our plan for the next phase in life.

My Book of Life

We are all unique, and the same episode or event can have varying levels of impact on those experiencing it. My own personal journey took me in all sorts of unexpected directions, some positive, others not. To help you chart your own progress through the earlier stages of your life, I have written down some of the key events that happened in mine. It might be useful for you to use as a comparison and to show

how different life is for each of us. This is, in other words, a template for the book of life you will compose for yourself, based on this chapter and the self-analysis in the next, 'Are you done yet?'

The First Chapter: 12–38 Years

1: Growing Up, 12–23 years

My home was a lodge in the Phoenix Park, where my father worked as gatekeeper and ranger, as his father had before him. You couldn't have a more magical upbringing than living in the Phoenix Park – the biggest city garden, right on our doorstep. In the early years my father sat in a hut opposite the house and various people would call on him as he policed the comings and goings through the North Circular Road's imposing gates. He would also open and close the gates to the People's Flower Gardens, ringing the bell loudly at dusk – usually to get his own brood home for tea. For us it was fantastic – a huge garden with cows and deer and so many unexplored jungles and ponds: the perfect place for a child.

I went to school at St Joseph's Convent, run by the Sisters of Charity, in Stanhope Street, near Stoneybatter. I wish I could say I studied hard, but I learned quickly that with little effort I could be average and, if I wanted to impress (rarely), I could push myself to excel. I regularly took notes home from the nuns for being distracted or talking in class. One note arrived to the house regularly: 'She does nothing but scribble all day long.' My mother laughs at that now (she didn't then!).

Those teenage years are about friendships mainly, but also about laying down a distinct personality: you are figuring out who you want to be. The key thing about this stage is the decision: 'When I grow up, I want to be . . .' I think we all have some notion of what we want to be during these years, but very often our lives don't follow that imagined path. I was sure that when I grew up I was going to be a vet.

Dublin Zoo was my second home, particularly the Pets' Corner. I would clean out the guinea pigs' house, hose down the rabbit hutches and de-louse the pigeons. I played with lion cubs, hand-reared a badger, collected privet leaves from the back of the elephant house for the stick insects – cleaning out their glass enclosure was not the most coveted job. We exercised the ponies in the evenings, and we had a very lazy donkey, Jenny, that we walked past the lion enclosure in the early mornings before opening to make her move a bit quicker. I learned how to milk goats and feed fledgling chicks with bread soaked in milk. I could clean out the llama enclosure without getting spat at by the cross ones, and I was adept at feeding the pet parrot, George, without getting my fingers clipped by his sharp beak. My mother eventually got used to me arriving home with some tiny or sick animal that I couldn't leave overnight in the zoo, so I often shared my bedroom with poorly hedgehogs, baby rabbits, broken-winged birds and even, on one occasion, a seal pup.

I was certain that my future lay in working with animals. When I left school I was still only sixteen (the joys of being an August baby), and instead of heading to college, I worked in the quarantine section at the zoo, helping to hand-rear the first two Western Lowland Gorillas. It was a blissful time for me – any young animal-lover's dream.

CHOOSING A CAREER IS RARELY
AN EXACT SCIENCE

What happened next was a bit of a curveball. I am still not entirely certain why, but I switched career track and enrolled in a nursing school. There weren't that many jobs around at the time and I wasn't entirely sure I wanted to head straight back into intensive studying at college. Nowadays going to university is an expectation. Back then it was the exception – especially for kids from an inner-city school. That said, my parents were keen for all of us to do well, whether we went to college or, like many of our peers, landed a solid job in the bank or the civil service. My mother had trained as a psychiatric nurse at St Brendan's in Grange Gorman and her sister was a district nurse in Sligo, so maybe nursing was in my DNA. But, to be honest, I think the decision to enter nursing had more to do with the fact that I was going to train in a small hospital on the banks of Loch Lomond, in Scotland. Just far enough away to be exotic, but it still felt a bit like Ireland.

My father's friend Paddy Mannion lived at the lodge at Parkgate Street and he had a daughter, Anne, who had gone to Scotland and married a policeman. She was working in Casualty at the Vale of Leven Hospital near Loch Lomond, and when she was home on holiday, she gave my dad a brochure seeking applications for would-be student nurses. It had travelled all the way from the banks of Loch Lomond to the Phoenix Park and I travelled all the way to Loch Lomond for an interview. I got caught up in it all – the heady journey on the aeroplane (the first time I had flown), stretching my wings, leaving the nest. My school-friends weren't doing anything remotely interesting and the civil service exams were looming. I figured anything that involved wearing a white uniform and *broderie anglaise* on your head couldn't be all bad.

THERE ARE PIVOTAL MOMENTS
THAT SET YOU IN A NEW DIRECTION

I think I was a good nurse. I loved it, for the most part. Yes, it was tough dealing with illness and death at such a young age, but it was also a great foundation for life. It gives you a healthy perspective: I have never stressed over business decisions. However, over the course of the three-year training programme, the bits I loved about nursing were slowly eroded by the petty rules that then beset the profession. When I trained, student nurses were part of the workforce and I was working in small hospitals in western Scotland, where we were often left alone at night in charge of a ward to cover mealtimes and shift changes. I remember vividly one night when a man had a cardiac arrest and it seemed to take the 'arrest team' for ever to get there.

I was up on the bed straddling the man while doing CPR when they eventually arrived, led by the night nurse manager. As I heaved myself to the floor, she pulled me to one side and reminded me that the dress code for student nurses did not include a chain and cross, then told me to remove mine from my neck. All I was thinking about was whether the man would live and how unfortunate he was to be left with only me to save him. (He survived, thankfully.) She stared me down until, hands shaking, I realized she meant me to take off the chain and cross – which I did, while they zapped the patient with defibrillation pads. I remember it vividly because it was a turning-point for me – not a dramatic moment, just a quiet acceptance that perhaps this wasn't what I would spend my life doing.

OVERCOMING FEAR IS NOT AN END IN ITSELF

All the way through my nurse education, if you had asked me if there was anything I was scared of, I would have told you categorically it was being faced with a burns victim. All those lonely nights in Casualty when we dealt with road traffic accidents and all manner of injuries, I lived in fear that a major fire would break out in one of the housing estates nearby and we would have to care for the survivors. It didn't happen, but I did something that was either foolish or courageous. I decided to confront that fear by doing a certificate in burns nursing at Bangour Hospital, near Edinburgh. The course was combined with plastic surgery (not to be confused with cosmetic surgery) and included reconstructive work.

It was a year of my life that changed me. I still remember seeing young children who had often been orphaned by serious house fires; they had been severely burned, but survived. As I went on to work in the outpatient department of Edinburgh's Royal Hospital for Sick Children, I saw teenagers who, after multiple operations, remained significantly disfigured – many suffered from serious depression, some had made multiple suicide attempts. At the end of that long year I knew without a doubt that I didn't have what it took to devote my life to this work. I overcame my fear, but learned something far more important about myself: I was not destined to be a nurse.

WHAT DO WE LEARN FROM THIS
CHAPTER OF LIFE?

People often ask me how I cope with the demands of my various jobs – but, really, how hard is it?

I respond with a litany of jobs other people do that are unbelievably tough, and chief among them is nursing: the teams who look after children in burns units, adults and children in hospices where they face death every working day; the nurses who care with patience and grace for dementia sufferers. As far as I'm concerned, nothing is ever going to be as hard as that in business, and no decision will ever be as serious as whether you should jump on the bed of the man who is in cardiac arrest, even though you're scared witless you'll do it wrong and he'll die. Nursing made me grow up, and it gave me the bedrock for my life and career. It remained important to me for many more years and even now I feel at home when I'm asked to talk to a group of nurses.

So, even when our careers take a meandering path, we shouldn't feel frustrated. Every job you undertake will teach you something – about life and about yourself.

2: The Decade of Indulgence, 23–33 years

At twenty-three you enter the Decade of Indulgence, so-called because it represents the ten years from the end of full-time study to the start of settling down – with the ties of a partner, family, mortgage and career. These years are meant to be all about you. You're free as a bird, not shackled with responsibilities, working to earn money and to have fun. Life should be carefree. Of course, it doesn't always work out that way.

I had applied for and won a position with the Royal College of Nursing in London as a professional officer, with responsibility for more than sixty thousand student nurses in Britain. It was quite a departure for me. I swapped Edinburgh for London, a white uniform for a business suit, and my working life was 9 a.m. to 5.30 p.m., like 'normal people'. My salary tripled, I had a company car, an office and a secretary – although I didn't know what to ask of the latter. She soon trained me, though, and before long I was travelling the length and breadth of the country, meeting student groups and producing visions, missions and action plans as if I'd been born to it. There were lots of other skills I was not born with and I will always be grateful for the intense training I underwent during my first year. I had never been in front of a television camera or sat in a radio studio, my only writing was in my nursing reports and I was far more comfortable talking one to one than with large groups. Yet my new job required me to be good in all those areas.

I went on one training programme after another – radio skills courtesy of a wonderful BBC presenter Peter White, blind since birth, who showed me how the spoken word can create wonderful intimacy and imagery. I went to the north of England to learn what to do, say and wear during television interviews. I did presenting courses that taught me how to deal with the unexpected, how to be natural and compelling, how to answer the question you wanted to be asked and, especially important for the audience, how to speak much slower, tone down my accent and avoid using peculiarly Irish phrases. I spent one week being filmed over and over again with a trainer who gave me brutally honest feedback as we reviewed the video tape. I got rid of the ems and ers and stopped fiddling with my hair. My voice became more neutral and I had a list of words to practise pronunciation. It was my own Eliza Doolittle experience. While these were accoutrements of my job, they made me into the person I am today. And they led me to another turning-point in my career.

At twenty-five I had enjoyed two good years of my Decade of Indulgence. I was living in London, socializing with new friends, learning new things – it was a rollercoaster and it was definitely fun. I knew I couldn't stay doing what I was doing because, in a way, I wasn't capable of doing just one thing. I was fortunate to be in a job that used my nursing and new-found communication skills, but I knew I would never put on another white uniform.

Through the wisdom of a male boss, who mentored me during my angst about what to do next, I decided to do a postgraduate programme in journalism at the UK's National College for the Training of Journalists (NCTJ). Believe it or not, I was by then a mature student and I really enjoyed mixing with the raw recruits who were just starting out in their careers; I felt I was on my third. Before qualifying, journalism students had to achieve an industry standard in areas like local and central government, interviewing skills and reporting at speed on a developing story. None presented a challenge and I passed with distinction. But learning to do shorthand at 100 words per minute (a standard requirement in test conditions for court reporting) was almost my undoing. Three times I sat that test before I passed. In any event, I was feeling much more at home in my new career and was learning to love the power of words.

Life, I was quickly realizing, is about weighing up the benefits or otherwise of a particular path and reaching a compromise. So, although I would have loved to stay in the cut and thrust of newspaper journalism, I couldn't afford to take such a steep drop in salary. I was by then living independently in one of the most expensive cities in the world and a rookie reporter was on less than half of what I had been earning. So I combined nursing and journalism and went to work for a weekly nursing magazine. I was the only one in the sector who had both qualifications, so I rose quickly through the ranks of the company. By the age of twenty-seven I was news editor, the following year I became editor of the magazine with a staff of thirty-five, then editorial director of the portfolio of magazines, and before my Decade of Indulgence was over, I was managing director.

That all sounds like it happened without effort, but the reality was that I gave up any notion of indulgence to pursue that career path. I worked hard and was continually learning. I went to Ealing College to study television production and direction, then to Ashridge College to study strategic management, and I started to do shifts at Sky TV in the evenings and at weekends. I was a regular contributor to the radio stations and got my own Sunday show with LBC and a Tuesday evening slot on Liberty Radio. There was almost no time in my life when I wasn't studying or working.

WHAT DO WE LEARN FROM THE DECADE OF INDULGENCE?

While I didn't get ten years of fun and freedom, as promised, it was an incredible decade in many ways. In my personal life, I met my first husband when I was twenty-five, we married when I was twenty-seven and separated when I was thirty-one. It was a difficult time for me personally, and this was why work and learning took centre-stage. I discovered something very important, even though I didn't know it at the time: enjoyment and success in your work life can compensate for trials in your personal life. My love of learning came to the fore and, without planning to do so, I rose fast through the ranks at work.

So, what I can say about those years, from twenty-three to thirty-three, is that they were transformative. I took some brave decisions to change career paths, an even braver one in my personal life, and I grew more as a person than at any other time in my life, apart from the last three years.

3: Settling Down, 33–38 years

Usually by the time we are into our early thirties, we begin to think about settling down. This could be with a husband or wife, or it could be that around this time you take on a mortgage or decide on a particular career path. For me, it was settling with a partner. I had already made one bad decision in my personal life and paid the price for that, so it was wonderful finally to fall in love. Meeting Richard and starting our life together was by far the most important thing that happened in the final part of the first chapter of my life. Everything else took second place. We knew after just a few months that we would spend our lives together, and we married as soon as my divorce was settled.

It was a magical time. I was running the publishing company and was comfortable with the familiarity of the business. Richard and I bought a house together and spent as much free time as we could making it a home. I don't remember feeling anything by way of challenge in my work life. I was studying for a PhD at the University of Wales, so I had my fix of learning when I needed it, and I went back to Ashridge College to study advanced strategic management. I was far from idle. But, for the first time, my focus was on my personal life.

We wanted children, which quickly became a focal point in our lives. When I didn't get pregnant naturally, we resorted to IVF. What began as an aspiration between us – to have a child together – grew into a bit of an obsession. I'm still not sure at what point that fervent wish metamorphosed into something that was all-consuming. Our happy post-wedding bliss was diminishing as that all-important dream eluded us. After many difficulties and miscarriages, we finally called time on the IVF programme, promising each other we would still live a great life without children and enjoy our time together. Amazingly, once we stopped trying, I got pregnant naturally and our son Dara was born in December 1998. I know that those experiences defined that period in my life and that having Dara changed the course of the next chapter.

WHAT WE LEARN FROM THE FINAL PART OF THE FIRST CHAPTER

Like most people, I was settling. My personal life was becoming more important to me and, apart from the enormous change that meeting and marrying Richard made to my life, the single biggest moment was when Dara was born. Our lives changed for ever in all the best possible ways. I know I could have lived a full life without a child, but I would have been regretful if I had not experienced motherhood and if Richard and I had not achieved that great dream: a child who was part him and part me.

As I left behind the first chapter of my life, I had already learned a great deal, chiefly that things often don't happen the way you expect them to. As you look back at that phase in your life, try not to be judgemental about your younger self – as you can see from my experience, we all make bad choices and face difficulties at this and every stage of our lives.

The Second Chapter: 38–58 Years

Generally we begin the second chapter in a more settled state, with life focusing on the routine of daily living. Going to work, earning enough to pay the bills, family issues all come to the fore, and learning takes a back seat. While you may still progress in your career, by now many people have found their work niche and are moving ahead in a familiar space. Earning potential becomes much more important, and reaching the milestone age of forty can have an impact on our perception of life, ageing and mortality. While some will experience the death of friends and relatives, the expectation during the second chapter is that we will say goodbye to members of the previous generation. We have already learned how to live our lives separately from our parents and siblings, but the final act of parting can be painful and life-changing.

1: The Settled Years, 38–42 years

Like most people, my thirties were for the most part quite settled. We had a child to mind, a mortgage to pay and there were never enough hours in the day. Sleep deprivation is a lasting memory of those early years of Dara's life.

My father passed away just a few months after Dara was born and we were heartbroken and bereft of his enormous presence. I was in London, but returning home when I could to see my mother and family. Although I had lost a close friend before this, nothing prepares you for the death of a parent. I couldn't imagine life without him. My dad was looking forward eagerly to his retirement and would regale us with the places he would visit and the things he would do. And then, without warning, he had a heart attack in his sleep on the eve of his seventieth birthday. We didn't get to say goodbye, and even though people said it was good that he went so quickly and didn't suffer, I regretted not seeing him one final time to say all the things I wanted to say.

I returned to work when Dara was twelve weeks old. I had started a new position with Smurfit Media and the *Irish Post* – going back to my editor roots. But I didn't last long as editor: pretty soon I was CEO of the business and back at the helm. For a period that was meant to be 'settled', I took on many new challenges. I was boss of a new business, and before Dara was much more than two, I was running three of Smurfit's publishing businesses – two in Dublin and one in London. I was commuting to Dublin from Monday to Wednesday (with Dara) and running the London business on Thursday and Friday. Life was busy. So busy, in fact, that I didn't really notice turning forty. Richard and I had a wild night in Enniscorthy (the *Irish Post* was sponsoring the Fleadh Cheoil), and he bought me a long-desired and heavily hinted-at Tiffany cross and chain. I don't remember feeling any sense of the passing of time or the fear of growing old. It was just another day in a packed life. I was on my way to completing a management buy-out (MBO), which would make me owner of my own business. Dara was a wonderful child, and Richard and I had decided to move back to Dublin. Life couldn't be better.

WHAT WE LEARN FROM THE SETTLED YEARS
I am conscious that my settled years were not that settled. I wasn't slowing down or plateauing. If anything, I was speeding up. Many of my friends were content to drift in their

careers and used to joke pointedly about my crazy work schedule, but it worked for us. While they looked in horror at the hectic pace of our lives, we were equally aghast at the routines they enjoyed: Sunday lunch in a particular restaurant, renting the same villa in the South of France each year, always Waitrose for the weekly shop and always on a Thursday evening. We lived in an opposite world that shunned routine and repetition. For us, the joy of something new, discovering different places and food was paramount. When we came back to Dublin, Richard had taken a break from the BBC and was doing more than his fair share of helping out with Dara and our home life. I had lost my father, and my career had taken me in yet another direction. But somehow it worked. I hadn't taken my foot off the accelerator and I wasn't drifting, but I could see that that was happening to the people around me.

In fact, I think that was what drove me on. When I talked with friends and heard their placid contentment in sameness, I felt stressed. They thought haring about between countries and having engagements day and night was horribly stressful, but to me, the alternative looked much more frustrating. I suppose one of the key lessons from the Settled Years is to be true to yourself and what you want. If you want hectic, live it, and don't apologize or feel guilty for that choice. Equally, if you really do enjoy a more settled life, don't apologize for it. Either way, do try to ensure that you are still learning and setting yourself challenges – no matter how small.

There is one other key lesson from this time: say the things you want to say to those you love. So often we behave as if time and death don't exist, but they are steady in their perseverance, and in this chapter of your life, you will lose some of those you love. I regret to this day that my father died without hearing the things I wanted to say to him – if it's in your power, don't let that regret mar your life, too.

2: The Middle Years, 42–52 years

At this time I owned my own business, Harmonia, and I was a Dragon on the TV show, *Dragons' Den*. It was a natural progression for me in terms of investment and I was comfortable in front of the cameras, not only because I had been a presenter in the past but because through all of the intervening years I had been a regular contributor to the BBC, ITV, Sky and subsequently RTÉ. It was a fantastic show and I loved working with the guys – the then Dragons Gavin Duffy, Seán Gallagher (who was later to stand for President of Ireland, with Seán O'Sullivan replacing him in the Den) Bobby Kerr and Niall O'Farrell. I wanted to invest in other businesses and, while I had dabbled a bit in the past, it opened my eyes to the potential opportunities in a wide range of ideas and inventions – from the mad to the ingenious. I invested in some great people and businesses from my time in the Den.

Harmonia was going from strength to strength: we were launching and relaunching new magazines and developing some of the areas of the business, particularly contract publishing and digital editions. Richard had joined me as editorial director and the long working hours began to ease a bit as the business became more stable.

Dara was a joy, and I stole as much time as I could to be with him. If I couldn't escape the office, he came and coloured at the table next to me or 'researched' children's comics – I kept a large batch under the desk. It was a great time, and if it hadn't been for the recession and all that it brought with it, these might have been more like my Settled Years. While we weren't hit as badly as other sectors of the media during the downturn, it was still a significant blow to certain areas, with contract publishing gone in a matter of weeks. At a time when I should have been pulling back and growing the business even further, I was working at the coal-face, sleeves rolled up, to secure revenues and refocus as quickly as possible. We survived those years, but for once in my life I was lacking that drive, that hunger – partly through the uncertainty of the economic outlook and where the business should grow.

We hatched a plan to take some months out – neither of us had had a break from work since school and I wanted to meet other publishers in other countries. Richard, Dara and I took off for four amazing months on New Year's Day in 2010. We spent time in Australia, New Zealand, China, Thailand and Cambodia, visited Richard's friend in Burma and met up with another great friend of his in Hong Kong. It was incredible for us, and for Dara. We took him out of school, but we did his lessons every day, following the official curriculum, and he sent a report back to the class every Monday on whatever adventure he had been on that week. Back in Dublin, they were getting a week-by-week account of visits to the Great Wall of China, the temples of Angkor Wat, the pandas in Beijing Zoo and the kangaroos in Australia. I don't regret a moment of that trip, and how amazing it was to have uninterrupted time together and experience so many incredible things. I sent boxes of magazines back from all of the publishers I met (more than thirty during the course of the trip), and returned to Dublin teeming with ideas and energy.

I split everyone in the company into groups, and gave

them piles of magazines in key areas to learn as much as possible about other publishers and other markets. Many were leading the way in high-end fashion, interiors and food. There was a real buzz in the business and I was back where I loved, with a great team of people.

Everything might have been different had it not been for what happened next. In September 2010 my sister passed away and while we were still reeling from that, just eight months later, Richard was diagnosed with cancer. The rest of that period is well covered in the earlier chapters so I won't dwell on it here.

WHAT WE LEARN FROM THE MIDDLE YEARS

Leaving aside the hard lessons from Richard's illness and death, when I reflect on the second chapter of my life I can see that the earlier part taught me a lot, too. I was very satisfied with my work life when I was inventing, creating and driving the business forward, but I was not fulfilled when I was required to shape, trim and maintain it to survive the recession. I used to joke that they were better off without me during those months when I was travelling because I am always tempted to tinker. I can't really stand still. Lots of people enjoy maintenance – keeping the status quo – but that's not my natural state. It's a great attribute when you have a balanced team and things are going well in the economy. It is not such a great trait when you need to batten down the hatches and wait for better times. The months we spent abroad gave us great respite. That time out and exposure to so many of my foreign peers gave me a new lease of life and the energy I needed to get the business moving again.

The most important lesson I learned was how crucial it is

to spend time with the people you love. When I look back now I am so grateful that we spent that time together and, in particular, that Dara has all those precious memories of those great experiences with his dad. It's a very simple lesson, but a good one: no matter how busy you are and how much you enjoy work, make time to enjoy your family.

3: The Empty Nest Years, 52–58 years

I have asked my mother, Margaret Casey (Mags to her friends), to help me with the latter part of the second chapter and to share with me her experiences of the third chapter. We are very alike and she is treading a path that I hope to follow. She epitomizes what the third chapter of our life should be like: she travels extensively, her iPad is a regular companion and she never stops learning because she's still curious about everything. At this point she is living beyond average life expectancy of eighty-one, but in the interests of us remaining good friends I won't reveal by how much! She walks every day and does Pilates and yoga. She follows me on Twitter and stays in touch with her many friends on Facebook. She shops and banks online and is a fan of audio books at bedtime. She loves fashion, getting her nails done and going to the hairdresser. She is always ready for an adventure and the unknown holds no fear for her. She doesn't dwell on her age, except to tell us regularly the music she wants at her funeral – at this stage, it will be going on for a week with everything she wants us to cram into the ceremony. She is the perfect person to take the reins now and it is through her voice that I write the final sections of this chapter.

MARGARET CASEY

A bit of background on me first. I grew up on a farm in Leitrim, in a remote corner of the north-west of the county. Pretty much like Norah, I left home at seventeen to do nursing, but I trained as a psychiatric nurse at St Brendan's in Grange Gorman (now closed). I was working there when I met Harry. We married within a few years and I moved into the gate lodge of the Phoenix Park, which was to be my home for the rest of my life. A wonderful place to live. I'm not a big fan of having too many neighbours, so it was perfect. I love the Park: it's the best back garden in the world. The elements and the seasons constantly change the landscape. In the autumn I look forward to the colours of the trees turning to shades of burnt orange and copper, and spring sees the cherry trees blossom and the arrival of the baby deer. Most mornings I wake to the booming sounds of the lions in Dublin Zoo, in competition with the chatter of the birds flitting around the feeding table in the back garden. It's hard to know which season is better. While sunny days see the People's Gardens filled with families and the noise of children laughing, there is a beautiful stillness and solitude to winter days. It was the perfect place to rear children and I had six – four girls and two boys. Harry was always with me during those growing-up years. Nowadays he would be considered a modern man, but he loved being among the hustle and bustle of the house. Eight of us in a three-bedroomed lodge ensured that it was rarely quiet.

Thankfully, I am picking up my story after the children were all but reared. I wouldn't like to relive some of those sleepless nights and teenage tantrums! The joy of motherhood. I had gone back to work at forty-eight when the children were older: my youngest daughter Carissa was still at school and Ciaran, the second youngest, was an on-off resident and at college. Norah had gone to Scotland to study nursing, Leo was at UCD, Catherine was working and my eldest, Betty, was married with a baby. Over the years I had tried to keep my hand in with night shifts at a local nursing home and I looked after an elderly lady with Parkinson's for a while, but it was difficult with the kids.

I suppose the toughest challenge I faced in my forties was learning to drive and passing my test. I really wanted to be independent and knew it would give me the freedom to go back to work. Harry encouraged me every step of the way, but in truth I was very scared at first. It was a long time since I had been that frightened and I was really nervous on the day of the test. I can remember my hands shaking and hoping the instructor wouldn't notice. I was sure I had failed, so when I saw that word 'Pass' my heart skipped a beat. Driving home in the car on my own was the biggest high I'd had for some time. It wasn't just the fact that I had got through the test, it was my passport to freedom – to go where I wanted, when I wanted and, more importantly, to get back to work. Public transport was not what it is now and nursing meant shifts, with even less chance that a bus would have me there on time and take me home. So, I was on the way back to a job I loved.

What happened next was a stroke of luck. Harry had seen an advertisement for a refresher course for nursing in St James's Hospital and I booked myself on to it.

Not long after I'd started, the tutor asked if anyone was interested in doing some temporary work at Cara Cheshire Home in the Phoenix Park. A fantastic opportunity for me and right on my doorstep. I volunteered immediately and never looked back. It was a place I wanted to work in. In those days any event or something new in the Park was a talking-point. I was there when John F. Kennedy visited – even got to shake his hand as he walked from the Áras back to the American ambassador's residence. I had seen the Pope say mass up at the Phoenix Monument. So, of course, I also remember when Cara opened its doors back in 1978 – it was the first purpose-built Cheshire Home in Ireland. I admired Leonard Cheshire and the ethos and values of the Home. It wasn't about nursing patients, it was about providing services for residents who had physical disabilities. It was their home and they decided how the place should be run.

Leonard Cheshire was a great man who dedicated his life to providing homes and services all over the world and he was inspired to do so because of one of the worst atrocities in human history. I was just a young girl in August 1945 when the USA dropped a nuclear bomb on Nagasaki – a place I hadn't even heard of before that day. Leonard Cheshire was a captain in the RAF and he was an official observer of the attack, which killed more than seventy thousand people, injuring as many again. He resigned from the RAF and devoted his life to good works. Thankfully, his reach extended to Ireland and the Cara Cheshire Home. He married Sue Ryder, who left her own legacy with a foundation to help disadvantaged and elderly people.

I worked part-time at Cara at first as I was still juggling family life, but I loved it from the start, and as soon as I was able to do so, I moved to full-time. There were times when it was hard working there. Many of the residents were young, some born with disabilities and others who had had tragic accidents; although they were resilient, it is hard to accept the dramatic change that disability brings. The frustrations, anger, disappointments and sadness of limitation were brought home to me on a daily basis by being around people who couldn't do all the things I took and still take for granted, like walking in the park, driving my car, being able to lift a spoon and feed myself. There were many rewards about working there, too, and some of the residents became friends. The family got used to them visiting or going out with me for social events or just a spin in the car to get out of the Home for a while.

There was one girl I really admired – she was so clever and had a great personality. Like Stephen Hawking, she was almost entirely paralysed but she didn't have a speech generator, like him. Instead she used an alphabet board and pointer, which she held in her mouth to communicate. I suppose she was my inspiration, in a way, not to allow the things you can't do to define you.

Home life was changing, too. Everyone was gone and the house felt empty. Harry was still working, of course, and I felt ready for a new challenge. The final years of the second chapter were transformative and I got to do something I had wanted to do since I was a young woman.

I had a hysterectomy when I was fifty-five – the usual reasons – and although it was tough getting over the operation, it didn't bother me that I was losing something important to me as a woman. My uterus had served me well and given me six great children. I'm pretty much a no-nonsense kind of person. If it needed to go, then fine. Get it done, get better and move on. There's no point in making an issue of something when there's no need to. In any event it gave me some time away from work to think properly about the next phase of my life.

While I love nursing I was always drawn towards

counselling – maybe that was what had attracted me to psychiatric, rather than general, nursing. In my mid-fifties I got to fulfil a dream of mine to become a counsellor. I wanted to spend some time doing something I knew I would be good at, especially as I grew to know the residents at Cara. It was hard sometimes to find the time to talk or even listen to them. Counselling would allow me to do that. It was a bit daunting, going back to college, but if you don't try something, you'll never know if you can succeed. It took a few years – two days a week at college, study and assignments in the evening and at weekends. I was one proud woman when I got my diploma. As a mother you spend all those years encouraging your children to do well in exams and attending their graduation ceremonies, but I'd never thought they would all be attending mine when I was approaching sixty. I am always grateful that I had the chance to fulfil that ambition.

LESSONS LEARNED DURING THOSE YEARS

I loved going back to work. Age has never been an issue for me – I sailed through the big four-oh and life was better than ever as I approached fifty. Working alongside people who couldn't always fulfil their hopes and ambitions gave me the push to do something I'd always wanted to do. I know there were times when I might have thought of giving up, but there was a bit of steel inside me that made me determined to get my diploma in counselling. It was something for me, not for the children or for Harry. And it made me feel so proud when I got the piece of paper that made it official. So, those years taught me a great deal about living life to the full and honouring the potential I had inside myself.

The Third Chapter: 58–81 Years and Beyond

The third chapter in my life, the Retirement Years, has been exciting and challenging. I have learned a great deal and I am still learning and enjoying life beyond the age of the average life expectancy, so my story continues.

1: The Decade of Retirement, 58–68 years

As I was approaching sixty I was happy doing a job I'd always wanted to do. Counselling was hugely rewarding and it felt right. I just knew it was tapping into something that I was good at. It is always more rewarding when you find a niche that's just right for you, and this was it for me. Cara was a very important part of my life and I think in some ways it was my 'other family'. It wasn't just a place of work. People lived there and I became part of their lives as much as they became part of mine. Some of my work colleagues became firm friends and remain so to this day. All of the small things and, on occasion, the big things tend to dominate your thoughts.

I knew it would be a wrench when I said goodbye at retirement. My only advice to people who are facing that challenge is to prepare for it and find ways to stimulate and challenge you outside work. I took the decision to job-share in the final four years at work precisely for that reason. I wanted to ease my way out and into the new phase of my life. I didn't want to be one of those people who hangs up their hat at retirement and drifts off into old age. That wasn't for me. So, while I had some extra time and space, I was enjoying some of the fruits of my labours. Harry and I started to take holidays and travel abroad. The children were older and we were enjoying spending time with them. Norah, Ciaran and Carissa had all moved to London, so we were regular visitors there. I love London and I still try to go at least once a year. We had grandchildren, who were a joy to be with (and hand back!).

I had some fun during those years. I had married young, spent much of my life being a mother, then worked long hours, so it was about time I had a break. We travelled all over Florida with Norah, then drove from Key West round the coast to New Orleans. It was a great adventure. Top of Harry's list was to see the *African Queen*, which was moored in Key Largo in the Florida Keys. It was the boat used in the movie of the same name, which he was a big fan of. It came out in the early 1950s and starred one of his heroes, Humphrey Bogart, alongside Katharine Hepburn. So the highlight of the trip, and what I remember most vividly, was the huge grin on his face when we stepped out of the car and saw the boat in all her glory in an unassuming backwater. He touched the weathered hull in wonderment and it was quite some time before we could lure him away. They were great times.

We didn't get a chance to do those things when the kids were growing up. We hardly ever went out and there wasn't the money for foreign holidays or special treats. When we went to London for the first time, we got a train into the city and hadn't booked anywhere to stay. In those days there was no internet – I don't even think we had mobile phones. So it wasn't that unusual to just turn up looking for a room, and we were certainly not going to be anywhere plush that would require reservations. But the problem was we didn't know anywhere in London. So we bravely hailed a black taxi, and when the driver asked where we wanted to be taken, Harry and I just looked at each other. Eventually, I remembered that there was a street called Oxford Street, so that was what we told him.

So, when I was very close to retirement I was living a pretty full life, but I wanted more. I wanted to continue to work as a counsellor, so I applied to ChildLine to work as a volunteer. ChildLine is now part of the ISPCC, but it was a charity that was started in the 1980s by the BBC's Esther Rantzen, initially to help children who were at risk of abuse; now it extends to all children who need support and help. It was set up in Ireland in 1989 and I wanted to give something back by using my skills to help children who were less fortunate than my own. I did the training and began to work shifts, at first supervised and then as a full-fledged counsellor. It really opened my eyes to the cruelty of the world and how children suffer. Sometimes I felt so hopeless, but there were also moments when I knew I had helped. It was a transformative experience in many ways.

Retirement from paid work was something I looked forward to because I had made those changes earlier in my life. I have always been a healthy, fit person, so walking in the Park is part of my daily routine. I hardly ever take prescription medicines, but I discovered the benefits of green tea and lots of other things that I added to my diet – I suppose you could call it alternative medicine. In any event, I saw the benefits of prevention rather than cure as I grew older. There were women my age and younger in my circle of friends who were trotting off to the doctor every week with one ailment or another. I used to dread asking them how they were as the list of what was wrong with them grew longer.

I went back to porridge for breakfast with lots of seeds and berries to give me a boost. I used to take this concoction (I don't any more) that was a dreadful mix of cider vinegar and black molasses before bedtime as I had read that it helped with arthritis, digestive ailments and gave you a good night's sleep. It worked for me because, as I was approaching my seventies, my doctor kept telling me that I needed my hip replaced sooner rather than later. I managed to live with it for a fair few years on all sorts of different homeopathic remedies, which is an area of natural medicine I have always been interested in. I remain quite strict about what I eat and I avoid processed food at all costs. I hadn't smoked since the babies came along, and my mother lived into her nineties. I'm lucky that I've never been seriously ill. For me it was a conscious decision to be healthy and mentally active.

There was, of course, the niggling anxiety about financial independence when I retired. I was fifty when I took out a pension, so I suppose I did worry about that a bit, but not unduly. The day I retired was a happy day and I enjoyed a farewell party with my work colleagues (which was a bit wild, but we'll say no more here), and I knew I would be seeing lots of them as my life changed for the better.

LESSONS FROM THE RETIREMENT YEARS

For me, retirement had no big psychological impact. I'd had a great ten years learning new things and had prepared for my retirement from paid work. There was no big strategy behind that – just an instinct that it was the right thing to do. I had been cocooned a bit as a mother in a busy home, and felt that those ten years taught me a great deal about life, about the challenges people face and how I could play a part, albeit small, in helping others less fortunate than myself. It was gratifying to do something good and I grew in confidence. In a way, I became an independent woman during those years and did something for myself. I wasn't somebody's mother or somebody's wife. I was myself.

2: Learning to say goodbye, 68–78 years

Something momentous happened when I was sixty-eight years old. Harry and I had enjoyed a couple of years of retirement together and life couldn't have been better. He was coming up to his seventieth birthday and my elder son was hitting forty around the same time. So they hatched a plan to have a 110th birthday party between them. Harry loved a party. The date was set between the two birthdays and it was a fantastic night – great fun, with lots of friends and family. Norah had had Dara a few months previously and couldn't make it to the party, so we went to London to see her the week before and toasted the big day.

It was a few days after the festivities that Harry went to bed and had a massive heart attack in his sleep – on the eve of his seventieth birthday.

That night will stay in my mind for ever. I knew that his breathing had changed and tried to lift him up, but I think even then he was gone. My daughter, Catherine, did resuscitation and mouth-to-mouth, and even when the ambulance took him away I thought there might be a chance, but he didn't regain consciousness. So, on 1 April 1999, I started the journey that many others, including Norah, have travelled – learning to say goodbye to the man who had been my constant companion for the whole of my adult life. It shook us all to the core and we were heartbroken. He was such a huge man – in every way. A big personality. When Harry walked into a room or you spent time in his company, you certainly noticed.

I knew his funeral would be packed, but I discovered that he had had another life – away from his family and many friends. He had worked quietly in the community with the

St Vincent de Paul Society, helping people in all manner of ways. People I didn't know came to shake my hand at the funeral: Harry had helped them at one point or another. We took him through the Park one last time, with outriders accompanying us. As we passed the lodge we stopped the cars and paused for a moment – one final goodbye. He left a big hole when he died. I was in shock – I couldn't believe he was dead. Just like that. No goodbye, no notice. He died in his sleep and I suppose I should be grateful for that, but I wasn't at the time. It was so unfair on him and on me.

When you have grown-up children with families of their own, life quickly settles back to 'normal'. Some women my age relied on their husbands to do things for them, but I was used to paying the bills and managing the house, so at least there was that. But life was very strange for a long time. Learning to live without someone is painful and difficult, and I had my own coping mechanisms. I got used to lots of phone calls and visits from my children, who were now overly anxious that they might lose another parent. But they stopped fussing after a while when they realized I was okay – shaken, but not broken, I suppose. I was lonely and Harry's death made me face my own mortality. I was displaced. Everything is totally different for a while and you don't know from day to day how strong you are going to be when you face the first anniversaries or hear a piece of music or glimpse a man in a crowd and, for a second or two, think it's him. But I had a life still to live and I had to get on with it through the hard days and the easier days.

There were two things that I knew would help me. Some company – and not of the family kind. They will forgive me for saying that because I tell them often that I love them but I don't want them living on top of me – I don't need minding.

I am very independent and I like to make my own friends as myself, outside the family. I decided to take in students as lodgers. I remember the first boy arriving – he was French and his name was Gaucci (I called him Gucci and still do). I bought a French–English dictionary so I could learn some words.

Since then I have had many lodgers and got to know young men and women from all over the world. They have been great company and have kept me young and interested. We had wonderful thought-provoking conversations, and although I was meant to do the cooking I quickly persuaded them to take over. I developed a love for all kinds of new dishes from their home countries. I stay in touch with many of them.

The second thing I knew that would help me was solved by the first. The money I earned from my lodgers went towards special treats and gave me the independence I longed for.

Learning has been one of the great joys of my life, and in the aftermath of Harry's passing, I hadn't thought about it much. I never would have pushed myself if it wasn't for Maeve Binchy: she nudged me in that direction, even though I had never met her – although I did later, when she and Norah became friends. She wrote a book called *Evening Class* the year Harry passed away, and I read it later on that year. It was about a schoolteacher called Nora who had lived in Sicily. When she came back to Ireland she ran an evening course to teach Italian. I loved the warmth and humour of the book, but it also got me thinking about learning a language. That autumn I got the list of courses from the People's College in Parnell Square and signed up to learn Spanish. Spurred on by some of my lodgers over the first few years,

I did French, too, and then Irish. I'd always wanted to speak Irish fluently and it was great going back into a classroom where I rediscovered the joy of hearing it spoken and learning it in a totally different way from my schooldays, when it was drummed into you, which felt like a punishment.

And I didn't stop at languages. I signed up to do practical philosophy with the John Scottus School in Northumberland Road. It was founded in 1986 by a group of parents studying philosophy and it had always intrigued me. It had a totally different approach to education using a philosophical base and a strong belief that all children had unlimited potential. At the time I thought that about myself. There was so much uncharted space beyond the limits of my life to that point. I did four programmes in practical philosophy and it taught me a lot about myself and my life – even though I had lived quite a bit of it by then. It got my brain thinking in all kinds of new ways – the mind has so much power and influence over our lives and it was important to me that I understood it better. If there is a thread running through me, it's the fascination I have with the mind and how it works, from psychiatric nursing, to counselling, philosophy and now mindfulness. It's a great way to clear your mind. It gives me inner peace and respite from the silly things that occupy me sometimes. I am not a slave to it, however, and my weekly session is just about right.

When I was seventy-one I finally succumbed to the hip replacement. I was in Boston visiting my son Leo, who had opened an office there, and I couldn't walk without pain. I had known that when it was limiting my abilities to do the things I enjoy, it was time to go for the operation. I don't know why I didn't do it sooner because I was a model patient and was back walking and living life to the full in no time.

I was pretty determined not to be on crutches or sticks for long, which gave me the drive to get active quickly. For some people that might be a big part of this chapter in my life, but for me it was something I had to get done and I'm glad I did it. It meant that I could get back to walking and driving and doing the things I wanted to do.

More importantly, I did something I'm very proud of. I hate not knowing how to do things. All the way through these years, when the internet was taking off and more and more people were using computers, it bothered me that I couldn't do that. It hadn't been a requirement of my job and I had never learned. Leo persuaded me to do the ECDL – the European Computer Driving Licence. I enrolled at Inchicore College of Further Education. I was in my seventies and became the oldest person then to do the programme. I admit that 'mail merge' nearly undid me – and when would I ever need it anyway? – but the course made me more confident with technology. You have to remember that beforehand I was afraid to turn it on. It was a whole new world and I didn't understand any of it at the time, so this was a big leap into the unknown for me. But I am my father's daughter and it frustrates me if other people know something that I don't. I also knew it was going to be important in connecting with people in the future. It was a great challenge and gave me a new lease of life. What a great invention!

LESSONS LEARNED FROM LIVING
BEYOND THE GOODBYES

This decade – 68–78 – was life-changing for me. At the start of it my husband Harry died suddenly, turning my whole world upside-down. I learned how to live my life in a different way. I rediscovered my love of learning and set myself unbelievable challenges (at least, to me they were). And I succeeded and did things I'd never thought I could do. I solved two problems in one go when I took in foreign students as lodgers, a big step. I was no longer lonely and I had my own financial independence. What I didn't expect was how much fun the students would be and how close I would get to some of them. They brought the world right to my doorstep and encouraged me to try new languages, eat new food and talk about all manner of things. I was interested in life again as I reached seventy-eight.

Conversation is a great way to keep your brain active, and staying close to young people outside your family gets you interested in new things.

3: 78 – the present

So, now you are in the final part of my story, my Mature Years. I am still here, beyond the years that people, on average, live. So that's good. I still don't think too much about ageing, but I will admit that I had started to, especially when I hit eighty. It took a conscious effort to intervene and call time on that line of thinking.

I hated reaching eighty. There was something okay about saying I was seventy-something, but as soon as I said 'eighty', people would say patronizing things, like 'Aren't you marvellous for your age?' For the first time in my life I started to hide my age. Not because it bothered me, but because of the effect it had on the people around me. I wasn't suddenly more frail or vulnerable, I hadn't lost my faculties and I wasn't a freak of nature. I was a healthy, active woman of eighty, who still enjoyed living. But, worse, I was beginning to think like an old person and that bothered me. I would find myself wondering what would be the use in getting a new car – I'd never get the years out of it. And I wasn't decorating the house because I mightn't be around long enough to get the benefit of the ten-year warranty on the new floor.

I stopped all that thinking and went in the opposite direction. I bought a new car last year and I just love it. I don't care how much use I get out of it because I love driving it now. The house is decorated – new blinds, new furnishings and walls painted. It looks great. I had moved on from the big slow computer to a laptop a few years ago, but I got an iPad last Christmas and it has revolutionized my life. I love Facebook and talk to my grandchildren and friends on FaceTime or Skype. I order my shopping on the internet and do online banking. I don't like to tweet, but I like to read Norah's tweets (a little insider knowledge!).

When I was eighty I went on an incredible journey and there have been many since. We all have bucket-lists and I have always had mine, although I didn't get to do most of the things on it until I retired. So, by the time I reached eighty I had stayed on a remote island in the Caribbean with giant land iguanas, I had travelled all over Italy, France and Spain and spent weekends in many great cities across Europe. I love going to New York and I have a grandson there to visit, and I have been to Canada twice to see my granddaughter. But I never thought I would go to the Far East. Richard, Norah and Dara had taken four months off to travel around Asia and Australia, and they suggested that I join them for the final weeks. Of course I said yes (even though I had to endure many mentions of how great I was at eighty going to the Far East!). I flew to Hong Kong and met them there. We travelled to Burma, which was incredible, stayed in a few

different parts of Thailand and then spent a week in Cambodia. The people, the vibrancy, the architecture – it was just
incredible. I suppose I'm blasé about friends who are surprised that I was still travelling to such an extent at eighty, but
I surprised myself a bit, too, to be honest.

I think I enjoyed it more because another painful period in
my life followed soon afterwards. When you go through your
older years, you get used to saying goodbye. Two of my sisters had passed away and all of Harry's family were gone.
You find yourself at more and more funerals, and you have
to try hard not to allow that to overwhelm you. But there is a
natural order to death, which makes it easier to accept if
someone has had a long life. But what shouldn't happen did
happen: my eldest daughter, Betty, died after a long illness,
leaving her four beautiful children and all of us devastated.
It's not natural to say goodbye to your own child. I try to be
with her children as much as possible and we all look out for
them, but I think of her often. Months after we said goodbye to Betty, Norah's husband, Richard, was diagnosed with
cancer. He was like a son to me. I had spent so much time
with Norah and him and we were all devastated by the news
of his illness. We felt like the unluckiest family in Ireland.
When Richard died a short time later, we found ourselves yet
again reeling from the shock. I know Norah often says
she learned how to live with that pain and loss by watching
me go through it when Harry died. Sometimes there are
things we learn from our mothers that we wish we didn't
have to.

Life continues for her and for me, and we owe it to those
close to us, who went before their time, to leave an impression and do our best with the time we have left.

LESSONS LEARNED FROM THE MATURE YEARS

So, what is my secret? I'm not sure there is one, but I do things that I know help to keep me active, healthy, and interested in pushing myself forwards. First, I am a great walker. I always have been. So, I walk for forty minutes every day. Some days I might need five minutes' rest halfway and that's all right too. I try to eat healthily. If my cholesterol goes up, I see it as a personal challenge to get it down through diet. I don't take pills unless I have to but I do take vitamins and supplements to help ensure I get sufficient nutrients. I love fish and I don't eat much red meat. I avoid processed foods and I still start every day with a bowl of porridge and maybe some blueberries or sunflower seeds.

I'm an avid reader and when I'm feeling lazy I let the iPad do the work: I listen to audio books. I try to limit the time I spend watching television, but as soon as I heard about Netflix and everyone talking about *Breaking Bad*, I had to get Apple TV installed, so I do some binge-watching on occasion – especially when the new season of *House of Cards* was released: I think I watched it all in one night.

I go out every day, maybe into town, usually by bus, to do some shopping or meet up with friends or family for coffee, lunch or dinner. I do Pilates and mindfulness yoga every week. At the moment I am dieting because I want to be a size smaller for my granddaughter Shauna's wedding, so I am doing a bit more than my usual exercise.

And I'm not done yet: there is lots more living to do and I still want to go to Argentina.

5. Are You Done Yet?: The Act of Auditing and Accounting

A question that resonated with me as I was going through my own search for a new future was 'Are you done yet?' Over and over again I asked it of myself in the hope that some blinding flash of the obvious would provide me with the answer. To be honest, I wasn't sure if I was or not. Done yet, that is. I felt instinctively that there was more to do, but I didn't know whether I should do more of the same or start again and face some as yet unknown challenge. What helped me reach a conclusion was spending time going back over my life and thinking through the various events that had led me to where I was at that time. In this chapter, I want to help you to do the same. A sort of audit and account on how well you've done up to now, and a reminder of some of the aspirations that were important to you at various stages as you grew up and older. Along the way it helps if you can see, from the benefit of time passing, why you took various decisions, especially the big ones that shaped your life.

There is no need for a pen and paper: this exercise is all about brain-time and allowing the memories to come naturally to you, rather than making a list in chronological order. Once you start, you will find that the important things rise to the surface and your mind will prioritize the critical from the not-so-critical issues. So, I don't want you to use notebooks, pens, smartphones or any other device: just sit down somewhere quiet, where you won't be interrupted, and think. How often do any of us allow ourselves the time to do that? But this is exactly what the audit and account in this chapter is about: thinking. I want you to take stock of where you are in your life and assess how well you have done in terms of what you wanted to do. The key here is to step back from the everyday pressures and tasks that distract you from seeing the bigger picture of your life, your as yet unfulfilled hopes and dreams, and to focus on them.

Why perform an audit and account?

I want to begin by acknowledging that there are exceptions to my belief that many of us begin to drift as we go through life. I'm not on a one-woman mission to fire up all those around me to be brilliant. But a year ago, when I was desperate to reignite my own life, I would have been eternally grateful to anyone who could have helped me find the way. I accept that some people are happy to drift into middle age without changing course, content to spend their subsequent years engaged in the everyday comings and goings of life. But I would like that to be a conscious choice, rather than a state of being that developed while you weren't paying attention. If you are still reading this, then I am guessing that, like me, when you are on your deathbed, hopefully many years from now, you will want to look back on the second half of your life and feel you acquitted yourself well, using the abilities and advantages that you had in life. I'm guessing that you've asked yourself: 'Am I done yet?' And that you've answered: 'No!'

Hindsight is all well and good, but it's no use here

There is a well-known syndrome among people who recall things from the past. It's called 'hindsight bias'. Another way to describe it would be: 'I knew all along that was going to happen'. Perhaps more than a few economists suffered from a dose of hindsight bias in the aftermath of the recession. I'm starting with it upfront because sometimes when we travel back in time to our younger selves, we're tempted to believe that events were planned or determined. There is only one person who knows the truth of those recollections, and that's you. No one else needs to know why things turned out the way they did other than yourself – this is a very private audit. Honesty might prove difficult, but you will learn far more from an honest autobiographical reflection than one that sounds better – even if it's only to your own ears. I can't emphasize this enough: in the privacy of your own mind, be perfectly candid and honest about why you chose to do what you have done. You never have to admit it to another living soul, but it's essential that you admit the unadorned truth.

A bit of background

This audit and account section is based on the many years I have spent giving talks to diverse groups of people, largely on the theme of personal satisfaction. I use this approach to encourage people to take a meaningful look at their lives. I haven't met anyone yet who has said they feel they have done all they set out to achieve.

The first time I used this approach was with a group of directors and CEOs in London, and it was eye-opening. It very quickly emerged that while they were all satisfied with their professional achievements, they were dissatisfied with their personal lives – it seemed as if one came at the expense of the other.

I remember one man in particular – let's call him Gary – because he became quite emotional about the loss of his dream to learn how to sail. He'd forgotten about it and got distracted when the kids came along and work pressures mounted. He was cross with himself because, instead of pursuing a passion, he had learned to play golf. Not because he wanted to, but because he was expected to. I think a quiet revolution was forming in his mind about the following weekend four-ball with the management team. I like to imagine him in the future, sailing solo in a beautiful bay, zig-zagging into the wind.

The lesson, though, and what surprised me about Gary and some of the others in the room was how angry they were with themselves and also how surprised they were that they had got to the age they were without having given a thought to the goals that were important to them. That was a moment of revelation for me: I realized that living can get in the way of vital living, and that it is crucial to be aware of it and watch out for it happening in your own life.

The other fascinating insight I have gained from performing audit and account in groups is the difference between men's and women's approach in terms of what they tick as 'done well' as opposed to 'not done at all'. For instance, women are generally far more accepting of derailment in their lives and the things they haven't achieved. I did one session with a mixed group, where the women were career-oriented, mainly late thirties and early forties, and all but one had children. The phrase 'you can't have it all' resonated strongly with them: there was a kind of shoulder-shrugging attitude to the things they hadn't got around to. Real women aren't super-women and this group, like many I've worked with since, had a quiet acceptance of life's ability to push you off-course.

The women were notably easier on themselves than the men, who were pretty uncompromising in their self-assessments. Almost all of them had regrets about not having spent enough time with their children. One man was on a second marriage and a second set of children and was determined to get it, as he said, 'right this time round'. With these men, and I have seen the same since, there was an unspoken 'Dammit, how did I let that happen?' They had got caught up with corporate ambitions and the heavy demands of being the main or sole breadwinner, and remained singularly focused on the next step or stage on the business ladder. It was the sort of 'tunnel vision' women often tease men over. In fact, one man said he didn't know why he wanted to get to the top of that particular ladder, admitting that he had never thought about whether it was right for him. He just got on, day by day, doing it.

When you undertake this sort of self-analysis, you are going to come face-to-face with your failures, which can be uncomfortable. We can spin business failures into helpful and necessary steps on the road to success, but it's harder to do that with personal failures – they usually cut deeper. Nevertheless, I'm going to invoke honesty and courage again because you'll need them to work through this process – just as all those participants in my sessions did. Perhaps this is why women forgive themselves more easily and don't dwell too long on what they haven't done: for the most part, their 'failings' are professional, often caused by circumstance, such as starting a family. It makes them more able to identify and own those 'failings', then articulate what they still want to achieve more clearly and more quickly than the men.

The men's regrets centred largely around personal issues, which made it more difficult to voice them – it was like an admission of neglect, or guilt. My advice to them was the same as I am giving to you now: look at the past candidly, but don't judge or castigate yourself for 'failures'. Remember, you're looking at what cannot be changed, so don't waste energy on what-ifs.

One final interesting thing to note from my self-analysis sessions is the difference in how people in each of the three chapters of life responded. I spend a great deal of time with teenagers – particularly transition-year students who want to develop entrepreneurial programmes. Young people invariably have great self-belief – that's what's so wonderful about spending time with them. They're setting out on a journey and they don't imagine for a moment that they won't get what they want from life. Sometimes I am the first person to ask them how they feel they're doing on the gameplan so far. And that's because they often don't have one. There are a few lucky ones who know from an early age that they want to be a doctor or a lawyer or play sport or sing in a band – but most sixteen-year-olds I've talked to were still confused and uncertain as to what they wanted to do. The conversation becomes much easier if you ask them what they want to do over the course of their lifetime. Then the big ambitions and dreams are revealed. In these sessions, I am always conscious to make it less about what they haven't achieved and much more about the great potential of the future.

A key milestone in life is reaching forty. As I ask groups how they feel about that birthday, the fear is naturally heightened for those who are facing it rather than those who have experienced it. There is a phrase that resonates with the over-forty responders: 'It wasn't as bad as I thought.' And, again, there are differences between women and men in how they perceive it. We are surrounded by clichés and assumptions about reaching what we believe is the halfway mark in our lives. 'Life begins at forty' sounds hollow to those who are dealing with all of the psychological, and sometimes physical, changes that are happening around that time. Busy people of both sexes tend to sail through it without consciously dwelling on any bigger meaning – other than it being another birthday.

Women in the various groups I have led tend to be more vocal about their anxieties. Sometimes they were linked to the combined pressure of work and home life, and sometimes it was the opposite – the perception of lost years spent looking after children who are now on their way to adulthood. Either way, those women expressed feelings of frustration about not having done enough with the years before their fortieth birthday, and spoke of their dread at being perceived as 'over the hill'. They also worried about lost looks, the impact of the menopause (and when it is likely to start), health – particularly weight gain – and a diminished career progression (with promotion going to younger candidates).

Interestingly, there was always a stark difference in those who had faced separation and divorce. The women who had been through a marriage break-up (particularly where their husband had found a new and sometimes younger love interest) were more likely to express anxiety about their physical appearance and self-worth. Some (not many) talked honestly about their disappointment at not having had children or not finding the right partner in life, with one woman speaking about that loss as almost like a bereavement.

Another key difference with women was that many had been proactive in staving off the ageing process. This ranged from investment in expensive anti-ageing creams to cosmetic enhancements and Botox, and some who hadn't were more than interested in learning from those who had. Others talked about particular diets and exercise regimes they followed or vitamins they took to enhance their nutritional status and improve their energy levels.

The men were less forthcoming about their feelings on reaching forty, especially in a mixed audience – either a mix of women and men, or of age groups. They were comfortable talking about health issues, physical exercise and their worries about work-related stress and health concerns. Some had been through divorce, had remarried and now had young children, which they described as both exhausting and wonderful. The all-male groups tended to joke with each other during these sessions, ribbing one another about new cars and changes to clothing/style. My perception was that always a lot was left unsaid and that the men tended to be more introspective about their thoughts on reaching forty. That said, there are always variations among people of all ages and both sexes, depending on background, career, personal circumstances and, above all else, how well they feel their life has gone up to that point. For some people, forty is not the major milestone in their lives – my own mother told me thirty was the worst birthday ever because she had four young children and thought she would never get beyond the piles of nappies and endless sleepless nights. For you, it could well be that your fiftieth year is the big event of your life, or maybe all those birthdays just pass without any big impact.

Out of the self-analysis sessions I have conducted and my own ongoing self-analysis, I have one key piece of advice I'd like to share. Whatever you choose to do in life, do it for yourself. I have learned that doing things for other people, even if they are the people you love most in the world, is never as powerful as doing it for yourself first and foremost. If you don't do it for you, then anything that happens to the precious people in your life will derail you. Although it may appear self-centred to think about yourself, it is the one true motivator in our lives – look inside yourself and work out what you want, rather than second-guessing what the people around you want and doing that. Do what you want to do.

Auditing and Accounting

How to start: an overview of you

Begin this process of recollection by thinking about all the elements that constitute you.

We all set out on our journey through life with parts of us that we inherited and parts that developed along the way. Set aside the nature versus nurture debate for now, because all that is important here is to try to identify something innate to you.

INHERENT TRAITS

First, it's worth considering which traits you believe are inherent and try to determine where they came from. If you believe that a particular attribute is genetic, then try to identify which parent or other relative you acquired it from. Often, it is only in later life that we see traits in ourselves that we recognize in one parent or the other. My drive comes from my father's side and my resilience from my mother. But I don't know whether that is to do with my DNA or the fact that I grew up under their guidance.

It could be that there is a stubborn streak in you, or an aptitude for a particular sport or pursuit that 'runs in the family'. There will be good and bad traits, but try simply to acknowledge them and trace them back. It's important to distinguish between traits you developed along the way as opposed to those you believe you inherited. It's not an exact science – sometimes we become great at something because our parents influenced us to concentrate on that area, for example. This part of your self-audit should help you to identify all the traits, good and bad, that you believe are intrinsic to you as a person.

LEARNED TRAITS

These are different from the traits you believe you inherited or that are familial. Learned traits are developed as you grow, for positive or negative reasons. I recently interviewed a man who had lost six stone in weight and asked him what he was like at school. I knew what he was going to say before he said it: he told me he had been the class clown. He had learned how to make people laugh to deflect hurtful comments from his classmates. He developed a 'big' personality and was popular because he was funny and entertaining. He has now lost weight, but that trait – the ability to make people laugh and command an audience – is still there, ingrained in him from his childhood experiences.

Other people develop their love of learning from a favourite teacher, or their passion for reading as a means to escape into another world. Learned behaviours almost always have a root cause so it's worth delving deeper to see what led you to develop those characteristics.

BEST AND WORST?

This is the part of the interview we all dread: 'What would you say are your best and worst qualities, Ms Casey?' As if by rote, I learned to say my best quality was working well in a team and my worst was intolerance of poor performance – thereby ensuring top marks from the interviewer. We all become adept at masking our weaker side with a more acceptable characteristic. But now you have spent some time thinking about all the qualities and characteristics that make you who you are, the next step is to rate them and consider the relative weight of one over another. A typical profile at this stage might look like the one that follows, and I offer it by way of reassurance that yours is bound to be a bit disjointed: we're complicated people. This is a real-life account from Angela (not her real name: she agreed to be recorded on the basis of anonymity), an administration assistant from Manchester with whom I conducted a one-to-one session. She's fairly typical in terms of how traits and characteristics are not easily assigned to particular sources or events. But you can see that she knows herself quite well – good and bad.

Angela's audit

What I know about myself now is that I am a forty-one-year-old woman with black hair and blue eyes, and although I am not pretty, I am not bad-looking either. I have a tendency to put on weight (from my mother) and my legs are too short for my body (from my father). I like my nose (father again) and my best feature is my lips (my own – can't figure out where they came from). It's in my nature to be happy and positive in life. I know I can drive people mad with my incessant optimism, but that's just who I am – I like to see the upside. I also know that I have a tendency to ignore bad things and I usually stick my head in the sand when things go wrong. I think I got that from growing up in a big family – I hid in case I got the blame in rows with my sisters and brothers. I am also a good negotiator because I am a middle child and I got used to proposing compromises between my two brothers.

I love fashion and my favourite activity is shopping – I learned that all by myself. Okay, maybe I was influenced by my mother and sisters, who were so competitive. I think I'm good at singing, too – I like karaoke and people say I have a nice voice. Not sure either of my parents was any good at singing, but I have a brother who sang in a band when he was younger.

I have a bad temper. I know that about myself and it's painful to admit it, but I fly off the handle sometimes and turn into a fishwife behind closed doors. It takes a lot to rile me, but when I flip, I do it big-time. It's my least attractive quality, and if I had one wish, I would get rid of that.

I'm a hard worker because I was raised to understand the value of money and the importance of earning your living. I'm not that career-minded, but I am reliable and you can trust me with a job to do. Dependable, I suppose. And I always turn up on time – it drives me mad when people are late.

I'm not religious – my parents weren't, and as I got older, I stopped going to church or praying. I don't believe in any of that stuff anyway – when we die, we die.

I'm tough on the kids – sort of stricter than I should be maybe. My dad was strict but my mum was a softie, so I'm not sure why I picked up the habit of laying down the law. I suspect it's because my husband would let them away with murder if he could, so I have to be the disciplinarian.

I don't make new friends easily. I was quite shy as a child and it took me a while to open up. I still find it hard to engage in idle chit-chat with strangers. I have one or two

close friends that I value a great deal and I don't need anyone else.

I am not the jealous kind. I feel comfortable being me and
I don't worry about my husband straying . . . but if he ever
did, that would be the end of that for me. I don't understand
women who stand by their men when they're unfaithful. I'm
quite black and white about that sort of thing.

Doing this session got me thinking about the things I
would like to be. I wish I was more generous – compassionate
may be a better word. In my house you had to fend for yourself: we didn't have much and my mother always said charity
begins at home. It stuck with me, and often when I pass a
homeless person in the street, instead of feeling sorry for
them I find myself ranting about why they don't go out and
get a job and work hard like the rest of us. I know that's not
a good way to be and I try to stop myself thinking too much
about why they are on the streets. I guess it's another bad
thing I don't like to think about.

Loyalty – that's really important to me. Growing up, you
always stood up for your sisters and brothers outside the
house, even when they were in the wrong. I would be a very
loyal friend – I don't like gossip and if anyone tries to
bad-mouth someone I know, I tell them to their face that I
am not prepared to listen to them.

Honesty? Yes, I'm honest – at least, I never stole anything
from anyone and I do try to tell the truth. If I lie, it's only a
white lie and usually to the kids to make them do something
they don't want to do. But when I think about it, maybe
sometimes I can be a bit too honest. I once saw a film about
a man who saw the wife of his best friend out to dinner with
another man – they were clearly having an affair. His
dilemma was whether to tell his friend or not. I wouldn't

have to think twice – I think you should always be honest and tell people the truth. In small ways, I can sometimes blurt out my opinion when a softer approach might have been better, but most people who know me know that's just the way I am. So that's me in a nutshell.

After this initial session, Angela and I got down to putting her traits into some kind of order, depending on whether they were dominant or presented themselves on occasion. A good way to identify the qualities that you believe aren't your best is to imagine throwing out the ones you don't want and keeping no more than three that you like in yourself. You soon see which you cherish and which you wish you had less of. Angela chose to keep her loyalty, reliability and positive attitude. She threw out her lack of compassion, honesty and, believe it or not, her work ethic (she said it was overrated!).

At the end of the initial phase of your audit, you should have some sense of the characteristics, behaviours and traits that combine to make you the person you are. Don't worry if it's still a work-in-progress because, as you continue, other aspects will come to the fore.

YOUR PERSONAL AUDIT AND ACCOUNT

I've told you about my own journey up to and through the analysis of my life, past, present and future, and now it's your turn. This only requires the will to be honest and reflect deeply on your life and choices. Think about what has made you who you are: how much comes from your family, how much from your own experiences? Think about the consecutive life choices you have made – did they make you happy? If not, why not? Think about your personality and what you feel most happy doing. Think about your future and how you would like it to be. Think about where you are now – what do you like and dislike about your current life?

I will use prompts and questions at each chapter of your life to encourage you to think about all the various aspects of that period. Don't worry if you find yourself going back and forward through the years: the same thing happened to me. Don't be overly concerned about exactly when things happened and what happened before that. That's really not important to this exercise. If some experiences stand out more clearly than others, follow your mind down that path until you feel ready to let it go. The intention is to prompt you to think more deeply about your progress through the three chapters of your life: 12–38 years; 38–58 years; and 58 years onwards. By the time you reach the end (stop at whatever age you are now), you should have a fuller understanding of your own life story and, importantly, the chapter you have yet to write.

The First Chapter: 12–38 Years

1: Growing Up, 12–23 years

WHEN YOU WERE GROWING UP, WHO OR WHAT DID YOU DREAM OF BECOMING?

You're not looking for the stock answer that we all gave to teachers, aunts and uncles. What did you really want from your young self? Whatever it was, no matter how ridiculous it sounds now, there was a purity in that aspiration that is deep-seated in your psyche. If you are lucky, the answer will come to you quickly without too much soul-searching. For those with fuzzier memories, you might need to have a conversation with parents or siblings to see if they can jolt your memory. What does the answer tell you about yourself?

I wanted to be a vet, which points to the softer side of my nature – the desire to help and make a difference. I never did achieve that goal, but my work now involves a huge amount of helping and making a difference; even though I went away from my original idea, I can see that I brought some of its essence with me. That might be the case for you, too – you aren't the thing you said you would be, but you might be a version of it. The question is: is that enough for you?

WHAT HAPPENED WITH THAT DREAM? DID YOU FULFIL IT OR DID YOUR AMBITIONS GET DERAILED?

Some people end up doing exactly what they aspired to do. They grow up wanting to be a doctor or a car mechanic or a dancer and that is exactly what they become. But for many others, those childhood dreams are not fulfilled and it is worth considering what went wrong.

It could be that your parents didn't want you to fulfil those dreams, or maybe you didn't achieve high enough grades to study a particular course. It might be that although you thought you would love to be a chef, you discovered during work experience or while studying at college that it wasn't for you. You may conclude that you simply forgot that was what you wanted to be. Teenage years have a way of derailing the best-laid plans. Maybe an event in your life took you down a different path.

The key question here is: how does it make you feel, knowing you didn't follow that dream? Are you glad that life took a different turn and you ended up where you are now? Are you surprised to remember what that original dream was? Or have you spent all your life since resentful that you never got the opportunity to follow your heart?

WHAT HAPPENED WHEN YOU LEFT SCHOOL?

First, have a think about what you were like at school. Can you remember what was written in the Comments section of the school report? Were you studious and attentive, or did you avoid homework and wing it when it came to exams? I interviewed two politicians recently and they told me they were both prefects at school – it didn't surprise me somehow. So what about you? Were you head boy or head girl material, or were you content to be one of the crowd? Did you have a teacher who inspired you or one who dented your confidence by predicting a bleak future for you? And what of those final exams – Leaving Cert or A levels? Did they make you feel stressed? Were you well prepared? Did you do better in some subjects than others? When you reflect on your time at school, how would you describe it – happy, miserable, mediocre, fun, stressful?

FURTHER STUDY OR WORK?

What happened next? Did you go out to work? Did you go to college/university? Did you learn a trade? Maybe you couldn't get a job or a place on the course you wanted. Did you go abroad to study or find work? If that was the case, did you feel forced to do so or was it a positive option for you? Did you take some time out to travel? If you did, were you happy you made that decision – was it a good experience? If you didn't take time out, do you regret not doing so?

If you went on to further study, think about whether it was a conscious choice after considering your options.

Sometimes we go on to study what we always wanted to learn more about, either because the subject interests us or because of our desire to join a profession or follow a particular career. For some people, however, the decision to work or study for a degree or other qualification is less considered. They go out to work because they have to, or maybe because they don't want to study any more. Often young people choose to do a course that their friends are doing or study at a college that is close to home – or, equally, choose one that's far away from home. For some the decision about what happens when they leave school is not up to them – it has already been decided for them by their parents. Whatever the case for you, spend some time thinking about why you ended up doing what you did: were you happy with that decision? Was it a good experience for you? This was an important stage in your learning years, and your perceptions and memories from that time are bound to be a bit hazy, so it's worth spending some time travelling back to that young man or woman and what life was like at the time. It could well be that, because of a decision you made then, you ended up doing what you do now, or perhaps not doing what you thought you might be doing now.

2: The Decade of Indulgence, 23–33 years

WHY DID YOU END UP DOING WHAT YOU DID
IN YOUR TWENTIES AND EARLY THIRTIES?

The Decade of Indulgence takes us from the end of study to the start of settling down. For most people, that's between about twenty-three and thirty-three years of age. During those ten years, generally speaking, it's all about you. There are no big commitments, you spend money and time on things you enjoy, and you have the freedom to move around and try out new things. It's during these years that you might choose to take time out to travel, you might dabble in a few different jobs without thinking too hard about career aspirations, or you might go straight into your chosen career path and start making a name for yourself.

This decade is the foundation for the next chapter of your life, so it's important to work out what was great about it and what was not so great: the freedom to do what you wanted versus the lack of money to achieve your ambitions, for example. It could be that jobs weren't available in the economy or in your area of expertise. Going abroad for experience or travel may not have been a positive experience. You might have lost that decade either because you chose to follow a career that was demanding and time-consuming or because you chose to settle quickly with a partner and/or had parental responsibilities.

Your analysis might include multiple factors, but look hard at your progress and the highs and lows of the period. It could well be that something that happened to you then shaped your future, so part of the process of taking stock of where you are now is identifying those elements, positive and negative. You can tell a lot about a person's level of satisfaction with that chapter by how they are living their next chapters. For example, I've met people in their thirties who are still attempting to claw back some of the fun they feel they missed out on in those years. This can be dangerous if you don't recognize and understand that behaviour in yourself. I have seen marriages wrecked and families deeply affected by it – when a woman or man decides they never had the indulgences others enjoyed and suddenly starts behaving like a teenager, flinging themselves into nightclubs and extra-marital affairs, forgetting their priorities and hurting those they love most. This is common enough behaviour, but it stems from lack of self-awareness. If you missed out in any way, then figure out how you feel and think about it and take good steps to get back what you need. Pinpoint the areas of dissatisfaction and do something positive about them.

3: Settling Down, 33–38 years

Now let's move to the commitment phase of your life, when you chose to commit to something – career, mortgage, partner, parenting (or maybe all four).

Sometimes we consider this phase very carefully. We meet someone, fall in love, and weigh up the best time for formalizing a partnership, whether through marriage or cohabiting. But it may also be the case that it happened without much thought. For lots of people the commitment phase is about settling on a career path or taking the plunge to enter the property market. It may be a tough or easy decision, but take time to assess what the key motivators were for you and how you entered that important part of your life.

It may be that you feel you have never experienced the commitment phase. I have some good friends who never married or had a serious relationship, who didn't enter the property market and who, although well into their forties, feel they are still deciding what they want to do with their life. There are exceptions at every stage of this review of your life, so don't worry if you don't fit the pattern or if things happened at a different time for you or not at all. The only issue to be concerned about is the recollection and review of yourself at that time.

ANALYSIS OF THE FIRST CHAPTER

After all that, you should now have a very good sense of your raw ambitions and dreams from childhood, and you should be able to see clearly the path you followed, or lurched along, from when you were a teenager to your early thirties. If dissatisfaction is buried in your past choices, you are now aware of it. So, do you need to make changes now to make yourself happier? Is there an ambition still burning away that you want to pursue? Identify and work out the steps that would be required to achieve it. Are you living a life that is true to your own personality or not? Again, answer honestly and work out what steps you need to take to get back to that true state. You have a lot of information about yourself now, so take it with you into the next chapter as you continue to tease out the complexities of your life.

The Second Chapter: 38–58 Years

1: The Settled Years, 38–42 years

For most of us, it is often during these years that we lose focus in our lives, albeit sometimes for all the right reasons. We become a parent, perhaps – a magical phase for most people. When you are auditing yourself, you are the only person who knows how you feel about certain milestones in any chapter. You might have wanted children and never had the chance to fulfil that desire, either because of difficulty in conceiving or because there was no significant other with whom you wanted to have a child. Or it could be that you decided having children wasn't important to you. You might have chosen not to have a child at that time and allowed other priorities to take precedence: your career, perhaps, or further studies, or just enjoying the freedom to do what you wanted when you wanted. It's also during these years that gainful employment becomes more important, as does the ability to earn a wage and to be in a position that will increase your earning potential. The commitments you've chosen to undertake – mortgage, partnership and/or family – often dictate that work assumes a new and ongoing importance.

When you look at your life during this chapter, think about all of those issues that you expected to happen – having children or not, the upward swing in your career path and the financial and personal commitments you took on. How well do you feel you did? Also, look at the sacrifices you've had to make. Did you give up work to look after the growing family or go part-time? Maybe you continued working and had to face the dual demands of home and work life. Perhaps you became the main breadwinner and didn't get as much time at home with the family as you would have liked. Did you miss out on holidays, special occasions, quality time and sports activities in order to work through this chapter?

Whatever the truth, consider it, analyse it and consciously weigh up what was good and bad about this period in your life – whether it's in the past or you're still working through it.

2: The Middle Years, 42–52 years

You hit the milestone of forty and begin a new phase in life. While some people sail through that significant birthday, many find it difficult – all of the negativity associated with growing old is magnified, and for many it is also when they come to terms with some painful issues. It could be that reaching forty is a reminder that you didn't or couldn't fulfil an ambition and now you feel it's too late. Whether you embrace it or fear it, turning forty and entering your forties is a chapter to be reckoned with.

The decade that begins at forty can be difficult because you are learning to say goodbye to loved ones – grandparents, parents or relatives, sometimes friends. The family home becomes less full as children move into their own circle of friends, activities, or leave to go to college. It can be a challenging time, often with hormonal changes (for both men and women) and psychological difficulties relating to ageing thrown in for good measure.

If you are going through those years currently or have passed them, spend some time thinking about the adversity you have faced. Try to divide the emotions you had about this chapter in order to define which ones relate to the perception of ageing and time passing, and which to the grief of parting with loved ones. Analyse the disappointments you might have felt around missed opportunities. There will inevitably be things you couldn't do anything about – like being unable to have children or not finding the right partner. Perhaps your marriage or partnership didn't work out and you went through separation or divorce.

Remember the good times, too – perhaps you did well in your career, or undertook some further study. Maybe you travelled somewhere you always wanted to go or became a grandparent. You might also think about the achievements of your children, if you have a family – or maybe the disappointment that they didn't do well. This chapter might also be called the Decade of Earning because at this stage you may well have reached a point in your career where you are/ were beginning to enjoy the fruits of your labour. Did your earning potential improve, and how did you feel as you approached the milestone birthday of fifty?

Ask yourself: during this chapter, did you branch out within your career, diversify and try new things? If so, why, and where did it lead you? If not, why not? Do you feel that has had an adverse impact on your career or earning potential? When was the last time you went beyond your comfort zone and tried a new challenge, something that made you feel exhilarated and fearful in equal measure? Did you/are you continuing to take care of your health in this chapter? Did things slide or are they sliding a bit out of your control, leaving you feeling less like yourself and casting about for things to make you feel better? In essence, do/did you feel in control of your life in this decade, or would you categorize it as a time of drifting away from yourself?

3: The Empty Nest Years, 52–58 years

For many people, the fifties are quieter years. The children may have left home, or it may be that you choose to spend your time doing quieter things – like reading or going to the movies or theatre. I spent some time talking to my mother about these years and for her they were the opposite to quiet. She went back to work in her late forties and was busy studying for her diploma in counselling while working full-time. It may well be that during this period you are/were busier than you have ever been, perhaps with different things. Spend some time reflecting on what life is or was like. Do/did you stay in touch with close friends or meet new ones? Has/had the daily pattern of life changed – either because you have/had more time to pursue the things you want/wanted to do, or perhaps you have/had extra responsibilities caring for a parent? Have/had you taken up any new hobbies or adjusted your routines in any way? Most of us aren't lucky enough to get through life without ailments, so perhaps around this time illness has/had dominated your life?

Although I have described this chapter of life as essentially dropping down a gear, I'm sure you know by now that my own theory is that it should be the opposite. Nonetheless, I have talked to many people in their fifties who have described life as a bit lower key and the kind of activities they enjoy as more sedentary. However, you could well be the kind of person, like my mother, who bucked the trend. The key question is: if you didn't, is that because you consciously shaped your life as you wished it to be by dropping down a gear? Or is it that you would like to buck the trend, but aren't sure if you can, or if you're allowed to? Perhaps there are family commitments that feel like obstacles to the life you'd like to lead. Or do you focus on ageing from a negative perspective and deny yourself the right to try new things and start afresh? If you are dropping down a gear, be absolutely certain it's a conscious decision and what you want. If it's happening and it's not what you want, admit that to yourself and start looking for ways to make the changes you need and want in your life.

The decade of your fifties is an important period of adjustment, and how you deal with the transition from active employment towards future retirement may dictate what happens next.

ANALYSIS OF THE SECOND CHAPTER

You have now thought back over the watershed years of your forties. These are years when we usually have a lot of expectations of ourselves, and also have many expectations foisted upon us. The commitments we choose come to define us, but they can also have a stranglehold on us that may cause problems. Privately, and honestly, assess your commitments, your feelings about them and where they have brought you in your life. If there are regrets, take them out into the light of day and have a good look at them. You will usually find there is something you can do about them – however tangential the action may seem. Knowledge, as they say, is power, so once you know your own mind with regard to these seminal years, you can use that knowledge to plan your next chapter – either opting for more of the same because you enjoy it, or committing to change the things that are extinguishing your spark.

That really is one of the key things to take from this audit and account: the ability and will to plan for the next chapter. Instead of walking backwards towards your later years because you don't want to see them coming, train yourself to turn around and not only face them head-on but anticipate them with plans, ambitions and new life goals.

The Third Chapter: 58–81 Years and Beyond

1: The Decade of Retirement, 58–68 years

So, you are now into the retirement years. I'm not there yet, so this is where I depart from personal experience, but in my work and in researching this book I have talked to many people who are living this chapter, and I have found their insights most helpful and encouraging.

For most people, this decade is one of significant change and adjustment. If you have been in active employment, you are probably beginning to see this milestone as a turning-point in your life. You may be looking forward to the end of the daily grind of getting up early and dealing with all of the ups and downs of the workplace. You may also be dreading it – the prospect of endless days looming ahead without purpose. If you have been a homemaker, the retirement of a partner or spouse will also signal some significant changes to your routine. Think about all of the emotions raised by these prospects – positive and negative. You may have received some good advice from people close to you, or maybe you have already given significant thought to your retirement years. What were your main concerns – financial, health, filling your time?

I spoke to a group of retired men recently – all well into their seventies – and they talked about the waiting as being the worst part of retirement. Work colleagues constantly reminded them that the 'big day' was coming – mostly in a jocular manner, but it grated on them. One or two said they were afraid of all that time yawning ahead, and the lack of purpose. Ironically, they were active members of a bowling club and all had other interests, but retirement had been a difficult transition.

For you, this might be a time of your life when lots of different emotions compete, with different pressures from family, work and yourself, with your own feelings about life and the passing of time. As always, there are exceptions to what happens during this chapter – self-employed people and members of some professions may continue to work so some of the emotions I am describing won't resonate. But the emotions relating to the passing of time probably will, if you take the time to reflect.

These years can be fruitful and energizing or draining. In this day and age, the sixties are no longer seen as old. For so many people, it is the decade of moving from parenting to grandparenting, which is far less onerous and, I'm told, even more enjoyable. Grandchildren can be a source of huge joy in this chapter but so, too, can the new-found freedom to travel, spend your own money and pursue new hobbies. After decades of hard work and possibly child-rearing, independence can be a heady cocktail. As with most things in life, there are things you can control in this decade and things you cannot. So, while you might fall prey to ill-health and grief, which you cannot avoid or control, you also hold the power of interpretation, by which I mean you assign meaning to your own life and ageing. You don't have to buy into the notion of age equalling weak and diminished. It has very little bearing on today's population. This is the time to decide to take the best care of yourself that you can, in order to maintain your health, and also to decide to live differently and vitally. It's in your hands to decide that course of action and make it happen.

2: Learning to say goodbye, 68–78 years

In a previous sub-chapter I talked about the pain of saying goodbye to loved ones who have passed on, but I was primarily referring to parents. During this decade, you could well be dealing with the loss of good friends, siblings and your life partner. I have a friend in this age group, who said she was shocked the first time one of her best friends died, in their late sixties: 'I realized they were taking them off my shelf now,' she said.

My own mother dealt with the death of her husband during these years and she also lost a sister. All of my father's siblings passed away in this decade. That is not intended to sound morose: it's simply that, as we all know, death is a fact of life. At a time when you are also dealing with your own ageing and the physical changes it brings, it is likely you are dealing with adversity through bereavement. What you need to think about, though, is how you deal, or dealt, with it. Did or does it overwhelm you? Were or are you able to find some coping mechanism? Sometimes people say to me that it is less of a wrench if they believe the person had a good life or if they suffered for some time before dying, making death a relief. During these years we all have to witness loved ones passing on yet find the resilience within ourselves to continue our journey. And that may well be the case for you. Did you or will you make other decisions during this decade – either to study again, or learn a new skill, or take up a new pastime? What about travel and other ambitions? If you have grandchildren, are they a blessing or a burden? What about friendship – are you still close to old friends or have you met new ones? My own mother was meeting new people from different cultures, age groups and backgrounds throughout this period and credits that for keeping her active, young at heart and in mind. Did you or will you make changes to your diet or physical activity? All of these things are part of this decade of maturity, and even though at times it is painful to remember, I believe that it helps if you face and consider them fully. Acceptance, perhaps, is the first step towards allowing yourself to continue to live life to the full thereafter.

3: 78 years and on

Although I have taken the life stages up to eighty-one – the average life expectancy – if you live to sixty, you can expect to live for another twenty-four years. That takes you to eighty-four and hopefully you will live beyond that. Again, I'm outside the scope of personal experience here, so I'm going to call on my mother again to add her perspective on this chapter of life, which she is currently enjoying to the full.

For my mother, life has never slowed down even though she is now past the age of life expectancy. She still does yoga and Pilates every week, she walks for forty minutes every day, she uses her iPad to stay in touch with her many friends across the world on Facebook, she follows me on Twitter and does anything she can online. She has a slight addiction to binge-viewing on Netflix, but that's one of her few sedentary guilty pleasures. She loves travelling – has been to Hong Kong, Thailand, Burma and Cambodia in recent years, as well as her annual trips to the Canaries, Spain, London and New York with friends and family. She has a keen eye for fashion and is currently on a diet because she wants to be a dress size smaller for her granddaughter's wedding this summer. She is, in short, what I want to be when I am her age.

Perhaps this resonates with you. I know that with many people it won't. But I found myself thinking about my mother and what makes her different a lot of the time as I wrote this book. What have I discovered? That there is nothing startlingly different about her. I'd love to give you her 'formula', but, try as I might, I can't identify one – other than, perhaps, resilience and a positive outlook. If you are fit, well and reading this, I hope you, too, can see that it is possible for you to live vitally until you die. From what I can see and learn, it's a matter of choice, resilience, effort and probably a smattering of good luck along the way.

ANALYSIS OF THE THIRD CHAPTER

Things will happen to you in the third chapter of life that you cannot control, and that you may well hate and fear. The key thing to realize and celebrate is that, in these years, your brain is your best asset. It is the part of you that commands outlook and anticipation, and it is also the means by which you can live a full and vitally interesting life, even during the periods when your body is misbehaving. (See Chapter 7 for brain fitness.) My mother's focus on acquiring new knowledge and skills has most defined her later years and has 'kept her young'. Her experience also shows the importance of maintaining friendships and making new friends – a diversity of people to talk to, of all different ages, ensures that your brain remains engaged and interested in life.

Yes, you will face death and grief, but always there must be the will to focus on life and your own journey through it. At times, that can be unbearably difficult, but there is one constant truth in life: in time, everything changes. The aim, the hope, is that, to whatever extent possible, you can help shape and conduct that change to match your ambitions and goals.

Conclusion

Auditing your life decisions and accounting for them may have been painful at times, but I also hope you remembered happy occasions and thought of some things with fondness and pride. The ultimate goal in doing this in-depth analysis of your life and yourself was to take you to your present – where you are now – and to help you understand the events and experiences that have made you who you are and brought you to where you are. The past is gone, the present is happening and ending all the time, so the next chapter in your life is always the most important. We can learn from our past experiences, but we cannot change them, so acceptance of all those moments across the years is the first step. I wanted to get you to this point so that, hopefully, like me, you could consciously decide what happens next. A sort of adult version of 'What do you want to be?'

We spend years as children contemplating that question when sometimes we have little control over whether we can fulfil our ambitions. At this stage, however, the future is yours to invent. You have the power to decide how you will spend the years that are coming. I cannot promise you will live them without adversity and challenges – but I can promise that if you make a conscious decision to live as full a life as possible, and make the kind of practical changes I propose in this book, you will lead a different and more vital life.

6. Vital Living, or How to be Zoetic

We have come a long way. I have set out my personal journey towards being a better version of me, and you have completed a difficult 'school report card' on yourself, your life choices, your achievements and disappointments. The point of what we are doing is to encourage you to move towards vital living. To me, this is a state of mind and being in which you feel fully alive because you are learning, growing as a person, enjoying what you do, enjoying your family and friendships and planning for more achievements in the years to come. It's a fully engaged, active and directed way of living your life, which is tailor-made by you to make yourself happy. This is what I feel I've achieved over the last three years, and I want to encourage others to do the same.

What we need to ask now, after all that soul-searching, is: how can I be the best version of myself? How do I live vitally? We are going to look at many different ways to help you to achieve this, but I'm going to start by suggesting what not to do. This may sound like heresy to many, but I believe the rise of 'mindfulness' as a way of living is not a good thing. Its huge popularity means it must be addressed, so I'm going to argue that vital living is the opposite of mindfulness, and encourage you to choose the more engaged way of living. That is not to say that I don't understand the value of taking time out of our busy lives for reflection and contemplation. We all need time to quieten our minds from the whirlwind of thoughts and emotions we experience. But

I see that as an occasional respite rather than as a way of living.

First, what is mindfulness? It originated in Buddhism but has now hit the mainstream, thanks to its adoption by psychologists and promoters of well-being. In its simplest form, it means keeping your attention on the present moment, being completely mindful of 'now' and staying in that now. You achieve that state through meditation. Personally, I don't think it's natural for humans to stay 'in the moment'. In fact, I believe the opposite. Humans – of all of the species on Earth – have the higher abilities of reflection and anticipation, hindsight and foresight, for a reason. Our genetic development is based on our powers to learn from past experiences, to process events and emotions, and predict what that may mean for us in the future. Mindfulness, to me, implies stasis. It's like dawdling in the slow lane while life races by. Instead, I love the idea of being vital, or zoetic, which basically means being possessed of life and energy. Being zoetic is about living with your eyes wide open, always looking to the future and the potential it holds.

It is worth considering the two common approaches to mindfulness. For some, it's a useful tool to cope with the stresses of everyday life, a quiet interval in the busy schedule of daily living. For others, it's the route to a higher plane – to enlightenment and spiritual wisdom. Meditation has its roots in spiritual practice and is not intended as a hobby but, rather, as a way to live a life of acceptance and in so doing to achieve a state of serenity. So can you do 'mindfulness lite'? Is it possible to use it as a hobby or as another set of useful coping skills to get you through difficulties? I think the reason it doesn't sit comfortably with me is because living a life of 'acceptance' is diametrically opposed to what I believe and strive for. I can see the benefits of ridding your mind of the clutter every now and again, so long as that's all you use mindfulness for. Life is meant to be lived full on. Seize it, shape it and drive it. You're your boss, and serenity is not the aim. Don't settle for being a bystander: get into the game and do your best.

My own view of life and the beauty of being vital is embedded in how we came to be who we are. Indulge me in a brief trip back in time to our evolution and what makes us uniquely human. In evolutionary terms, we have spent most of our history (90 per cent) as hunter-gatherers. Twelve thousand years ago agriculture took over and we farmed for our food. Our success as a species owes much to the ability of our predecessors to engage in an early form of reinforcement learning, in which future decisions are based on past experiences. Hunter-gatherers didn't stay in the moment: they learned, appraised and moved forward. There are two opposing views of humans as a species: Charles Darwin believed we have inherently the same cognitive abilities as other animals but have developed them to a greater extent through evolution; other scientists believe that humans are distinct from other species by virtue of their intellect and abilities.

Many traits have been cited as uniquely human – some stand up to scrutiny better than others. Humans uniquely enjoy humour, can appreciate beauty, and we understand our own mortality as against an animal's survival instinct. We have complex communication skills: verbal, through language, and writing, through sophisticated symbols. We have a sense of right and wrong, and the ability to abide by personal values or spiritual beliefs. We also understand time and the connection of the past to the present and the future. We have foresight. We become wise by learning through experience. We also have the capacity to love and form deep emotional bonds.

While other animals, and especially our closest relations in their world, the great apes, have the foundation blocks for some of these traits, our understanding of time and the connection between past, present and future sets us apart, according to one of the world's leading experts in this field. Thomas Suddendorf is professor of psychology at the University of Queensland, a fellow of the Association for Psychological Science and the author of *The Gap: The Science of What Separates Us from Other Animals*. After extensive research over twenty years on human evolution, apes and children, in this seminal work Suddendorf reviews and tests the abilities regularly cited as uniquely human. Of all of these, he narrows the list down to just two traits that make our minds distinct from other species'.

First, our ability to review future scenarios and determine how we wish to reach them. Nowhere in the animal world do we find evidence of goal-setting or anticipating future scenarios. Our 'free will' is based on our ability to see possible future outcomes, weigh up pros and cons and decide which way to go. And although we know to our cost that this is an inexact science, it does give us the guide ropes to achieve our goals. Second, our need to link our minds together: in order to ensure that we make the best possible decisions based on the best possible information, we connect with other humans. According to Professor Suddendorf, these traits make us unique: 'These two attributes appear to have been essential to our ancestors' transforming common animal traits into distinctly human ones – communication into open-ended

language, memory into strategic planning and social trad-
itions into cumulative culture.'

This means that we are genetically designed to think ahead,
to plan for the future and to develop goals that we aspire to
achieve.

How do you take your mindfulness?

I used to think there was something wrong with me because
I can't do mindfulness – until I found others who shared my
inability to remain connected to the present. Every time I try
to concentrate on the moment, my brain flies off into the
future, weighing up the pros and cons of a particular course
of action, or mentally writing a speech, a radio script or an
article. The moment just never seems compelling enough to
remain within it – there's so much else to think about and
enjoy. Yet the concept of mindfulness has swept through
Western civilization as the next BIG thing, and marketers
have been busily labelling everything 'mindful' – teas, apps,
learning courses, weekend retreats, yoga, books, music. I am
drowning in mindfulness. It's coming at me through every
medium and in everyday conversation. And, of course, when
you take a simple idea to extremes, its true meaning often
gets lost. Mindfulness is just another word for meditation,
despite those who are trying to create an enormous industry
out of it. But it's become a movement for some, helped along
by high-profile celebrities getting on the bandwagon and
claiming (retrospectively) that their success is all down to
mindfulness. The list of ailments it now claims to cure is
endless – high blood pressure, addictions, eating disorders,
skin conditions, digestive problems, headaches . . .

I am not naturally a sceptic, so I didn't develop my opinion on mindfulness out of cynicism. I read up on it, quizzed friends who are fans and read articles written by its exponents and experts. And then I tried it out. Anything that promised that my life would be transformed was definitely worth considering. I felt nothing. I achieved nothing. To me, it was the emperor's new clothes.

The problem with mindfulness is its definition: it is meditation. Anyone deciding to adopt mindfulness as their coping mechanism ought to be told that loud and clear. Studies are being conducted into the disadvantages of meditation, which we can only surmise increase when the person doesn't know that that's what they are engaging in. For example, Sarah Bowen, a researcher at the University of Washington, warns that people with depression or trauma issues should only meditate with experts present who can offer emotional support and guidance.

Neuroscientist Dr Willoughby Britton, at Brown University, Rhode Island, has researched the positive benefits of meditation for those suffering from depression, but she is now working on a project she calls 'The Dark Night' about some of the dangers of mindfulness. Dr Britton decided to carry out the research after she had treated two patients who were admitted to the psychiatric hospital she was working in for symptoms they had developed during a meditation retreat. She was very surprised: 'This hardly ever happens, but this was two in one year. So I thought this was interesting.' She explained where the impetus for her research came from: 'And then, ironically, I went on a retreat at the Forest Refuge, and actually had all kinds of difficult, challenging [emotional] states come up. And it was years before I ever realized, before I learned what they actually were. And I had a lot of the same reactions . . . I thought that I had gone crazy. I thought I was having a nervous breakdown. I mean, I really had no idea why I was suddenly having all these, like – terror was a big symptom of mine. And I found out much later that these were actually classic stages of meditation and I was woefully uninformed. Which I think is actually pretty representative of a lot of people. So we're trying to sort of correct the lack of education.'

Dr Britton set out to discover whether 'this might be something that's new in America and maybe Americans are just meditating their way into insanity or states that just aren't relevant'. According to her research, symptoms of anxiety and fear are well known to Eastern practitioners as 'classic stages of meditation'. While we have many reputable mindfulness experts, this is an unregulated space, and where there is money, there are profit-seekers. Unfortunately, amateurs – well-meaning or otherwise – rolling out mindfulness in the West, without knowledge or experience, have the potential to cause harm to vulnerable people. In time, perhaps, we will understand more about the science, but there is no harm in putting the brakes on the mindfulness 'gurus' who over-promise in books, weekend courses and online lessons. The people who are most at risk of experiencing the downside could well be those most attracted to a quick-fix solution for their illness.

Aside from research like Dr Britton's, I believe there are other reasons why mindfulness might not be the best course for us humans. First, it is important that we experience emotions, good and bad. We evolve as humans because we learn how to deal with difficult feelings. Bad experiences often make us stronger. Segregating our minds from negative emotions gives only temporary relief and represses feelings we should work through. An important part of experiencing anger, hurt or loss, for instance, is processing it and learning to overcome or live with that emotional state. Life is not easy, and while mindfulness offers a useful respite, it is not a panacea. It might alleviate the symptoms, but not the underlying cause.

Unfortunately, there are no quick fixes that allow our minds to bypass these complex and intrinsically human challenges. The mind needs time. But we are also, as humans, connected to one another: we are driven to communicate and learn from each other. One of the downsides of meditation taken to excess is that it is a lonely way to deal with life's problems. 'A problem shared' plays no part in a process that teaches you to meditate the emotion away and to remove yourself from upset. We develop our relationships by talking things through with friends and loved ones. Being angry and vulnerable, hurt and anxious is part of our humanity, and we form deeper emotional attachments with others by having an honest relationship based on truth and reality.

Back, then, to my initial argument, which is that living vitally, being zoetic, is the best way to conduct a life. I firmly believe it is, having tried some alternatives. The key to making this a successful strategy for living is our fundamental urge to link our minds together, to look to one another for useful information. We ask questions and give advice. We bond through sharing experiences. We can use our imagination to entertain the perspectives of others as well as to consider entirely fictional scenarios. This allows us to take advantage of others' experiences, reflections and imaginings to guide our own behaviour prudently. It's about always learning, always thinking, always acting. It's most definitely not about standing still.

Our extraordinary human powers do not derive from our muscles and bones, but from our collective wit. Together, our minds have spawned civilizations and technologies through which we have changed the face of the Earth, while even our closest animal relatives live quietly in their dwindling forests.

The basic thesis of this book is that you can live fully in every chapter of your life. When people ask me how, this is my answer: live vitally. Relish the good and don't fear the bad. Keep your brain active and hungry for new information and feed that hunger every day. Keep your body vital, healthy and active, too. You can choose to stand still, or you can choose to keep moving. When I was hit by adversity so huge it threatened to engulf me, this was my only way out – it was the life-belt I clung to in those desperate times. I chose life. And that means something. It is a choice that spawns another hundred choices: if you choose life, you choose movement, engagement, feeling, thinking, loving, hurting, learning, failing and succeeding. That's the key to vital living: choose it all.

7. How to Age with Vitality

From the moment we are born, we are growing older. Yet my guess is that most of us spend our lives in denial about the ageing process. It is partly to do with that ageist view of young being better and the obsession with keeping youthful looks at all costs, but older people also remind us of our own mortality. We don't dwell on a future where we might be old ourselves, so we avoid thinking about it or planning for it. But what if you could change that and believe that your third chapter, from the age of fifty-eight onwards, may be the best period of your life, the time when you can achieve all that you ever wanted to achieve? Instead of seeing a future based on your largely negative perceptions about what ageing might mean for you, create a future in which it is a backdrop to a great adventure.

I believe we might naturally progress through the chapters of life, without fear or anxiety, if it wasn't for an arbitrary age that we see as a key milestone in life – a portal that transports us from useful and active to a burden on society, friends and family: the retirement age. We have determined (particularly in developed countries) that there is a point beyond which we stop growing in knowledge, competence and skills and start to decline in all of those areas. For most workers, the cut-off point for paid employment is sixty-five, an age set in stone 125 years ago. In 1889 Germany's chancellor, Otto von Bismarck, designed a social insurance programme for older people, making Germany the first country in the world to do so. Eight years earlier, in 1881, he had requested that Emperor William I write to the German parliament to promote the idea. In the letter he states: '. . . those who are disabled from work by age and invalidity have a well-grounded claim to care from the state'.

Initially the standard retirement age was set at seventy (Bismarck, by the way, was seventy-four at the time). In this there may have been a touch of cynicism, given that life expectancy at the time was seventy-one. In 1916, the age was lowered to sixty-five. The USA moved to a social insurance system in 1935 and similarly set the retirement age at sixty-five – not because the Germans had done so, but because some precedent had been set in private and state pensions at the time so it was more about pragmatism. In Ireland and Britain the Old Age Pensions Act 1908 intro- duced a non-contributory pension for people aged seventy or over, based on eligibility. There was widespread take-up, particularly in Ireland, where poverty was rife. We still have significant poverty in the older population, but my point is that the age at which people retire was set up for different reasons and in a different era. Nonetheless, for most people their retirement age is written into their contracts of employ- ment and it is generally taken as sixty-five.

My father's pre-retirement course was to teach him how to do nothing. I'm exaggerating, of course, but the purpose, he told me at the time, was to prepare him for a life with lots of free time that he might fill with gentle hobbies. He couldn't think of anything worse and was looking forward to being done with the day job so he had time for all the things he still wanted to do. Retirement is inextricably linked to the post-work benefits people may have earned throughout their working life. It is not about a state of mind or the cessation of usefulness: it's about reaching an age where the state, your employer's or your own pension kicks in. So, any change to the retirement age impacts on a benefit that people feel they have earned or have a right to. Putting that to one side, what if there was a different way of looking at how you earned a living post-retirement – moving from paid employment to self-employment or enterprise?

Ageing often leads to an unfavourable judgement of competence and ability in the workplace and in society. My own experience is that age has nothing to do with an employee's performance or an entrepreneur's ability to start or drive a business. On some levels, it's an advantage. We may be moving beyond marketers' 'golden years' products and services targeted at older people, but we still perceive age and, in particular, post-retirement as a diminution of faculties and competence. We like to treat our 'elders' in society with respect and we feel a duty to care for them, while at the same time lowering our expectation of their achievements or worth. A newspaper headline is far stronger with the word 'pensioner', especially if it feeds off the idea of vulnerability and infirmity.

Similarly, the wow factor comes into play when we see a news item about someone we perceive to be beyond competence achieving something we see as extraordinary – the eighty-year-old marathon runner or the seventy-five-year-old PhD student. It makes news because it is considered to be the exception. But the fact is that, over the next two decades, they will no longer be the exception. The first of the Baby Boomers (born in the post-Second World War baby booms of 1945 and 1964) began to retire in the last few years and will continue to join the ranks of retirees until at least 2030. This is a very different generation from what has come before – both culturally and in terms of wealth. In the USA and in Europe, we perceive Boomers as privileged and affluent. While many commentators believe that most have been in denial about planning for their ageing years, they will be an entirely different demographic sub-set from the current one. The subsequent generations – Generation X (early 1960s to early 1980s) and Generation Y (also known as the Millennials – early 1980s to 2000) will have an even bigger impact.

As the Boomers come to terms with the fact that ageing arrives with a new set of 'brand values', most of them negative, they will have a unique opportunity to change some of the fundamentals, if not for their own generation then for generations to come. The system is currently designed to encourage people to believe that the end of the active phase of their lives comes at the age of sixty or sixty-five and that from then onwards they are 'pensioners'. Whether you agree or disagree with a defined age of 'retirement', the cessation of work for your full-time employer should not dictate your own game-plan. Your life, your worth and your potential are much bigger than how you earn a living and the chances are that if you reach the age of sixty, you will be around for another twenty-four years or so, according to the experts. More importantly, you have the opportunity to dramatically change that phase in your life so that you remain as healthy and active as possible, able to do all the things you ever wanted to do.

Given the change in life expectancy, the ability to earn a decent pension pot, the sense of energy and vigour new retirees are exhibiting, we will have to learn a new vocabulary for the final chapter of life. The word 'retirement' belongs to a different era, one that is past. After reading this chapter, I hope you will stop using the word 'retirement' and substitute a whole new bunch of achievements and aspirations. Forget about 'getting older', in terms of the final chapter of life. Instead, think: getting smarter, getting wealthier, getting wiser, getting more rounded as an individual, getting more empathetic, getting to become a grandparent, getting more free time, getting more choices. Now, isn't that a life worth aspiring to, planning for and anticipating?

Facts and figures: the evidence for vital ageing

The world is ageing fast, and that's good news. There are already more people over sixty than children under five, and by 2030 there will be more people over sixty than under ten. By 2060, one in three people in Europe will be over sixty-five. Developed countries are recognizing the need for speedy reform in this area: unless there are significant changes in budget planning and policies around ageing, the next big crisis to push government budgets way off kilter may be the demographically driven costs of age-related health and social care. Despite the consequent economic challenges we face globally, countries like Japan are showing us how different the future could be.

A worldwide monitoring programme, the Global AgeWatch Index, rates countries by how well their ageing populations are faring in terms of four key areas: income, health, employment and education.

How well do we fare in Ireland and the United Kingdom compared to other countries and continents? Just over 17 per cent of Ireland's population is over sixty, and it ranks twelfth in the Index, just above the UK at thirteenth. We score highly in certain areas: for instance, the overwhelming majority of people (95 per cent) over fifty feel they have friends and family they can rely on if they were in trouble; and 97 per cent are happy with the freedom of choice they have in their lives. We don't score so well when it comes to employment, with only about half of those between fifty-five and sixty-four working, and almost the same number (54.6 per cent) of those over sixty have had secondary or higher education. The UK, on the other hand, with 23 per cent of the population over sixty, ranks highest in income security, at number ten of ninety-one countries, with life expectancy at sixty above the Organisation for Economic Co-operation and Development (OECD) average of 23.5 years. The USA, with 19.1 per cent of the population over sixty, that's just over 60 million people, comes in eighth position on the Index, but while more than 82 per cent of older people in the USA are covered by a pension, some 23.6 per cent live in relative poverty. No surprise that it ranks second in employment, with at least 60 per cent of people between fifty-five and sixty-four working.

Life expectancy

Before we leave the figures behind, let's look at three more key indicators of age: life expectancy at birth, life expectancy if you survive to the age of sixty and, the most important of all, how long can you expect to live a healthy life? For comparison purposes we will use the same three countries, according to the World Health Organization.

Life expectancy at birth is not always a useful indicator because it includes child mortality, and life expectancy rises after childhood, which is why the average life expectancy if you survive to sixty is a more useful indicator. These are averages, of course, and I am using the figures for both sexes combined, even though women have higher life expectancy in all three countries: Ireland, UK and the USA. In Ireland and the UK, at birth we can expect to live for just over eighty-one years, and if we are still alive at sixty, we can expect to live for another twenty-four years, that is until we are eighty-four years old. If we are born in the USA, the predictors are not so good: seventy-nine years' life expectancy at birth, and twenty-three more upon reaching sixty. Japan continues to lead the global indices. Life expectancy has improved dramatically – especially in the past decade – through health and lifestyle changes. If you are fortunate to be born in Japan, your life expectancy will be eighty-four, and twenty-six years when you reach sixty.

There is an even more important indicator than life expectancy, however, and that is how many years you can expect to live a healthy life. None of us wants to grow old in a vulnerable or frail state. The Global AgeWatch Index looks at healthy life expectancy at birth (HALE), which is the average number of years a person can expect to live in 'full health'.

Japan is top of the list again, with an expectation of full health until the age of seventy-five. For the UK it's seventy-one, in Ireland it's seventy, with the USA trailing at sixty-nine. As a shocking reminder of the divide between rich/poor and developed/underdeveloped nations, a baby born in Sierra Leone has an average healthy life expectancy of just twenty-nine years.

Should we let statistics rule our lives? Yes: these figures and averages are real, but the older people of Japan are showing us that how you choose to live can make a very positive impact on your life expectancy and the length of your healthy life. It is also a fact that we have the power to create a longer, healthier life for ourselves. It is more than possible that our final chapter can be our most productive, where we become who we want to be and make a difference.

Smart age technologies

In October 2013 I was asked to join a workshop as part of the Global Irish Economic Forum on smart age technologies. This is the development of intelligent, age-friendly systems from automated environments to computers, robots and other devices. Many technology companies developed products and services aimed at the younger market and are beginning to realize that they have missed out on a rapidly growing demographic group. But, once it got started, the aim of the workshop was much broader. It opened my eyes to the challenges and opportunities of global ageing and the need to think radically differently about the accepted wisdom around it. The workshop was led by Washington-based Susan Davis, a major player in this field, the chairwoman and founder of one of the most highly sought-after international public-affairs companies (Susan Davis International). Heads of universities, representatives from technology companies, key industry figures from the pharmaceutical world, government ministers and senior civil servants sat around the table with me, all having a vested interest in planning for the demographic upheaval that is coming our way. The premise of the workshop was to position Ireland as a global hub for smart age technologies and services, based on the belief that the country had many of the essential elements to take advantage of this significant gap in an emerging market.

After the Forum, the government took on board many of the recommendations of the workshop and included the need for progress in this area in the subsequent Action Plan for Jobs 2014. It sets out the reasons why:

> As a proportion of the population, over 65s are growing faster than any other group and are expected to double in numbers by 2040 to 1.3bn from 7 per cent to 40 per cent of the population; and those over 80 will treble.
>
> In four years, for the first time in human history, the number of people over 65 will outnumber children under 5. Governments, corporations, health services, transport providers and others have responded, but when the population structure is literally turned on its head, incremental, single-dimensional solutions are inadequate.

While Ireland is working to position itself as a magnet for smart age technologies, one country is already leading the field in this area. You've guessed it: Japan.

Out of necessity, Japan has been leading the way in terms of tackling an increasingly ageing population. It is a 'super-ageing society', with the highest ratio in the world of older people as a percentage of the population, at 24.1 per cent. The total population in Japan began to fall from 2004, but the percentage of older people continued to rise – a by-product of lowered birth rates. One of the foremost experts on ageing is Professor Hiroyuki (Hiro) Murata, who is head of the Smart Ageing International Research Centre at Tohoku University. Japan's population is ten years older than that of the USA, and by 2025, the country predicts it will have to double the long-term care insurance budget, which is already at 10 per cent of the country's total spend. Through a concerted and integrated approach, Japan is transforming its efforts and spending from reactive to preventive, in order to maintain people's health and well-being for as long as possible. Smart ageing is making a real impact on perceptions of and the reality for Japan's elderly population.

Professor Murata's work is focused on changing perceptions so that people believe they can become smarter as they age, if they continue to make an effort. As he preaches his smart ageing philosophy around the world, he emphasizes ageing as a stage of ongoing human development rather than as a period of decline, with the loss of physical or mental acumen. Smart ageing involves remaining as healthy as possible for as long as possible and keeping your brain active. It requires effort and planning; it doesn't happen by default. But as a strategy for your life it is much more worthy of effort and attention than, say, applying anti-wrinkle creams or taking daily multi-vitamins.

Dementia is perhaps the biggest challenge facing all of us as we reach the age of seventy. In Japan, for instance, seventy-five is a pivotal turning-point where the body and brain change. Within three years, almost 60 per cent of people in this age group need care. For those of you reading this who plan on sticking around for as long as possible, that's a frightening thought. It's in our own interest to take action much earlier in our lives to ensure that we stay healthy and well. I know that for many people the idea that they might plan for old age is an anathema – let it just happen and hopefully I'll be one of the lucky ones. But luck has very little to do with it, despite the odd exceptions, like the ninety-year-old who smoked cigarettes all her life and drank like a fish. Most of us need to put in the effort, the earlier the better.

Practically speaking, as we grow older we need to do four things to stay healthy, according to Professor Murata's research: physical exercise; pay attention to what we eat and our nutrition; stay connected and maintain our contact with other human beings; and keep our brains active. It all sounds like common sense, except that for many people as they drift towards their middle years, all four of those areas are already compromised. We stop watching what we eat; our lives become more sedentary; we stop making new friends and often lose contact with existing ones; and we rarely push ourselves to learn new things. But the research and proof are out there: you can age smarter and healthier, if you choose to do so. What can you do?

Train your brain

Dementia is a very significant problem for people over the age of seventy-five yet it is not inevitable. Japan has proven that training your brain staves off dementia. In fact, one extraordinary study showed that a woman who was bed-ridden for three years was rehabilitated through low-tech intervention of brain skills training. This has to be one of the least costly preventive and treatment measures you can take: no drugs, no technology, just simple exercises to stimulate the part of your brain – the pre-frontal cortex – that keeps you happy and healthy.

So what doesn't work? Ironically, the one thing that homes for elderly people tend to use to excess. Your brain does not get the right kind of stimulation by watching television. In fact, it accelerates dementia. The only senses that are stimulated when you are watching the box are auditory and visual – your brain has to do very little to process what you see and hear.

What does help? The good news is that your brain does

not need to do difficult calculations to stay in peak condition. It needs regular quick, simple challenges. Simple maths helps – even calculations that you may think are too easy; the quicker you have to process a sum, the better. Reading aloud is a great exercise because you have to read and speak the words on the page at the same time.

Professor Murata uses the example of a village in Japan where the average age is seventy-eight and only two people need nursing care. The village became a living experiment through an entrepreneurial project that has kept the inhabitants active and well. The village has a 'leaf business' in which older people forage for highly prized leaves to sell to Japanese restaurants. They sign up for whatever amount of time or effort they want to put into the business and the profits are shared.

This idea was ingenious for a number of reasons. It involved walking – maintaining physicality. It required some brain activity in working out what to pick and what to leave – a simple challenge, neither too easy nor too hard. It also ensured that there was a degree of competitiveness because each participant was paid for what he or she collected. Professor Murata says that competition is very important for humans as we age. It also allowed for flexibility: as we get older, we may not always be able to work set hours or for a set period in the day. The business idea itself was ingenious – low tech, a niche market and a product that was very different and couldn't be replaced easily. If you imagine that project being replicated closer to home, you envisage a totally different future for rural towns and villages struggling with an increasingly dependent elderly population.

Smart ageing in action

Japan is actively dealing with a rapidly ageing population right now, but the reality is that most countries in the world are facing into a super-ageing society. For you, it means that hopefully you will be around a lot longer than your parents and grandparents were. Whatever age you are now, you need to start thinking about ageing. In the same way that in the first chapter you were preparing for the second, i.e. getting an education, a job and perhaps choosing a life partner, you should use the second chapter to prepare for the third. Our aim is to live vitally all of our lives: planning and preparing have a huge role to play in achieving that. You can't expect to be the lucky one, who gets to drink whatever, eat whatever, not exercise and still be dandling the grandkids on your knee at seventy-five. It takes effort. To my mind, that's not difficult. It's effort I enjoy putting in because I'm getting so much back. And if I can push that return into my sixties and seventies, I'll be very happy with my achievement.

We are going to move on now to look at concrete steps we can take towards living vitally, but I want you to take the key things from this chapter with you:

- Retirement is not the end of your useful, enjoyable life
- Ageing happens throughout life, not just after sixty-five
- Your brain's health is your responsibility and you can make a difference
- Your body's health is your responsibility and you can make a difference
- You are the one who assigns meaning to the chapters of your life, not marketing companies,

government agencies, TV programmes or
anything else
- You can age smarter, stronger and better than any
other humans in history to date
- It is worth investing in your future self now – the
returns will make you very happy.

8. Brain Sparks 1: Dopamine

We evolved from risk-takers, intrepid explorers who set out on journeys into the unknown and learned how to survive and thrive in the harshest conditions. Modern humans usually take fewer risks as they go through life, and instead of being fuelled by the brain's powerful engine to move into the fast lane, we're more comfortable in the middle lane, on cruise control. In this chapter I want to explore the power of the brain to motivate you to be a better version of yourself. If we treat it right, our brain is our best asset as we age and can serve us well. Imagine the brain running at full throttle, pushing you to be the brightest you can be. Most of us experience that at some point in our lives, so we already know we can be better than we are. My search led me to find out why that is and how we can reignite the brain, creating the drive to push us beyond the limits we have set for ourselves, consciously or subconsciously. And the good news is that we can.

The dopamine effect

You are going to hear a lot about dopamine in this chapter, and I hope by the end of it you will be as fascinated as I am by how this amazing chemical can influence so much about your zest for life. This is, in effect, the 'spark' that holds the key to living life to the full – in the fast lane, on full throttle and right there at the outer limits of your potential.

Dopamine is a neurotransmitter, or brain chemical, that was 'discovered' in 1958 by Arvid Carlsson and Nils-Åke Hillarp at the National Heart Institute of Sweden. Dopamine is critical to all sorts of brain functions, including thinking, moving, sleeping, mood, attention, motivation, seeking and reward, although recent studies point to dopamine more as the driver towards a reward rather than the reward itself. In other words, dopamine fuels the engine of your being and your life.

I have been intrigued by this neurotransmitter for some time, and the more I read about it, the more intrigued I become about the power it wields over our lives. I also think that I used to have reasonably high levels of it and that, after Richard's passing, it diminished. When I started researching it seriously, my mission was to find out why that had happened and what I could do to get the level in my brain back up to where it should be. Now that I have researched it closely, I can look at my friends and colleagues and, without testing them, I know instinctively if they are running on high, medium or low levels of dopamine – and by the time you have finished reading this chapter, you'll be able to do the same.

Searching for the spark to reignite my life

Let's look first at what it felt like to have low levels of dopamine. I was at a stage in my life when I was feeling pretty disinterested in what was going on around me, and the rewards I was getting from work were no longer motivating me. I knew that the latter years in business had shaped who I had become. I was the person who helped others to be better than they had been, who shaped and moulded people and teams, and satisfaction came from working with someone I knew I could develop. It had worked really well for me. At some point, though, I began to feel I had drifted into the middle lane – not challenging myself too much, relying more on the knowledge I had than seeking new learning, and maybe the rewards from other people's success aren't as high as those you get when you succeed in something yourself. I might have continued in that way and not questioned it too much, had it not been for Richard's untimely death and the aftermath. I think people like me, who are used to being in control, who feed off the energy within teams and shared successes, struggle in the face of personal challenges. While the rational side of me knew that no amount of wishing would bring Richard back and return life to what it had been before, I still couldn't move on from the incessant litany of questions about why this had happened and, if we had taken a different course of action, could we have avoided it?

I knew that the solution was not in the fruitless replaying of past events, but I was stuck in a vortex of apathy, with little or no motivation to move on. The only motivating influence in my life was Dara and I knew that, for both our sakes, I couldn't remain maudlin and listless for too long.

I have been blessed with strong self-belief and that, coupled with the ability to work hard and to learn what I don't know, has stood to me throughout my career. I also learned very early on as a woman in business that success was never going to be as simplistic as 'leaning in', as Sheryl Sandberg, chief operating officer of Facebook, would have the world believe. Women haven't progressed in the work-place because of systemic inequalities: it is far more complex than a simple lack of perseverance. That said, whether you are a woman or a man, and whatever your age, race or culture, we all share one thing: the spark that motivates us to lean in, dig deep, push harder or get on in life is more difficult to find when you are faced with the traumatic aftermath of loss. Life-changing events are named as such because they are. So this, then, was my personal starting-point. I felt disengaged, disinterested and disinclined to continue in my current course. I was searching for the trigger to get me back to being my usual full-on, high-speed self, and the obvious place to look for it was in the brain. I wanted to be busy, to fill my life with challenges and learn to make up for the absence of Richard, the life we had led and were going to lead together. I had identified the problem – a lack of engagement and energy that was dragging me down and keeping me there – and I knew I needed to find a solution. I started to search for the spark that might reignite my life.

Dopamine and the world's biggest risk-takers

First, let's look at the more extreme end of dopamine production. The planet's biggest risk-takers have higher levels of dopamine than the rest of us. Adventurers and explorers, who push themselves to do things we would fear and avoid, have high levels of dopamine coursing through their bodies. Unlike adrenalin, which is released in response to danger and protects us through the fight or flight response, dopamine urges us forward to face danger and overcome fear. And it's not just the big-name adventurers who operate on high levels of this brain fuel: some of the biggest risk-takers in business or those who stand for public office also have higher than normal levels of dopamine. Lower levels of dopamine lead to apathy and lack of motivation, and play a key role in conditions such as Parkinson's disease and schizophrenia. The more we get to know about dopamine, the greater our understanding of what motivates us to be as we are. It introduces a whole new dimension to the debate about whether leaders are born or made. Quite possibly it has nothing to do with DNA or management learning and all to do with this powerful neurotransmitter.

An article I read in *National Geographic* fired my own journey of discovery about this amazing chemical.[1] In it, *National Geographic's* award-winning writer Peter Gwin explorer the area of risk-taking and why explorers face danger, get from on when others would turn back. The article includes an interview with one of the foremost researchers on dopamine, the University of Washington neurobiologist Larry Zweifel and this is his view:

> When you're talking about someone who takes risks to accomplish something – climb a mountain, start a company, run for office, become a Navy SEAL – that's driven by motivation, and motivation is driven by the dopamine system. This is what compels humans to move forward.

When I read that, I felt a bolt of recognition – it spoke to me of my past self and my current self and the vast difference between the two. To me, the article held the key to my own apathy at the time and why I longed to experience moving forward, setting goals, facing and overcoming fear and taking risks again. Zweifel identifies dopamine as a neurotransmitter that is 'crucial to the risk-taking equation'. Thankfully, not all of us have super-charged dopamine levels,

---

1 Peter Gwin, 'The mystery of risk. Why do we do it? What makes an explorer face danger and yet press on when others would turn back?', http://ngm.nationalgeographic.com/2013/06/125-risk-takers/gwin-text.

urging us to take life-threatening risks. The amount we have is controlled by molecules (autoreceptors) on the surface of our nerve cells, according to a study conducted by Vanderbilt University, Tennessee, neuropsychologist David Zald, who discovered that the fewer autoreceptors you have, the freer the dopamine flows.[2] And that is not always a good thing. In this study, Zald was looking at novelty-seeking behaviour and levels of dopamine – the dangers of too much dopamine. He discovered that when dopamine flowed freely, people took greater risks, sometimes to their own detriment. Rodents, for instance, who engage in novelty-seeking behaviour are more likely than other rodents to self-administer cocaine when they can access it. The study concludes that 'Novelty-seeking personality traits are a major risk factor for the development of drug abuse and other unsafe behaviors.'

So, while dopamine is a powerful motivator, it also has the potential to be destructive. One of the most interesting studies in this area was also carried out by a team at Vanderbilt, which also included David Zald. This time, he was engaged in research that questioned why some people are highly motivated to get on in life, while others are happy to avoid pushing themselves too hard. The study was published in the *Journal of Neuroscience* in 2012[3] and one of the scientists involved, post-doctoral student Michael Treadway, commented that 'Past studies in rats have shown that dopamine is crucial for reward motivation, but this study provides new information

2 D. H. Zald *et al.*, 'Midbrain dopamine receptor availability is inversely associated with novelty-seeking traits in humans', *Journal of Neuroscience*, 28, no. 53, December 2008, 14372–8.
3 Michael T. Treadway et al., 'Dopaminergic mechanisms of individual differences in human effort-based decision-making', *Journal of Neuroscience*, 32 (18), May 2012, 6170-6, http://www.jneurosci.org/content/32/18/6170.short.

about how dopamine determines individual differences in the behavior of human reward-seekers.'

The research found that, at its best, dopamine helps you to push limits; at its worst, it pushes you over the edge of the cliff and leaves you for dead. It's the driver, not the brakes; dopamine has no stop button. Adrenalin works to escape danger, but dopamine encourages us to face it. Professor Zald puts it best: 'An Arctic explorer who's slogging through ice for a month isn't motivated by adrenalin coursing through his veins. It's the dopamine firing in his brain.'

What's interesting about some of the latest research into dopamine is that the link between high levels of this chemical and pleasure is not as strong as previously thought. In fact, John Salamone, professor of psychology at the University of Connecticut, has spent most of his academic life researching dopamine, and he believes that more and more studies are pointing to dopamine as the motivator, rather than the pleasurable reward it offers that was the traditional view to explain why we liked and obeyed our dopamine triggers.[4]

In his work, Salamone has been trying to find out why dopamine is sometimes linked to anything but pleasurable experiences – post-traumatic stress, for instance. One of his research studies looked at dopamine levels in rats, how motivated they were to achieve a particular reward for a varying amount of work. The rat was offered a choice: head down one corridor where there is a pile of food; or choose another corridor where there is a pile of food twice the size of the first but there is a small fence that must be scaled to get to it.

4 John D. Salamone and Mercè Correa, 'The mysterious motivational functions of mesolimbic dopamine', DOI: http://dx.doi.org/10.1016/j.neuron.2012.10.021.

His findings show that rats with lower levels of dopamine will almost always choose the easy path and go for the lower-value reward, while the rats with normal levels of dopamine will go to the extra effort of jumping over the fence to get to the larger pile of food. According to Salamone, 'Low levels of dopamine make people and other animals less likely to work for things, so it has more to do with motivation and cost/benefit analyses than pleasure itself.'

I have learned that when we don't push ourselves dopamine diminishes, and because it's diminished, we don't push ourselves. In Chapter 4 I wrote about the three chapters of life and how we grow phenomenally in the first chapter as we are learning new things and exploring the unknown. I don't need a study to tell me that dopamine is flowing during those years. As we get to the second chapter, we start to do less of the things that involve risk and novelty and would rather not face fear or the unknown; often we are far more attracted to the comfort of familiar things and people. Again, it doesn't require a lot of research to determine that our dopamine levels are tapering off. This means that in the second chapter, from the age of thirty-three to fifty-eight, the fuel is low and the engine is not firing as much as it should be. The challenge is to work out how we can get it to spark again.

Love conquers everything

Most of us will never experience the high of reaching the summit of Everest or the thrill of exploring uncharted territories, but even the least likely Indiana Jones among us will have felt the power unleashed by high levels of dopamine. Sadly, it sometimes happens just once in our lifetime, and we spend much of the rest of our lives trying to sample it again.

I believe most of us have experienced our brains in a higher gear because anyone who has fallen head over heels in love will know what it is like to be a better version of themselves. This has far more to do with the brain than the heart. So, imagine the moment (if you were lucky enough to have one) when you met the love of your life across a crowded room and your eyes connected. The look you exchanged – eye to eye – set off triggers in your brain that immediately took you to a higher level in terms of your personality and abilities. When you connect or focus on someone you are in love with, it sparks off a chain of actions in your brain. Externally, you are also changed – your eyes, hand movements, body language are all different from how they were moments before. Your heart rate has increased, your sweat glands might be active and your tummy is doing somersaults. Sometimes even touching the other person feels like a bolt of electricity. While all of this is lovely, what's happening inside your brain is much more interesting.

When you want to be attractive to the object of your affection, you put forward the best version of yourself: you smile and laugh more readily, you're animated and interested, you listen with rapt attention. We often say that people in love are 'lit up', 'glowing'; they have a bounce in their step and they appear more alive. Love also makes it possible to stay up all night (talking, among other activities) and still appear at work the next day energized and smiling. Love makes you run faster and take bigger risks than you would normally take. It inspires poetry, music, books, art, not to mention all manner of crazy stunts and almost herculean endeavours. It even turns the most prosaic of us into romantic, imaginative artists, poets and, some would say, fools. For some people, being in love is the best state of mind they will ever experience and they spend a lifetime mourning the loss of the heady feeling that they could take on the world – and win.

Let's explore the science behind the sensation of falling deeply in love. I think we can all easily agree that it would be great to capture that feeling of invincibility and happiness and make it last. One researcher who has spent much of her life delving into the brains of loved-up people is Dr Helen Fisher, who is a biological anthropologist at Rutgers University, New Jersey, the author of five books and also, interestingly, the chief scientific adviser to the internet dating site Match.com.[5]

Through her research Fisher discovered that falling madly in love sparks off all sorts of changes in the brain. When you gaze at the person you are in love with, the primitive part of your brain – the caudate nucleus – lights up first. This is quickly followed by the area that produces dopamine. She points to the fact that it 'bestow[s] focus, stamina and vigor' and is the reason why we love being in love. Dopamine is therefore all-important in terms of the addiction to being in love, and also why breaking up with a loved one is painful and difficult.

Take a mild craving – chocolate, for instance – then deny yourself the pleasure for a while. It's difficult, but not insurmountable: perhaps the brain finds another way to reward you for denying a mild craving. When it comes to the big stuff, however, the release of dopamine has a powerful effect on your body. The pleasure and excitement it releases is the root cause of addictive behaviour. So, at its most benign, the dopamine effect is the kick you get out of eating something

5 Helen Fisher, TED Talk, http://www.positscience.com/pop-up/video/video-helen-fisher.html.

nice, while at the other end of the spectrum it's linked to drug and alcohol addiction. We yearn for the reward that dopamine gives us in terms of the feel-good factor without the withdrawal symptoms when it's taken away. A bad break-up with someone you love can cause as much destruction in your life as kicking any addictive habit. Indeed, some argue that it can be akin to breaking a drug or alcohol addiction.

So, what's the solution? How do we keep dopamine flowing beyond the 'head over heels' phase of love, ensuring a steady stream of motivation and a can-do attitude? I suppose one solution is that we should find a way to make love last and to stave off the often inevitable decline of that madly-in-love feeling. There is some research in this area among long-term married couples.[6]

We all know couples who have been together for a lifetime, still hold hands and appear loved up. When you scan the brains of couples like that, you find the same activity as when you first fall in love. So it's possible to stay 'in love', even though we don't fully understand how. People who feel most satisfied in relationships often feel more positively inclined towards their partner, attributing certain traits to them that may be exaggerated. I know men and women who have a skewed view of each other. The wife will tell me how handsome the husband is or how he makes her laugh. To me, an outsider, I wonder whether she needs her eyes or hearing tested. The same is true of men in a similar state of delusion. One friend recently asked me to buy a present for his wife for their wedding anniversary and told me her dress size,

6 Bill Hendrick, 'Still madly in love? Brain scans can explain', http://www.webmd.com/sex-relationships/news/20110114/still-madly-in-love-brain-scans-can-explain.

which was two sizes smaller than her actual size – to him, she will always be the svelte girl he married. I am not sure this is a good way to go through life but, according to the research, it makes for a happier relationship. Good sex helps, too, apparently. But for the rest of us mere mortals, who see all the bad and irritating habits of our loved ones over time, there might be another way.

Dopamine-inducing behaviour

There are some activities we know help with dopamine production and all its positive benefits. As well as falling in love and staying in love for as long as possible, here are some ways to induce your own natural high.

1. Newness: doing something new is a great way to get the dopamine flowing.[7] While we may not want to be intrepid explorers, we need to challenge ourselves regularly with new things. I talked in Chapter 3 about facing fear and embracing it. While I am not suggesting that you head for the nearest bungee jump, it's good to do something different. As we get older we tend to do the same things: we like routine and get 'stuck in our ways'. The brain prefers you to get out of your comfort zone – learning to dance, walking in the hills, going skiing, riding a bicycle – and the reward is a nice hit of the pleasure chemicals that make us feel good.
2. Food: eating nice food gets the dopamine running – but only in moderation. Dark chocolate high in

7 Michael Merzenich, TED Talk, http://www.ted.com/talks/michael_mer zenich_on_the_elastic_brain.html.

cocoa solids, for instance, gives you a great kick, but if you eat too much, it can work in the opposite way: dopamine levels drop and it's harder to satisfy your craving.[8] For some people, a certain food or drink gives them that quick kick – bacon, for instance, fine wine or maybe a type of dessert. Your treat-food makes you feel guilty and happy at the same time. I once sat next to a home-made ice-cream stand near Lake Garda in Italy and every single person who was persuaded to sample its delights smiled as they took their first lick. It seems impossible not to feel happy on a sunny day doing something you imagine is a bit illicit.

3. Music: another great way to get dopamine flowing, which we will look at in more detail in Chapter 10. Music can bring us great pleasure, whether it's the empathetic crooning of a love song or a beat that sets our hips on fire and forces us to move. I don't think you can underestimate the power of music to heal and enhance, so factoring new types of music or dance classes into your 'newness' schedule makes sense. It will give you a dopamine kick that will set your spirit soaring.

4. Personal motivation and reward: anticipation of a reward triggers dopamine so a daily challenge, no matter how small, gives your brain the dopamine nudge. If you can put a simple reward system in place in your own life, you can help to increase your

8 Peter Delahunt, 'Junk food and addiction – how cheesecake and bacon are like heroin and cocaine', http://blog.positscience.com/2010/04/26/junk-food-and-addiction-how-cheesecake-and-bacon-are-like-heroin-and-cocaine/.

dopamine levels. But first ask yourself, 'what motivates me?' Once you understand the triggers that push you to do things – even to get out of bed in the morning – you will begin to work on how to create scenarios that reward you in a way that is meaningful to you. There is no deep psychology here, just the basic principles of why we all do what we do. What motivates us to seek a reward? A compliment, a salary increase or a promotion at work, a holiday, new clothes or just the satisfaction of achievement? Our drive to do well comes from one of three things or a combination of them. First, the reward itself – eating a piece of chocolate because you like it. Second, the satisfaction you get from achievement and earning the reward, such as passing an exam. Third, the motivation of learning can be a reward in itself, like learning to drive a car.

The reason why personal motivation and reward are particularly important is because knowing what drives us helps us to understand how to bring it back into our lives when it's missing. I read some early research about introducing unexpected rewards into the classroom to help motivate children to learn, and I have worked in more than one company that used unexpected rewards to boost sales performance. As humans, we like the feeling of doing well and we like the high we get when we achieve something. When we're growing up and facing new things, we're often bolstered in our efforts by our parents, teachers, siblings and friends, telling us how great we are and how we can achieve the goals we set ourselves. As we grow older, we receive fewer motivating compliments – and maybe we feel we don't need them any more. We're adjusting all the way through our lives to the changing nature of our relationship with parents who are less likely to tell us how amazing we are and how we can do anything we set out to achieve in life. The learning starts to move in the other direction: we become the motivator and the booster in keeping our parents active and interested in new things.

We are also less likely to get those rewards in the workplace if we have moved up the career ladder. Leaders are people who give of themselves: their role is to motivate and mould people and teams so their reward is far more likely to involve seeing someone else develop and progress. I know that, for me, the best feeling in the world is seeing someone blossom in business acumen and skills. It is one of the best parts of mentoring emerging entrepreneurs. For those who become parents, often our rewards revolve round the achievements of our children, sporting, academic or artistic. I guess this is why you need to be a bit selfish in determining your rewards because this has to be about you and not about basking in the reflected glory of others.

I came to that realization myself some time ago and it was a revelation. I thought that leading, motivating, mentoring new talent was enough. It isn't. I found that I, too, need to be developing and pushing myself, even if I don't have a circle of people urging me on with morale-boosting compliments. We can only give so much before we have to seek out new goals and achievements for ourselves and make them happen. That's being alive.

One side note that may resonate with those who are obsessed with social media: science tells us that dopamine is the cause of your addiction. The instant gratification we get from texting, tweeting, posting to Facebook and checking out stuff on the internet can lead us into a 'dopamine loop' so that we can't put the phone down or ignore the ping that tells us a new email or text message has arrived.[9] This is the dark side of dopamine and it's good to be aware of it.

The best way to avoid becoming addicted to dopamine is to understand how it works. I've done some of the hard work for you, but the real search should come from you. This is a complex area, the subject of numerous research studies that evolve our thinking. The most important thing I learned from my own tour of the brain is that dopamine is incredibly important in terms of our ability to succeed and to live our lives as fully as possible, for as long as possible. I wrote earlier about Hiro Murata's research in Japan where, through brain training, he was able to rehabilitate a woman who had been bed-ridden for three years. No pharmacological intervention, no technology, just the simple act of doing brain exercises. That's pretty phenomenal. Just imagine what a bit of brain stretching can do for you and your zest for life.

9 Susan Weinschenk, 'Why we're all addicted to texts, Twitter and Google', http://www.psychologytoday.com/blog/brain-wise/201209/why-were-all-addicted-texts-twitter-and-google.

9. Brain Sparks 2: Serotonin

The reason I want to encourage you to learn more about these essential neurotransmitters is so that you can take some practical steps to try to ensure that it's not the chemicals in your brain that are holding you back from being your best self. What I have learned is that understanding the brain is an important dimension in the decisions we make in our lives – as we are always told, information is power. Serotonin is a powerful neurotransmitter that influences our moods, motivation and drive for life. Of the forty million brain cells we possess, most are influenced directly or indirectly by serotonin. My research into this super-brain chemical unearthed lots of myths and misconceptions, but where there is evidence that can be relied upon I've shared it, along with practical ways you can try to keep your serotonin levels in balance. One thing is very clear from the science we can rely on: when your serotonin levels are depleted, you're not going to feel like taking on too many of life's challenges.

Mirrors in the valleys

Late in 2013, for the first time ever, the sun shone in the winter months in Rjukan, a small town three hours north-west of Oslo, in Norway. This momentous event made headline news around the world. Why? The town is nestled between the mountains, in a narrow valley that was once home to the world's largest hydro-electric power plant (it's now a museum).

While nature made it the perfect backdrop for this enter-prise, the steep mountains meant the town was without sunlight for half of the year. While most Norwegians get used to winter grey, and even darkness, Rjukan's inhabitants lived in the shadow of the mountains for six months each year. Then something amazing happened. On the opposite side of the town, way up on the mountainside, three enor-mous solar-powered mirrors were erected, perfectly placed to follow the movement of the sun across the sky and reflect its light on to the town. Bright sunlight flooded the town square and the world's press captured the moment, beaming the images around the globe.

The idea was inspired by an artist, Martin Andersen, who had moved to Rjukan in 2001. As September approached he found himself having to take his young child further and fur-ther away from the town and down the valley to catch the sunlight. During the following six months, he described how he could see the sun and the blue skies but no light shone on the town. He started to wonder if a mirrored installation might change that. His search led him to Arizona, where a stadium was using mirrors to keep the grass growing; then to the Middle East, where mirrors were used to deflect the hot sun to heat steam turbines; then to Viganella, a village in Italy, where a sun mirror had been erected in 2006. While Rjukan's mirror had been conceived as an artwork, technol-ogy brought it to fruition, and it has transformed the lives of the town's inhabitants. In 2013 they spoke with wonder about the sun's light and its effect on them. But one comment, reported in the *Guardian*, from a woman called Ingrid Sparbo, struck a chord with me. Ingrid had lived in Rjukan all her life and she said that the townspeople 'do sort of get used to the shade. You end up not thinking about it, really. But this . . .

this is so warming. Not just physically, but mentally. It's mentally warming.'[10]

There is probably more truth in that statement than she intended: people who live in the far northern hemisphere suffer twice as much from seasonal affective disorder (SAD) as those in more sun-soaked regions of the world. In Alaska, for example, SAD affects almost 10 per cent of the population, whereas in Florida it affects less than 2 per cent.

Most of us feel a little down as winter approaches. Sometimes we feel sluggish and have difficulty sleeping. We can feel a bit deflated in spirit; we talk of needing a 'boost', but find it hard to get one. The science behind those feelings – which for some people can be extreme – points to decreased levels of serotonin. Scientists know that people who are sad or depressed have low levels, but the research cannot as yet tell us conclusively why, or how it is caused. But it has come up with some helpful points, which add up to a picture of serotonin and its role in our brains and bodies.

In search of the science of serotonin

Like dopamine, serotonin is a powerful neurotransmitter that has far-reaching effects on risk-taking, decision-making, mood and motivation. When we have decent amounts of serotonin, it boosts our sense of well-being. When the levels drop, however, it's a very different story. Serotonin deficiency decreases libido, reduces appetite and tolerance of pain. Extremely low levels of serotonin have been linked to

10 Jon Henley, 'Rjukan sun: the Norwegian town that does it with mirrors', *Guardian*, 6 November 2013.

irritability, impulsivity, aggression, disordered eating and sleeping problems, and also to depression and lethargy. In fact, many anti-depressant drugs work by increasing production of serotonin in the brain. It is also linked to decision-making and learning from adverse experiences. These are all areas that influence your ability to feel energized and motivated, to lead a full and active life. Is there anything we can do to ensure that our serotonin levels stay in balance?

You will read lots of myths, suppositions and science about serotonin, as I have, and the myriad of influences it has, or in many cases may have, on the body. The truth about serotonin is hard to find and my search proved frustrating and intriguing in equal measure. I eventually had to content myself with making well-informed assumptions, some based on robust research studies and others on findings that were less clear cut, as to why serotonin is important to how we lead our lives and what we can do to help keep our levels where they should be.

DON'T PUT YOUR HAND IN THE FIRE — AGAIN
Much of the research supports theories around serotonin as a key influencer in how we make decisions, how adept we are at learning from past mistakes, the level of reward we expect and how soon we expect it, and the all-important impact it has on mood and energy levels.

Let's explore motivation first. Take a moment to think about what motivates you. Not the everyday drivers like work and study, but the bigger pushes and pulls in your life. The truth is that our perceptions of reward, accomplishment, mood and motivation are far more likely to do with the duo of dopamine and serotonin (with rewards from the opioid system)[11] than with the 'nurture' factors of education, social-ization or peer influence. While serotonin and dopamine are often partners in our decision-making, motivation and moods, they have two different roles. They are, in essence, at opposite ends of the spectrum. Dopamine is the driver; serotonin is the inhibitor – they are yin and yang; comple-mentary and contrasting.[12]

It's better to consider serotonin more as a protector than as a defence. At the right level, serotonin stops us doing something where the outcome might be negative, like not putting our hand in the fire again once we have felt it burn. If we have learned in the past that a certain action is damaging to us, serotonin uses that learned experience to prevent us doing it again. But it also plays a role in balancing the reward we might get from taking a certain action versus the punish-ment we might receive as a consequence. So, in the same scenario, if my serotonin levels were not as they should be, I might put my hand in the fire to retrieve a €100 note, even though I know it will burn me. Low levels of serotonin are linked to impulsive behaviour, where that balance is out of kilter and the lure of the reward becomes more important than the damage that might follow. Alcohol and drug addic-tion have been linked to low levels of serotonin – and perhaps that's why people talk about the 'self-destruct' mode that we see in people with alcohol dependency. Aside from those with harmful addictions, I'm sure we all know impulsive

11 J. Le Merrer, J. A. Becker, K. Befort and B. L. Kieffer, 'Reward processing by the opioid system in the brain', http://www.ncbi.nlm.nih.gov/pubmed/19789384.
12 Jeromy Peacock, 'The role of dopamine and serotonin on motivation: implications for academic advising', http://jeromypeacock.com/academic-writing/the-role-of-dopamine-and-serotonin-on-motivation-implications-for-academic-advising/.

people who want to win at all costs – even when they will pay a high price, either through the break-up of a marriage, loss of friends or of their home. It's a cautionary note about the importance of perspective and balance. Dr Robert Rogers, professor in cognitive neuroscience at the Department of Psychiatry, Oxford University, is interested in the characteristics of gamblers. A few years ago he reviewed the evidence around the roles of dopamine and serotonin in decision-making in humans and how the two chemicals worked together.[13] Among the evidence he unearthed was that when serotonin is depleted, we are less patient about waiting for a larger reward. While serotonin levels influence impulsive and risky behaviours, the reason behind this is complex. Our ability to balance the reward versus the punishment associated with the outcome of high-risk decisions is impaired when levels are low, but it also has an impact on our notion of 'fairness'.

There is a game, popular among economists, called the Ultimatum Game (UG). One morning, our resident economist on Newstalk *Breakfast*, Pete Lunn (senior research officer at the Economic and Social Research Institute), tried it out on Chris Donoghue and myself. In the game, one person offers to split an amount of money with another. So let's say I have €10 and I offer €3 to Chris. Chris has the choice either to accept or reject my offer. If he accepts, he gets €3 and I get €7. If he rejects my offer, neither of us gets anything. It may appear to be a straightforward challenge, but the outcome is often surprising. According to Professor

13 R. Rogers (2011), 'The roles of dopamine and serotonin in decision-making: Evidence from pharmacological experiments in humans', *Neuropsychopharmacology*, 36 (1), 114–32, doi:10.1038/npp.2010.165.

Rogers, lots of studies of the UG show that people will often act irrationally when faced with this choice and will reject unfair offers – particularly those of less than 30 per cent; this decision-making is related to activity in the brain. The building-block necessary for the production of serotonin is tryptophan and, according to the professor's review of the evidence, when trytophan is depleted, unfair offers are rejected. So, when serotonin is low, we are more likely to see things as unfair – even to the point of making an irrational decision. We would rather see another person do without something even if it deprives us of a benefit.

When I read this evidence, I was reminded of the many irrational decisions we make in our lives, from childhood onwards. A row over sharing a favourite toy will often lead one child to break the toy in a tantrum, ensuring the other child won't get the benefit – even though the tantrum child won't either. As we grow up, do we make similar decisions? I find myself thinking about an ex-colleague, who worked hard to ensure another colleague didn't get a promotion, even though it meant she would have to continue to work alongside him. For me, it became an important internal checklist when I made any crucial decision as a boss: a pause to reappraise my motivation for making a particular choice or deciding on a particular path. I know that it is very easy to get sidelined by perceived slights. I have met many people who put their success down to a teacher at school or a previous manager who told them they would never amount to much. They believe that their drive to do well is linked to proving that person wrong. I'm not so sure. I think sometimes we like to use that as a way of repairing our ego (which undoubtedly took a bruising at that moment). But my motivation has to be positive.

Serotonin helps us to be patient about rewards when they are worthwhile, and although the research is not conclusive, Professor Rogers's review also points to a role in our perspective of good and bad outcomes to decisions – including risk-seeking and risk-averse behaviour. And in between the science there is this nugget of wisdom. This is how Professor Rogers describes it in his summary:

> Moreover, if serotonin activity can influence the activity of positive vs negative cognitive biases, it should not surprise that tryptophan depletion and other manipulations that enhance such biases find greater expression in the processing of negative choice outcomes as aversive events more frequently warrant reappraisal.

Admittedly, you might not see it at first, but 'aversive events more frequently warrant reappraisal' is the key. When things go wrong, they require more consideration than if they go right. So, learning more about serotonin took me right back to learning from failure and how important it has been in my life, both work and personal. I was gratified to find that the time I had taken to learn from it had been well spent. The important message I took from this review of the evidence is that the weighing up of the outcome in terms of doing something again is all important. Just because I failed once or I had a bad experience doesn't mean I won't try again. The difference is that a healthy brain will allow you to consider the consequences and face the decision knowing that the outcome could be good or bad. Another lesson learned from serotonin is that impulsive behaviour is not the same as taking risks. While I encourage people to step outside their comfort zone and take a risk, it's not about a spur-of-the-moment decision regardless of the consequences.

What does it all mean?

Serotonin is a powerful chemical that exerts an enormous influence on you – your motivation, impulses, moods, decision-making, perception of rewards and feelings of well-being. It is sometimes dubbed the 'happiness hormone', but I feel that is an over-simplistic label. Along with dopamine, it has the potential to be the brakes or the driver on your journey through life, depending on whether you allow the levels in your body to decrease or maintain them. (See Chapter 10, 'Design Your Future Self', for practical ways to boost serotonin levels in your body.) Understanding the brain and the triggers that determine so much about why you are as you are will help you to come up with strategies to cope with the effects of these neurotransmitters, control them where you can or, at the very least, dent their power over you. Your aim is to maintain balance: too much or too little serotonin leads to problems. Remember, you have the power to use those neurotransmitter sparks to boost your drive to succeed.

10. Design Your Future Self

Who do you want to be?

There is no such thing as eternal youth. There is no elixir, no secret, no formula. We all know that the 'age-defying' bandwagon is a multi-billion-euro industry that feeds off our desire to look younger than we are. We know it, but we still fling ourselves into all the creams, hair dyes, make-up and cosmetic enhancements that money can buy. Why do we do it? Because we are part of a society that is obsessed with youth and tightly defined notions of 'beauty'. It's very difficult to swim against that particular tide because the current is so strong – it's society-wide and pretty much worldwide. For women, it's particularly difficult, but men are subject to similar pressures and attacks on their self-esteem as they get older. If age has taught me anything, it's that society as a whole has to change its perceptions, and we as individuals have to challenge and change our own. Instead of wasting our lives chasing our youth, we need to embrace all stages of our development and learn to live them as fully as possible.

When we're young we don't really understand how foolish it is to want to be older – even though we spend our first twenty years sometimes wishing we had attained more years than we have. As we age, we waste a good proportion of our lives hankering after what we had instead of embracing what we have and what we can look forward to. While we can forgive the ignorance of youth, we need to stop making excuses for our own behaviour as we drift towards middle age. We have to shift our focus to what matters: it is possible to stay healthy and feel energized for all of our lives; age is not a barrier to wellness. And, more importantly, you can also continue to learn and grow as a person throughout your whole life – not just in the early stages.

Ask yourself: do I want to expend a huge amount of time, energy and money chasing a mirage? Or do I want to embrace the person I am, at this age, and work towards being the best person I can be in all my future years? We have a new focus now: living vitally in every decade.

Do I believe in a mid-life crisis?

I believe that our bodies go through changes as we age, but I think that the psychology of mid-life is almost entirely based on the false premise that our best years have passed. We are bombarded with marketing messages about staying younger, looking younger, quick fixes to avoid the spectre of ageing. We blindly accept that young is good and ageing is bad. We consume material that reinforces the stereotypes of old age. Those stereotypes regarding the limitations of old age are built from foundations in history: culture, music, art, film, reading and our own experiences of elderly parents and relatives. But this generation is different. You are part of something that is new and you have the ability to design your own future and your own future self.

Charting the course of your life

As the Japanese experience tells us, some of what we need to do is, sadly, not up for discussion. If you want to have the foundations to build a great future in the latter part of your life, then you have to be smart about the effects the ageing process has on your body and your mind. Apart from the all-important matter of keeping your brain active and constantly challenged (see Chapter 7), I found these things worked for me:

1. Exercise: keep your body in healthy condition
2. Diet: food for your body and your brain
3. Brain training: maintaining brain fitness
4. Absorbing the light: the effects of light exposure
5. Less LED screens
6. Massage/hug: the power of human touch
7. Faking it . . . until it's real: the necessity of smiling
8. Fear: being afraid is good
9. Simple pleasures: music, reading, laughter
10. Staying connected to other people

1. EXERCISE: KEEP YOUR BODY
IN HEALTHY CONDITION

The first, and key thing, you must do is to work at keeping your brain and your body in healthy condition. You know the areas you need to work on, but those are the very least of what you need to do to maintain yourself in good working order. The life plan has to be much bigger than that. I am not a nutritionist or a personal trainer, but I know what worked for me. And, by the way, I'm no poster girl for fitness and diet, but I did change my lifestyle and habits and I do feel much more alive for doing that.

A vital body: regular exercise

One of the key changes that happens to us as we move through the different stages in our lives is that we neglect to

keep our bodies in tune. It is another way of resigning ourselves to the decline in our physical abilities. As we grow
older, our reward system often involves very little physical
effort. In fact, it becomes sedentary – a sit-down with a glass
of wine is probably the number-one 'reward' we promise
ourselves when the working day is done. When I spent time
in Sydney, I marvelled at the Australians' healthy attitude to
after-work activities: Cockle Bay was often dotted with sailing boats, beaches full of people having a late-afternoon
swim, cycling, walking, jogging – their reward system was
much more geared towards fresh air and getting their bodies
moving after a day in the office. I was reminded that in Ireland our after-work activity is often indoors and sitting down,
having dinner, watching TV, going for a drink in a pub, sitting in the cinema, all requiring little effort. We often perceive
exercise as something we did when we were younger or
which is reserved for sportier folk. But the truth (however
much we dislike it) is that we need to keep exercising our
bodies – not slavishly, I hasten to add, but it must be part of
our daily routine.

I don't think I'm very different from other people in admitting that I was far from being in peak condition when I hit
forty. The effort of juggling home and work life had taken its
toll on physical activity: other than the walk from the door to
the car and the car to the desk, not much else was happening.
Of course, the odd spurt of walking or climbing a hill or
sporadic visits to the gym helped to reassure me I could still
do it for that indeterminate time in the future when I would
make the decision to be more active. I have enormous sympathy with anyone reading this who already feels drained by
the time they get home in the evening. When the kids are
finally in bed, you lunge for that bottle of wine and the

remote control. Frankly, life is bloody hard sometimes and it is more than understandable that at the end of hectic, stressful days we crave some 'me time'.

I'm not great at joining things – it works for some people, I accept that: I like to do things at my own pace and in my own way. One evening, instead of opening the fridge, I headed out for a walk. As I started to get into the rhythm of the steps (and, frankly, stopped working out when I could turn around to go home to the sofa), I realized something. While my body was doing something by rote, my brain was freed up to think. It sounds corny, but it was a revelation. A small, personal revelation about where I was at and what I ought to be doing. After that, I signed up for personal training sessions.

For fear you might imagine that I gave myself a stern talking-to one day, I want to fess up to the truth here: all of these changes were evolutionary, happening slowly, over months. The springboard, however, was the absolute conviction that I needed to live a fuller and more active life without any endpoint – perceived or otherwise. What I have learned since is how important physical activity is to my well-being. It helps me unwind. I can process things during a long walk and I return feeling physically tired, which helps with sleep – and it costs nothing. I also learned, sadly, that walking isn't enough and that I need to do some cardio work on a regular basis. I tend to use spinning at the gym for a cardio workout, but that's mainly because of my busy lifestyle. When I have the time, real-life cycling and interval running make me feel much better.

If you have left daily exercise behind and feel unmotivated, don't focus on that. Just start with one walk – leave the house and walk. It's an excellent place to start.

2. DIET: FOOD FOR YOUR BODY
AND YOUR BRAIN

I've long been fascinated by the various personality types in the world – especially the difference between the dreaders and the doers, as I think of them. The dreaders are those people who can suck the energy from a room just by walking through the door. I think we all know at least one person like this – full of doom and gloom, always seeing the cloud behind the silver lining, the kind of person who leaves you feeling deflated after every conversation. Sound familiar? And then there are the doers, people of resilience and fortitude who keep going, usually with a smile on their face.

I mention this because, thinking about the difference between the dreaders and the doers, I began to wonder why some people are wired differently from others, why they hold a different outlook and also, if you were one of the unlucky ones who saw all the gloom and doom in the world or, as in my own circumstances, were feeling flat and lacking in spark, how could you create that good mood, that strongly positive outlook? It was a question that bothered me.

My search for an answer led me to the amazing neurotransmitters, dopamine and serotonin (see Chapters 8 and 9). We need dopamine and serotonin to boost our mood and make us feel vital, so my research revolved around a particular question: if your levels of those two chemicals were temporarily depleted, could you trick your body into producing more, and what were the dangers associated with doing so? What's interesting about dopamine is that it can have a negative and a positive effect on eating patterns. Dopamine reward pathways are linked to many addictive substances – some relatively benign, like chocolate, sugar and caffeine, and others having more harmful effects, such as alcohol, nicotine and narcotics. When people are giving up cigarettes they tend to eat more because cigarettes and food share the same dopamine reward pathways.

Serotonin, as we have learned, is also a very powerful neurotransmitter with a wide range of influences, including the regulation of mood, appetite, perceptions of pain and sleep patterns. Whatever we think about the science and what it suggests in terms of diet, there is enough there to convince me that, if possible, I don't want my serotonin levels to go down if I can help it. Not only are depleted levels linked to feeling sad, research conducted at Macalester College, Minnesota, links low levels of serotonin to more aggressive behaviour, eating disorders and sleeping problems. While the jury might still be out in terms of what you should eat to help the body produce serotonin naturally, at Princeton University, New Jersey, researchers have identified non-pharmacological ways to make the body produce serotonin, including exposure to light and regular exercise.

During my own dark times, without knowing any of the science, I was aware that something had to change in terms of my diet, not just for the positive physical benefits but because I was sure, in my own case, that my diet was contributing to the lethargy I felt and the sedentary lifestyle I had adopted. When life doesn't give us many natural highs, we fall back on some of our basic feel-good activities and top of the list is often eating – especially the wrong kinds of food. At least, that was my experience. Only those of you who have been there will understand the comfort of a carb-fest while mindlessly watching some trash on TV. The pleasure is always short-lived because it doesn't make us feel good afterwards – in fact, there were some days when I felt so bad about eating an entire pizza, laden with cheese and salami, that I had to eat something equally unhealthy an hour later to make me feel better.

I know I'm not alone in this. I have met so many people who have empathy with the eating thing! That's the only way I can describe it because sometimes when we lack pleasure in our lives, just putting a forkful of something yummy into our mouths is the least we can do to make life good. In the past, I ate my way through every emotional state going. I would eat when I was happy and all was right in the world, and when I was stressed and had had a difficult day – well, dammit, I got through all that so now I deserve to eat what I want. During the early stages of grief, you feed your body to make up for the emptiness in your life. I did it. I'm just reminding you that I'm not one of those people who preaches about this stuff without ever having suffered it or understood it. I am no zealot about exercise or diet. I just knew that my life needed to change and some of that change centred on intellectual things, but a lot of it was about how I felt physically.

When I read about dopamine, I understood more about our desire to create the feel-good factor it induces and how it can, in turn, lead to overeating. Binge-eating when we feel low kick-starts the neurotransmitter and gives us a short-term reward – a temporary high – but over time that eventually leads to lower dopamine levels and a decrease in the receptors in charge of satiety, which means you end up craving more and more food while feeling less and less satisfied. The classic vicious circle of a dulled life.

A number of years ago I worked, on occasion, as an adviser to the World Health Organization's European office, and I was always struck by how that august body defined health in its Constitution: 'Health is a state of complete physical, mental and social well-being and not merely the absence of disease or infirmity.'

I really like this definition because it is cognizant of the need to feel good – not just to be without ailment. So what's the secret to well-being, to increasing your energy and zest for life? It certainly isn't about giving yourself a good talking-to. I tried that and found that I could quite easily ignore myself. Nor does the answer lie in well-meaning colleagues, who try to buck you up with the odd pep-talk. But given I truly believe that living life to the full relies on feeling great to start with, I knew that I had to make fundamental changes to my lifestyle and undo all the bad habits I had tangled myself up in.

My natural starting-point, then, was my diet. We eat food every day, so I reckoned it had to be an essential part of feeling bad or feeling good. Not being an expert in this area, I started to keep a record of what I was eating and when, just to find out what my intake actually looked like when I was honest about it. Lots of well-meaning friends – some more qualified than others – began to give me their perfect recipe for healthy eating. I can't remember them all, but some included not eating after 6 p.m., starving for two days and eating what you want for five, the low GI, the low GL, the no carbs, the shakes, the juicing and so on. I tried lots of things and worried most of the time that I had chosen the wrong formula and that something else would work better for me. I was right in one sense. Everyone is different, and slavishly following the next diet fad is a waste of time.

The secret to healthy eating is to change your diet and eat less food more often. I began to read nutrition books as avidly as others might read *Fifty Shades of Grey*. The new erotica in my life was any research that might point me in the right direction. I am a complete nerd about most things and try to uncover all the facts before making a change – some people might call it procrastination, but to me it is making a well-informed decision. At any rate, I embarked on a level of research worthy of a PhD on nutrition.

Okay, okay, I'll admit it. Before all that healthy research and decision-making, I fell prey to the promise of a quick fix. I was drawn to a controversial book called *The 4-Hour Body: An Uncommon Guide to Rapid Fat-Loss, Incredible Sex, and Becoming Superhuman.* You can see the attraction. (And do not drop my book like a hot stone to go online to buy it!) Someone bought it for me as a Christmas present when it came out in December 2010 and I found it buried on the bookshelves when I was clearing the office. It was by the American writer Tim Ferris. His first book, you may remember, and the one that put him on the map, as it were, was *The 4-Hour Workweek.* Anyway, what the hell? It was bound to give me a few pointers to get me started. By the way, just so you know, the book promises that within thirty minutes you will learn a number of incredible things, including how to lose lots of weight, stay trim even while bingeing, how to feel great after only two hours' sleep and how to produce fifteen-minute female orgasms! Well, maybe I wasn't the best subject for the book because I failed at most of these aspirations, but I did learn one thing (and, no, it had nothing to do with sex). Tim writes that he spent more than a decade learning how to 'hack the human body', interviewing lots of doctors, high-performance sportspeople and conducting personal experiments. And it was one of these experiments that I adopted into my life after reading the book.

Ferris conducted an experiment on himself using blood-sugar testing to find out if any of three substances anecdotally named by people to curb food cravings and control blood-sugar levels could, in fact, do just that. The aim of the experiment was to discover if he could stay in fat-burning mode longer. The three substances were lemon juice, vinegar and cinnamon, taken prior to eating. He attached to himself a blood-sugar meter, with probes into his abdomen, so he could measure his blood-sugar levels. The outcome was bad news for vinegar because in Tim's experiment it didn't work, but lemon juice and cinnamon did. He took three table-spoons of freshly squeezed lemon juice before meals, which he claimed lowered his blood-sugar response to meals (com-pared to his controls) by about 10 per cent. Cinnamon also had a positive effect. He tested three types of cinnamon and the most effective was Saigon cinnamon (also known as Viet-namese cinnamon), then cassia cinnamon and finally Ceylon cinnamon. All helped blood-sugar levels to some extent, with a warning that four grams per day (about 1.5 teaspoons) is probably the maximum amount of cinnamon anyone should consume.

In any event, from then onwards lemon juice and water became part of my diet, especially during the morning, and my cupboard always contains Saigon or cassia cinnamon to sprinkle over yoghurt. Cooking with lemon also emerged in some interesting studies around blood-sugar levels and advanced glycation end products (AGEs), substances which are linked to ageing and degenerative diseases, like diabetes and Alzheimer's. These studies have shown that lemon can help reduce the body's blood-sugar response to food, which in turn helps keep insulin levels stable. (See Reading List, Food and diet, page 298.)

While I was seduced by the quick fix that could never be, I had at least made one change for the better – lemon juice and cinnamon. But I was only just starting. While my new natural appetite suppressant was battling to change a year's worth of bad behaviour, I continued to read anything I could about who might help me to feel better. For me, what I ate had to help my brain as well as my body. I wanted to eat more healthily, yes, but I also wanted the drive to maintain that change in my life over the long term.

I've reported over the years on the miracles of various food substances to enhance your brain power, and although I regurgitated various new research findings as they were produced, I had never really explored what the underlying science points to in terms of brain food. If you put something into your mouth, it stands to reason that it might have an impact on your brain as well as your body. So the key question was: what is the best brain food? The answer I found was this: amino acids, which help sharpen the brain; fats, in particular polyunsaturated fatty acids like omega-3; antioxidants, found, for instance, in vegetables; and glucose, of course, to provide the fuel. Of those essential components of a brain-food diet, the two I wanted to learn more about were amino acids, because they work on neurotransmitters, and antioxidants, because they help preserve brain cells. I am very aware that the science surrounding these findings is not entirely proven, but my own attitude is that if it helps my brain in any way, I want it, and even if it doesn't, I know these foods will help my body, so I still want them.

Amino acids

Almost every expert who promotes a dopamine-inducing diet does so on the basis of recommending foods that contain amino acids (a building-block of protein), particularly tyrosine. Tyrosine is an important amino acid that some nutritional experts and other health professionals believe encourages your brain to release dopamine and norepinephrine. This theory is based on the view that high levels of dopamine can curb food cravings, especially impulse eating or overeating. So the claim goes that by following a diet high in micronutrients, especially tyrosine and the amino acid L-tyrosine, your dopamine levels will rise and your satisfaction and pleasure in eating the right portion of food will be enhanced. (For foods rich in amino acids, see Table 1, page 191.) What we do know is that when your brain naturally produces dopamine, it makes you feel good – it's a reward pathway, remember, so pleasurable activities, such as eating and having sex, give you a rush of dopamine. When it's absent, you can feel low and lacking in energy or interest. If there is a way of getting your body to give you that boost through diet or other interventions, then it is worth exploring and experimenting. So, the mantra is to eat foods rich in tyrosine, which is an essential trigger for making dopamine.

Another amino acid regularly mentioned is phenylalanine, which is found in tofu and other soy-based foods, as well as in fish, dairy and meat. And the really good news is that dark chocolate is a really good source of L-tyrosine – the higher the cocoa content, the better. I keep a bar of the best 80 per cent cocoa chocolate I can find and have a square most evenings to boost my mood. It works!

Antioxidants

Blueberries, which are high in antioxidants, are now a daily part of my diet. I also take a daily supplement of spirulina, but you can also eat broccoli, carrots and spinach to boost your intake. Lots of teas, by the way, have antioxidants.

My focus now is on the right kind of eating – meals that leave me feeling satisfied, with energy levels restored. That's what eating should be about – foods that make you feel vital and alive, light and energetic. (The direct opposite of how simple carbs and saturated fats – junk food – make you feel.) Accordingly, I now eat a diet rich in amino acids and antioxidants. I think carefully about my diet, which is a huge change for me, and I try to adhere to the old adage: eat to live, don't live to eat.

One important facet of my diet is the fatty acid, omega-3. While I had heard a bit about it – mainly that it was in oily fish and was good for us – I didn't understand how important omega-3 was to the brain and, in particular, the ability to make new brain cells until I studied it. It was very good news to me that you can, according to the experts, replace your brain cells: we make them throughout our lives and they affect our memory and ability to learn. It is claimed that omega-3 helps trigger the production of serotonin. I'm not sure that the evidence is entirely done proving the claims about eating oily fish, but at least one study has shown that it slows down the rate of decline of brain function. (*Archives of Neurology*, October 2005, showed that eating oily fish slowed cognitive decline by about 10 per cent in older people.) I now try to have one omega-3 source (found in many fish, especially oily species, and in walnuts) at least once, if not twice, a week. Good sources include tuna, herring, salmon or mackerel, which are high in B vitamins as well. Another reason why fish became part of my diet is because of the trace mineral selenium. Low levels of selenium have been linked to depression, so to maintain a good level I eat fish and whole-grain cereals.

Table 1: Sources of vital brain food.

RECOMMENDED BRAIN FOOD	SOURCE
L-tyrosine	Fava beans, duck, chicken, ricotta cheese, oatmeal, mustard greens, edamame, dark chocolate, seaweed and wheat germ
Amino acids	Protein such as fish, eggs, chicken, turkey and red meat
	You can mix certain other protein sources, such as root vegetables with grains, to make stronger amino acids
	Vegetables, such as artichokes and avocadoes
	Fruit: strawberries, blueberries and prunes
	Nuts and seeds: almonds, sesame, pumpkin seeds
	Wheat germ (amino acid phenylalanine, that's converted to tyrosine).
	Lima beans, herbs (often in teas), nettles, fenugreek, ginseng, milk thistle, red clover and peppermint
	Supplements: tyrosine, vitamins B, C and E, iron, folic acid and niacin
Betaine (an amino acid that is important for the functioning of heart and blood vessels)	Beetroot

Tyrosine	Ripe bananas
Antioxidants	Apples (quercetin – said to be ridding the body of free radical molecules inhibiting the production of 'bad' cholesterol)

Complex carbohydrates help the brain in a number of ways, especially those like wholewheat bread and pasta, which are rich in tryptophan, the amino acid that converts serotonin in the brain. Root vegetables, such as sweet potatoes and carrots, are also brain-enhancing, nutrient-rich foods. Of the recommended vitamins, the one that comes up time and again from experts in this area is B6, which is said to help elevate feel-good serotonin levels – it's found in fish, poultry, wholegrains and leafy green vegetables.

It is also recommended that you maintain sufficient levels of folic acid in your diet, to prevent decrease of serotonin levels. A folate-rich diet would include starchy beans, such as kidney (cook thoroughly) and black beans (don't overcook), chickpeas, and raw green vegetables.

While there is lots still to be done in terms of proving the influence diet has on the brain and, in particular, on dopamine and serotonin levels, it's still good sense to make your diet the best it can be while the science is catching up. Food for your brain is more about harnessing the power that already exists and helping to maintain its function for as long as possible. Smart eating may not make you clever, but it will help to keep you as clever as you are already!

3. BRAIN TRAINING: MAINTAINING
BRAIN FITNESS

It is essential, for a full and vital life, that you keep challenging your brain, feeding it information, and giving it new experiences to process and learn from. Our brains are our best asset, and are worth investing time and effort in to ensure we get the best results from them. Don't settle for a sludgy brain, for a TV-soaked lazy brain: do the things necessary to stay sharp and get sharp.

We have to take our brain health seriously in order to maximize and extend its function. There are things you can do to keep it in good working order and always improving: I recommend that you start them today and don't give up. This sort of conscious living and self-maintenance is a necessary part of vital living and, of course, the potential rewards are tremendous.

- Your brain needs challenges: you need to learn new things and you need to put in place a training regime to ensure it still has to work to figure things out – not big maths formulae, but regular quick and simple challenges; the less time you have to process them, the better.
- Stay competitive: either intellectually or physically, because it helps to keep the brain motivated to succeed.
- Don't watch too much television: no matter how interesting it is, it's not good for your brain because you are the passive recipient of information.
- Read: a far better brain activity than TV-watching, and reading aloud is even better because you have

to read and speak the words on the page. Volunteer your reading services for children or perhaps older people of your acquaintance – you might be surprised at the reactions and outcomes.

- Meet people: make a conscious effort to talk to them, especially if they are different from your normal circle of friends or work colleagues.

- Make great conversation: this can be the best brain exercise of all. I'm not talking about an argument with the same well-worn paths of defence, but a real conversation, one that challenges you and makes you think. Being interested in other people's views and knowledge is something we often lose, along with our tolerance for people who are different. Open your mind and get talking.

- Do something new: the brain loves novelty and it gives you that great feeling of accomplishment when you do something for the first time. Make yourself proud.

- Set goals: our understanding of time and the connection of the past to the present to the future sets us apart from all other animals. We were given foresight for a reason, so look ahead and set some challenges that will push you out of that comfortable space you're lingering in.

- Put a reward system in place for yourself: even everyday challenges should lead to rewards because anticipating the reward is what fuels the brain and motivates you to succeed.

4. ABSORBING THE LIGHT: THE EFFECTS OF LIGHT EXPOSURE

Light is an important trigger for well-being all year round, as important in the depths of winter as it is in June and July. Taking into account all of the science and advice about sun-protection and the dangers of over-exposure to UV light, sunlight plays an important role in the production of vitamin D, which in turn promotes serotonin production. And don't always be tempted to put on your shades when you're out-side because sunlight on your eyes also boosts serotonin – but only short exposure, please, as overdoing it could cause dam-age. As autumn and winter approach, you have to try harder to find those rays on gloomy days, but any daylight is better than none.

The general malaise that most of us feel as the days get shorter and the light gets gloomier has to do with our circa-dian clock – the natural daily rhythm of the body. Sometimes we become less active, we lose a bit of our vigour, and it's not uncommon for us to eat less healthily, craving carbs and sugars. You may notice that you feel a bit flatter in the after-noon. It can affect how well we sleep, and lack of sleep in turn leads to lack of energy, an impulse towards binge-eating . . . and a cycle is already developing. So it's in our own interests to work on our serotonin levels so we don't spiral down-wards. My own experience tells me that getting outside as much as possible makes me feel better all year round, but especially as the days get shorter. Maybe take a leaf out of the Norwegians' book: add more mirrors to your house and angle them so that the sunlight reaches gloomy corners.

In fact, the Norwegians provide some great ideas when it comes to light exposure and seasonal affective disorder (SAD). Unfortunately, you'd have to travel to avail yourself of them, but the Scandinavian countries have embraced the concept of light cafés, which are proving very popular and, by all accounts, very effective. It's a simple idea: as you enjoy a coffee or a meal, you are bathed in high-intensity light, which has a therapeutic effect. The idea has spread to the USA and London's Science Museum. Let's hope this is one notion that skips on to our island – a lot of people would welcome it, no doubt.

5. LESS LED SCREENS

I once did a piece on radio about how reading your tablet or smartphone just before bedtime made it difficult for you to switch off and sleep. I don't need to retrieve the research paper to know that is certainly the case. I had got into the habit of checking the news bulletins last thing before sleep and doing one final run-through of emails and tweets. Now my tablet stays on the bedside locker, on silent, until it fulfils its function as an alarm clock each morning. It's also worth noting that, although light is important during daytime hours, you should try to sleep in a darkened room at night. Light helps to create serotonin, but while we're sleeping it can prevent it from converting into melatonin, which is important for a good night's rest.

I don't need research to know that it's not good for my teenage son to spend the day on his computer, games console or watching television. It gives him headaches, makes him tired and lacking in enthusiasm for much else. So now we agree in advance the amount of time he can spend on each activity on free days, with plenty of time in the park and out on the bike to counterbalance the screen time. In your own life, perhaps it's worth thinking about how much time you're spending in front of an artificial screen – television, laptop or smartphone. How much time do you spend in man-made light as opposed to sunlight? Try to balance the two and, in any event, ensure that a day at the computer involves plenty of breaks.

6. MASSAGE/HUG: THE POWER
OF HUMAN TOUCH

I have read lots of articles on the therapeutic benefits of regular massage, particularly its effects on serotonin levels. Either convince someone in your life to take it up as a hobby or swap it with something you currently spend money on as a treat. I know I always feel great after a really good massage, but it's not just your muscles and aches that are getting relief: several research studies have shown that regular massage helps alleviate depression and anxiety. There are even studies that show regular massage on babies helps them sleep better and cry less often. Most of these studies showed significant increases in serotonin levels following a period of regular massage.

If you can't afford a massage, a good hug every day helps. Get in the habit of giving those special people in your life lots of attention, hugs and hand-holding. The power of touch is immeasurable – especially the loving kind.

7. FAKING IT . . . UNTIL IT'S REAL: THE
NECESSITY OF SMILING

Smiling releases serotonin, but when our levels are low, we probably don't feel too much like smiling. There is a way of faking it, though, and achieving the same results. I have often cited the theory that we can trick the body into being happy by fake-smiling, even when we don't feel too happy. I have tried it myself on many occasions and it does work. But I wasn't sure what research supported that theory – until I learned about a man who has spent a lifetime proving that we can make ourselves happy just by smiling. Dr James D. Laird, professor at the Department of Psychology, Clark University, Massachusetts, has been on a mission since college to discover which comes first: happiness or the smile? He explores his 'self-perception theory' and the connection between feelings and behaviour in his book, *Feelings: The Perceptions of the Self*.[14] If you are interested in human behaviour, this book is a must-read: it will change your thinking about why you feel the way you do and how much power you have over those emotions.

In the book Laird discusses the hundreds of studies he has conducted to prove that feelings are the consequence, not the cause, of behaviour. It sounds wrong, it should be the other way round, but Laird's work has proved he's right. He was following in the footsteps of a most influential thinker in philosophy and psychology. His name was William James, and in the late nineteenth century he became the first educator in the USA to offer a course in psychology, leading many who followed to call him the 'father of American psychology'. Way back in 1890, William James published *The Principles of Psychology*, in which he explained that

> Common sense says we lose our fortune, are sorry and weep; we meet a bear, are frightened and run; we are insulted by a rival, are angry and strike. The hypothesis here to be defended says that this order of sequence is incorrect . . . and the more rational statement is that we feel sorry because

14 J. D. Laird, *Feelings: The Perception of the Self*, New York: Oxford University Press, 2007.

we cry, angry because we strike, afraid because we tremble . . .[15]

Fast forward to 2007 and James Laird begins his book with that passage from William James, who inspired Laird to continue the work he had started. But before that, a simple interaction with a man who had a peculiar smile started Laird's journey as a young graduate student. That strange smile played on his mind and he started to think about the nature of smiling. Laird did an interview when his book was published, in which he explained what happened next:

> For some reason I tried smiling the way that guy did. It didn't help. So I asked myself, "How do I smile?" I smiled in my way and then I thought, I feel happy. Then I tried scowling and gritting my teeth and that made me feel angry. Then I frowned and that made me feel depressed. So I thought, That's funny. It's not supposed to happen that way. We all know the feeling is supposed to cause the behavior not the other way around. But that's not what I was experiencing.[16]

Back in 1974, he had conducted two experiments in which he tested whether fake-smiling, as opposed to authentic smiling (also known as a Duchenne smile), would make the participants feel happy.[17] He needed to trick people during the experiment so that they didn't know what he was up to. He attached electrodes to the corners of their mouths, the

15 W. James, *The Principles of Psychology*, New York: Henry Holt, 1890, p. 449.
16 Clark University website, at http://www.clarku.edu/faculty/jlaird/ Publications.html.
17 J. D. Laird, 'Self-attribution of emotion: the effects of expressive behavior on the quality of emotional experience', *Journal of Personality and Social Psychology*, 29 (4), April 1974, 475–86.

corners of their jaws and between their eyebrows. He pre-
tended that he was measuring electrical activity between the
electrodes and got them to relax and contract their facial
muscles. What he discovered was the participants had the
same experience as him – when he simulated fake-smiling
and asked them how they felt, they reported that they felt
happy. He went on to conduct nearly a hundred more experiments to prove his theory and discovered that it's not just
emotion that can be manipulated in this way. Critically, his
experiments showed that people felt the emotion after they
had performed a particular behaviour. For example, he says
participants in various experiments '. . . report low self-esteem
after they have been made to stand in a slumped posture, and
high self-esteem after they have been made to stand up
tall; . . . report feeling they deserve a bad outcome after they
had "lost" an apparently random coin toss that they agreed
would determine the outcome; . . . report being romantically
attracted to strangers into whose eyes they were required to
stare.'

Along the way, Laird also found that the area of feelings
and self-perception is far more complex than he had envisaged. He also discovered that there is a link between facial
cues and a wide range of emotions and feelings, such as pain,
confidence, feelings of liking and disliking, panic disorder,
post-traumatic stress disorder and taste sensitivity. Stick with
that theory for a minute and consider how much control you
have over the way you feel and how you perceive your mood.
You already know that when you look good you feel more
confident. Laird takes that a step further: if you can fake a
smile to make you happy, frown to induce anger, then how
much more can you change the way you feel through your
own behaviour?

And just so you don't have to rely on Laird's work alone, another study in 2002 also set out to explore the emotional experience of fake-smiling. On this occasion the participants were told not to use any facial muscles, but to hold a pencil in their mouths to create different kinds of smiles, from pursed lips to wide upturned smiles, while they watched funny videos and pleasant scenes. Other participants used the pencil to induce a frown. And guess what? The ones with the upturned mouths laughed more at the funny clips than the ones who faked a frown.[18]

The results supported Laird's theory that making the face smile – even using a pencil – makes people feel happier. Other studies, by the way, have tried the same method but using chopsticks, so if you don't feel like making your facial muscles do the work, use whatever's handy to push your mouth upwards in a big wide smile. Before long, you will begin to feel better and your smile will be genuine.

In 2012 another study explored the idea of holding a smile on your face to reduce stress and, astonishingly, the researchers discovered that not only did it do just that, it also helped reduce the heart rate of the participants.[19] Psychological scientists Tara Kraft and Sarah Pressman at the University of Kansas said they wanted to see if the old saying 'Grin and bear it' had any scientific merit. They found that smiling, whether you feel like it or not, helps you cope with life's stresses. So the old saying holds some truth after all.

18 Robert Soussignan, 'Duchenne smile, emotional experience, and autonomic reactivity: a test of the facial feedback hypothesis', *Emotion*, no. 2, March 2002, 52–74.
19 Tara Kraft and Sarah Pressman, 'Grin and bear it: the influence of manipulated facial expression on the stress response', http://www.psychological science.org/index.php/news/releases/smiling-facilitates-stress-recovery.html.

8. FEAR: BEING AFRAID IS GOOD

It may be an odd notion, but fear provides impetus and energy in your life. Not the paralysing, limiting fear that puts years on you but the kind of fear that makes you realize how long it has been since you stepped outside your comfort zone and took a risk. When we are young, we are almost always doing things for the first time – sitting significant exams at school, going to college, attending interviews, start- ing a new job: it's part of growing up, to face things that scare us and overcome that fear. Nonetheless, there is a per- ceived wisdom that we should avoid situations that make us feel fear. We fear fear itself – that it will debilitate us, embar- rass us or even destroy us. It's not true. Fear keeps us alive and, more importantly, makes us feel alive.

I talk all the time about how I have learned far more from failure than success in my business life. Way before the cur- rent trend towards embracing failure in leadership growth, I was preaching to young entrepreneurs about the importance of failing and the lessons you can learn from things going wrong. If everything I had ever tackled and every risk I had ever taken had paid off, I wouldn't have achieved what I have achieved in my business life. So how does failure relate to fear? For me, they come hand in hand: being afraid to be afraid limits us in terms of risk-taking. We grow up to fear failure – in our exams, relationships, etc.; if we set goals, we want to succeed. That's a healthy aspiration, but where it becomes limiting is when, as we grow older and have more control over our lives, we choose goals we know we can achieve. We can determine how high to set the bar so that it remains attainable for us – worse still, we stop setting the bar at all.

Our fear of fear becomes so ingrained that, as we go

through life, we automatically shun activities and situations that might frighten us. But remember your fearless younger self, who took a risk on meeting someone new, who made new friends and learned how to live away from home. Remember that, and then remember how energizing and liberating it feels to face something daunting and win through. It's fantastic, and it makes us feel we are really living life to the full.

I was helping someone recently who was painfully shy and deeply uncomfortable about speaking in public. Mathew (not his real name) had spent his life avoiding having to put up his hand or take the lead during company presentations. In all the time I have known him, I can count on one hand the number of times he has spoken in public – at meetings or conferences. He came to me because his daughter was getting married and he wanted to do her proud on the day with his speech. It took a lot of courage for Mathew to come to see me because we are business associates and he had to admit something deeply personal to me in terms of his fears and worries. He told me he was spurred on because his daughter was already finding ways to excuse him from his father-of-the-bride duties. He really wanted to impress her and the rest of the family and prove that he could do something he had spent a lifetime avoiding.

We painstakingly worked through hours of practice, honing the script, the delivery, the pauses, the humour. It took weeks to create the perfect ten-minute speech that hit the right note in terms of tone and delivery. It was important that the speech sounded like it was his, not Norah Casey's. There were times when he would throw down the pages in frustration if he forgot his lines or stumbled over words, and on those days he would threaten to give up. But he came for the next session with renewed determination. Now, unless you understand the gut-wrenching anxiety of someone who shuns the spotlight, you won't really appreciate what a challenge this was for him. Not only was he confronting those fears at a very significant event, he was also going to be talking to the most important people in his life – who are sometimes our harshest critics!

When the big day arrived Mathew had managed to keep his preparations secret; his daughter and wife were anxiously asking him if he had a speech ready. Mathew had no notes and no written speech because he was rehearsed to within an inch of his life and needed no paper to remind him of what he was going to say. When I called him that day, he was full of self-doubt, imagining all kinds of terrible scenarios, from forgetting his lines to being stilted in his delivery. But he also had the determination to see it through – he had worked hard and he wanted to succeed.

I was in the room that day as a wedding guest. When he stood up, I could see his daughter and his wife glancing anxiously at him – they were being protective and were worried for his sanity, no doubt, especially as he didn't have a single note in his hands. What followed next was amazing – Mathew delivered his speech with confidence, pausing at all the right moments, glancing around the room to include everyone in his eye-line; he smiled warmly at his daughter and pulled off a nice tongue-in-cheek joke about his new son-in-law. When he finished, the applause was thunderous and his daughter leaped to her feet to hug him. He was the talk of the day. And what of Mathew himself? I have never seen him look more alive: he was pumped up, animated, talkative – there was a vibrancy about him that almost made him a magnet for people. His energy was phenomenal. I asked him later in the evening how he had felt, and he told me he hadn't felt so alive for a long time.

For Mathew, facing his fears in that way changed his life. He didn't go on to become a motivational speaker or to run for the presidency, but there was a significant change in his behaviour. He is now much more comfortable interjecting in boardroom conversations, I have heard him make excellent points at public events and he has even been an expert commentator on a radio current-affairs programme. He knew his fear was holding him back so he pummelled it into submission – and he has never regretted it.

Mathew is just one of many examples I could use to illustrate this point. We all have things that scare us, but it's not acceptable to sit back and never tackle the fear. If you do that, it holds sway over you and is likely to become bigger and more irrational as you get older. You can take a key piece of advice from Mathew's story: prepare to tackle your fear. If you are well prepared, you can achieve anything. You'll have to put in the hard work beforehand, but if you set yourself a difficult goal, which involves risk, you will get a huge sense of achievement from conquering your fear and attaining that goal. We spoke earlier about the worldwide obsession with youth, which fuels a head-spinningly huge cosmetics economy: wouldn't it be truly revolutionary if we all became obsessed with the really good things about youth, like taking risks, doing new things every day, ignoring the fear and achieving the goal?

9. SIMPLE PLEASURES: MUSIC, READING, LAUGHTER

I started to listen to music during my evening walks as I tried to plan a better self. Music has been a great companion throughout my life, but never more so than in the past couple of years. As well as the body and the brain, you need to look after your mind – or perhaps I mean your soul. Music does that for me. My gentle music-filled walks became a regular feature in my life and I felt so much better because of them.

There is magic in music – it transports us, lifts us up, changes our mood and, unbelievably, it also makes us move. While it never enhances our ability to survive, music is intrinsically part of our human make-up. We used music and song before we could speak – even day-old infants are soothed and captivated by lullabies. Sometimes when we listen to music it goes straight to the brain for processing, while at other times it goes to our spinal cord so we just have to dance, tap our feet or sway along in spite of ourselves. Music was and still is an important part of my rehabilitation and evolution as a person. I see it as another vital ingredient for my mental and physical well-being. In those early weeks of rediscovering physical exercise, I used to play anthems or songs that made me feel good. I was in Scotland as a nurse and loved the Proclaimers, so of course 'I'm Gonna Be (500 Miles)' was on the playlist, and while not really reaching that milestone, it certainly got me round the park a few times! When I felt lonely I played The Lumineers' 'Ho Hey' or Outkast's 'Hey Ya'. To me, these were modern anthems that made me feel I was part of a larger group, that I belonged to a club – even if it was limited to people who loved that song, too. On melancholic evenings, when I wanted to be kind to myself, I listened to the beautiful 'Be OK' by Ingrid Michaelson. If I wasn't writing this book, I might be tempted to write about how magical and powerful music is in our lives. It's something I had forgotten until Richard passed away and I had to learn a different way.

Similarly, I think the ability to read and lose ourselves in a good book is one we should nurture and aim to retain all of our lives. Reading can deliver a very important side-effect in the shape of empathy, perspective and understanding. It is another way of walking in someone else's shoes and encourages us to stretch our viewpoint wider to encompass new experiences and thoughts. It's good for our brain to keep reading and I think it's good, too, for the development of our emotional and social intelligence. Too often I hear people say, 'Oh, I don't really read any more. No time. Used to when I was younger, but no time now.' To them I can only say, 'Make the time. It's worth it.'

On one edition of *MindFeed* (my regular weekly radio show on Newstalk), I set about trying to find out the science behind laughter – quite simply, what makes things funny. I know that watching something that makes me laugh lifts me out of myself on even the most difficult days. In the months after Richard's death, I bought the top hundred funniest movies of all time online, and Dara and I would watch one each evening – a treat for getting through the day. Anything with John Candy in it would have us both laughing heartily (*Uncle Buck* was a big favourite). *Dirty Rotten Scoundrels, Airplane!*, all of the Monty Python films (Dara could recite whole sections of *Life of Brian*) – they were great therapy for our bruised souls. So, my quest was to see why we find some things funny and others not.

I read a lot about the science of humour, if you can call it that, for that *MindFeed* programme, and it's all fascinating. It has been calculated, for example, that children laugh about four hundred times a day, while adults laugh about fifteen times. Isn't that striking? But think back to your childhood: you were quick to laugh – often silly, even normal things were inexplicably funny and you were always giggling with friends. Later on, we get serious, focused and we can forget to see the funny side. I don't want to sound trite, but I do think in the low times, we need humour more than ever, but that's usually when we shut down and don't allow ourselves to laugh. But you *are* allowed to laugh – give yourself that licence. Science has shown that laughter is good medicine. There is also evidence that happy people live longer, make better bosses, better employees and stay healthier. So don't forget to laugh! Keep company with people who have a capacity for fun and happiness. Make a point of watching a funny movie as regularly as you can and support the great comedic talent we have by going along to live shows and festivals. It makes things seem better somehow.

It's common, during difficult periods, for us to turn away from music, novels, comedy – the simple enjoyment that allows us to lose ourselves in other worlds. I wonder if, perhaps, we deny ourselves permission to enjoy those things because we are so trapped in ourselves during the difficulties, so trapped that we can't lose ourselves in other worlds. We should try to avoid or overcome that: losing ourselves in something else is healthy, and it helps.

10. STAYING CONNECTED TO OTHER PEOPLE

One of the words we most often hear associated with old age is 'loneliness'. Charities emblazon that word on posters, urging people to remember the older people around them who may drop off the edge of our fast-paced lives until we realize we haven't seen or talked to them since last Christmas. Anyone who has experienced loneliness – no matter their age – can attest to how debilitating it is. Physically, it often traps you in your house because you've 'no one to go out with'. Mentally it traps you in numerous ways: it locks you into your own thoughts; denies you fresh perspectives on life; shuts you out of conversation and laughter; decreases your self-confidence and self-esteem. I haven't yet conducted my usual level of research into the phenomenon of loneliness, but even a cursory read is enough to tell you that it can be a very serious condition. Studies have linked loneliness to depression, suicide, increased blood pressure, obesity and sleep problems.

It's essential, throughout our lives, that we seek out company, make new friends and involve ourselves in hobbies, groups, activities that bring us into contact with people regularly. Often we can be our own worst enemy in this – 'I couldn't go along', 'I'm not a joiner', 'They wouldn't want me in that group', 'But I've never done it before, I'd be the worst one there.' All of those excuses mean one thing: 'I'm scared'. That's fine, be scared, but go out and do those things anyway. No one is going to come knocking on the door, pleading for you to do something new. This is where resilience and determination come in because you've only got yourself to fall back on – you are the driver of your own life.

My own mother is a good role model in this regard. We, her children, were quietly worried when she decided to take in young lodgers, but we were completely wrong. As she described in Chapter 4, those young people brought new life into her home and she benefited hugely from it. It's a case of putting yourself in that position, even if you're not entirely comfortable with it, because human contact, the support of friends and shared conversations are the basis of a vital and happy life.

As I look back over this chapter, the list may seem strange, but as I said at the start, I've just set out what worked for me.

Sometimes the simplest thing can strike a shaft of light through a dark day, or ignite a new passion in you, a new quest or goal. I would urge you to keep trying things – don't stop. This is all part of living fully, being alive to the opportunities around you for fun, learning and laughter. It isn't always easy and you won't always feel like it, but aim to keep moving – don't stand still.

11. Bright Sparks – Inspirational People Who Live Life to the Full

Back at the start of writing this book I found myself in Penguin Ireland's offices on St Stephen's Green in Dublin. In the room were Michael McLoughlin, the MD, Patricia Deevy, Editorial Director, and my agent, Sheila Crowley from Curtis Brown in London. It was our second meeting to talk about *Spark!* Most business gurus pontificate on the importance of simplifying and streamlining a proposal into a few succinct sentences, but I always find it difficult to do the 'elevator pitch' when it's something I care passionately about. There was a book inside me bursting to break free and I took the floor to sell it with gusto. When I drew breath Michael said, 'There is only one problem, Norah. I can see how persuasive you are when you are here before me talking so fervently, but can you translate that into words on paper?'

He had a point. The whole landscape of communication and the power of the spoken word versus the power of the written word is the subject of my long-running PhD which I began many years ago at the University of Wales. How indeed could I use the limitations of words on paper to convince you that it is possible to live life at a higher plane, to be the best version of yourself and to unleash that powerhouse of potential inside you?

So this is my back-up plan.

I figured that if you got to the end of the book and were still not convinced of the sense or otherwise of what I wrote that I could rely on the stories of ten inspirational people to prove my case.[1]

For the past while I have been doing a weekly show on Newstalk called *MindFeed* – morsels for the brain on Sunday mornings. What I loved about the show was the indulgence (in today's media world) of talking at length to one inter-viewee each week who agreed to take the '*MindFeed* Chair'. What they signed up to was an honest appraisal of their lives. So no matter how famous, rich or successful they all shared their humanity – the strengths and weaknesses, the pitfalls, hurdles and achievements that made them who they are. In Chapter 5 I urged you to do a self-audit – to look back at your life and assess the highs and lows but I encouraged you to do it just for you – a private audience with yourself. My guests on *MindFeed*, however, signed up for a very public self-assessment that uncovered some startling truths about them – for many of them the revelations were a first.

Not many interviewers want to delve into the minds of their guests, and few get the chance to spend as long as I did talking to interviewees. I have talked to rock stars, pop stars, some of the world's wealthiest people, great entrepreneurs, explorers, writers, people who earn their living making us laugh, politicians, selfless charity campaigners, heroes of sport and creative geniuses. And you know what they all have in common? They were just human like you. And without exception they faced many of the challenges shared by the rest of humanity – grief, adversity, personal and professional

1 My thanks to Newstalk for their permission to transcribe the following interviews from *MindFeed* and use them as the basis for the profiles that fol-low: Joanne O'Riordan; Cecilia Ahern; Pauline McLynn; Michael Carruth; Adam Clayton; Roma Downey; David Essex; Pat Falvey; Jocelyn Bell Burnell; Fionnula Flanagan.

failure, mental and physical challenges, humiliation, fear, anger, loneliness and more. But what set them apart is that they found a way through. They figured out how to seize life again and again despite the knocks, and they not only learned to live life to the full, they discovered how to be the best version of themselves. So all the way through this book I have been using the limitations of words and my own personal story to share that message with you, and now I am unleashing the most powerful weapon of all — the life stories of my real-life heroes who epitomize what living a vital life means to me. So now you don't just have to take my word for it.

Joanne O'Riordan

There is an awe-inspiring young woman I'd like you to meet. Before I introduce her, I have a little exercise for you first. I'd like you to cast your mind back to when you were sixteen. Remember how it felt. Exciting, perhaps. Overwhelming, too. Lonely, for many. One thing I think we all felt as teenagers was that we were somehow different, that the world couldn't begin to understand the unique constellation that was us. We may even have written terrible poetry to that effect. To discover what fitted you, you pushed against boundaries: you tried on new emotions for size, tested your family to their limit and probably broke a limb or two, just to find out what your body could and could not do. You felt different, yet so desperately wanted to feel the same as everyone else. And those terrible, terrible clothes? You're forgiven. At sixteen, you most likely wanted to look like everyone else, too.

Today you realize that whatever made you different as a teenager was to be your greatest asset. Geek then? Technology Titan now . . . There are a thousand other examples. If I were to write a letter to my teenage self, it might read: 'Dear Norah. Try not to worry. You are exactly who you are supposed to be.' Had my teenage self read it, I doubt she would have been convinced! Because it has taken me, and everyone I know, decades to appreciate that being unique is the most powerful, precious gift we possess.

Meet Joanne O'Riordan. At eighteen, she is no different from any other teenager. She loves One Direction, is a passionate football supporter and a self-confessed iPhone addict. She has dyed red hair and, when we meet, is preparing to sit her Leaving Certificate. Joanne is smart, funny and ambitious. Like any teenager, she gets angry sometimes . . . and no more so than when someone won't allow her to speak. She's very good, incidentally, when it comes to speaking. Joanne O'Riordan is a typical teenager in every sense, but two. In 2012, aged sixteen, she delivered a stunning keynote speech to the United Nations. And in 1996, by virtue of her birth, she entered a very tiny group of individuals diagnosed with tetra-amelia syndrome.

'Tetra-amelia syndrome means that you were born without your limbs,' she explains. 'And there's no real explanation as to why that happened. There are only six [correct at time of interview] other people in the world like me, so that's what makes us pretty unique.'

I'm talking to Joanne on the eve of the release of a documentary entitled *No Limbs, No Limits*. Created by her big brother, Steven, it chronicles her life to date and includes home footage of Joanne's tireless attempts to beat the odds. It shows how each day for her has been an uphill struggle, how incremental improvements in her quality of life have demanded a preternatural strength of will. 'I'm unique,' she says. 'But I'm not different. I have overcome many barriers and obstacles that may be inconceivable to any able-bodied person. It never matters how long it takes to get there. All that ever matters is that I try, and try again . . .'

Joanne grew up in a modest house in County Cork with her parents, Ann and Dan Joe, three brothers and one sister. Her early years, as recounted in her brilliant TED Talk (www.ted. com), featured various contraptions, each designed to improve her mobility. One, a 'flowerpot-type thing' worked: it allowed Joanne to sit in it and 'bop around a bit, explore my environment . . . look at something other than the ceiling'. Next was a 'little jacket' with fake limbs attached. This was less successful.

'My brother said it made me look like a plastic doll. My family, like me, preferred me as I was – natural.' Following that, a micro-electric hand was created, but proved too heavy for the little girl to use. Meanwhile, Joanne's parents had decided to encourage her to walk – which in Joanna's terms meant learning to balance upright and propel herself forwards unassisted. Their daughter smiles at their optimism even now.

'There were many times I fell and cried,' she says. 'But eventually I, like so many others, took my first "step". This was a step into the realization that my life would no longer be on the floor, or in a pot, restricted.'

Restrictions lifted, Joanne really got moving. Aiding this was her 'car', a motorized wheelchair allowing her to move in any direction she pleased, and at speed (she likes speed). It was in this car, in February 2011, that she squared up to a politician named Enda Kenny, who was then on the hustings trail in her hometown of Millstreet, County Cork. There he made her a promise: should his national leadership campaign prove successful, she could be assured that government disability allowances would not be cut.

Enda won. Joanne was delighted, describing him to school-friends as a 'legend'. She and her family knew that daily life with government allowances was challenging enough; reduced assistance was an unthinkable prospect. So a 2012 budget announcement came as a crushing blow: disability allowances were, after all, to be reduced. Enda had reneged on his promise. As for Joanne? She was angry.

Using her chin to type, she wrote the nation's leader a letter. 'The next time,' it read, 'do not tell people like me something that you are not going to do.' She upbraided him in the press, speaking of how disabled people have a voice, yet are not listened to: 'You have to shout out louder to make sure you are heard.' Her shouts were heard. The Taoiseach reversed his decision and Joanne found herself an unintentional heroine. News headlines carried her name. National awards followed. Invitations to address the world came next.

'I never thought it would become this big, entire situation,' she tells me. 'When he came to Millstreet, I was just having a general conversation with him.' In retracting his decision, Enda Kenny has, she says, regained her respect. 'I still like Enda Kenny, even if people find that hard to believe. I met him at the People of the Year Awards in 2012. He told me that he had done his research and found out that we share the same birthday . . . but I already knew that!'

I ask a simple question: how is life today? 'I have always wanted to be independent,' she responds. 'As a teenager now I want to feel like I'm taking on the world, and I can win, and all that jazz . . . I try to do everything by myself.' Joanne is very funny, upbeat company, but I wonder if she has always been such a positive person. Growing up, was she conscious of her differences? 'No, not really,' she says. 'I grew up in an area where everyone knew me from birth. I was lucky in that no one ever picked out the differences, but if you'd go outside of Millstreet, you'd have the odd one or two toddlers saying, "Look at her, she has no hands and legs." But that doesn't bother me, because they're just inquisitive. I know, if I was in their situation, I would probably be the exact same.'

We talk on, and to appreciate her personality, you need to eavesdrop . . .

How do you deal with it, Joanne, when children make comments about you on the street?
Well, their mother usually takes them away before anything more is said! It's fairly awkward that way . . . but if

they do hang around, I would sometimes talk away to them. They're kids at the end of the day. They don't have any malice in what they're saying.

I've spoken to your mum, Ann, before and I know how much your family believes in you. You grew up believing you could be anything you ever wanted to be in the world. So what did you want to be?
I wanted to be a Pokémon trainer or a firefighter. I thought I could do anything! Now, I'm hoping to become a sports journalist, covering GAA or Spanish soccer. The big aim is to have my own TV show, so hopefully that will happen soon.

Are you mad about sports?
Ya – it's a slight obsession! Since I was about three years old my father said I had an obsession with sweaty men!

You're a very lovable young woman, but if Ann were here would she talk about the rebellious side of the teenager?
Ann would tell you about the hormonal teenager who's having mental breakdowns every hour of the day . . . No, I'm joking! I suppose I'm a regular teenager. I have good days and down days and whatever. I was reading this thing about 'what tree you are' the other day. It told me I'm a nutwood – that I have a really bad temper and that I'm an egotistical maniac and always have been . . . It described me pretty well, I'm not gonna lie!

You might be a regular teenager, but you're no ordinary young woman. You were invited to the UN to speak before the International Tele-communication Union. How did the invite come about?
It came about after one of my appearances on *The Late Late Show*. An Irishman named Paul Conneally – who is based in Geneva – was organizing a conference for girls in

technology . . . He saw my interview and saw how obsessed with technology I was, and how much it made an impact on my life. I often say that technology is one of my limbs. So I went over, did my speech, and it all happened on the week of my sixteenth birthday, which was pretty cool.

Were you nervous?
No, not really. They're just regular people, only in fancy suits!

You used the occasion to challenge the tech community to produce a robot for you, to assist you in daily life . . .
They asked me what my personal wish was, and I said it was for them to build me a robot. I remember writing the speech with my brother, Steven. When we got to the robot bit, he said, 'You can't say that . . .' And I said, 'I can and I will.' So we put it down. And I suppose we were naïve because we thought a robot might be built and given to me on the spot. What happened was that Trinity College offered to begin the build, and we started working closely with them . . . and then we saw that it's a long process!

Robbie the Robot was unveiled by Trinity engineers in March 2014 . . . Have you had a chance to try out the prototype?
Well, Prototype 1 is the physical shape of him . . . It doesn't really do anything yet, so the next stages are about getting it to do the things I want it to do. My father says it's like a shopping list . . . You upgrade it every so often.

What do you want him to do?
He's going to do all the basic things that you would take for granted. He would pick up things that I drop, open doors, get me a drink from the fridge . . . small things like that.

So Robbie will exist independently of you, obeying your instructions . . .
Yeah, I call him the 'slave without emotions' – I think
that's the best way to phrase it!

I think every woman would want something like that in her life!
I know, right? But seriously . . . in fifty years' time,
everyone will have one. They'll look back at me challenging them to build me one at the United Nations and
think, That's not much of a challenge!

Joanne, what things can you not do that frustrate you?
Well, I suppose I never really look at things I can't do.
Because that would put me down, you know, make it
into a bad day. I try never to focus on that aspect,
ever . . . and if I do start thinking that way I consider it
a small blip. I don't know, I suppose the worst thing is
not being able to play sport, but I exorcize that by being
an obsessive sports fan . . . some would say stalker!
There are always ways around everything.

*No Limbs, No Limits is about you, but it speaks to everybody.
Does that weigh quite heavily on your shoulders . . . your very personal
life up there on a big screen for all to see?*
Well, we never really saw it as that big of a deal . . . For
me, it's more about that awkward moment where I can't
go to the cinema because I might have to see my own
trailer and I'd be cringing with embarrassment. But as
my father would say, 'Pressure is only for tyres!'

What do you do to take the pressure off? Are you a TV addict?
Well, I like the soaps and *Keeping Up With the Kardashi-
ans*, because I enjoy seeing that kind of life. People give
out about it, but if you're having a down day, you can
watch it and have a nice feeling after it. And I always

have this joke with my father that I'm gonna be fairly famous myself one day and I'm going to have fans lining up on the street wanting my picture or my autograph . . .

But you're famous already, Joanne! People must regularly stop you on the street . . .
They always do, actually, which is fairly funny . . . and I love it when people my own age stop me. I like being famous among my own peer group. My big hope would be that if I went abroad I was recognized there. Then I'd feel I'd really made it!

The last time we talked you had a bit of a crush on somebody. Who's the current crush?
The last crush – that's so 2012! Em, I don't know. I think I'm too busy to have a male species in my life . . . They're weird anyway. I mean, come on, who really wants them? I have Robbie – he'll do me fine for now!

Joanne O'Riordan is eighteen. She can type thirty-six words per minute. On her phone, she stores a list of ways to phrase sentences more positively. She is a columnist with the *Irish Examiner* newspaper. She has changed how people with disabilities are perceived, not just in Ireland but globally. She stands twenty inches tall.

Facing a blank page and creating something out of nothing –
now that's what I call spark. This is even more the case when
you use that blank page to create stories that resonate with
people all around the world, regardless of race, religion or
creed. Cecelia Ahern makes it look easy. She is internationally famous as the young woman responsible for twenty-two
million book sales, the woman who, at twenty-one years of
age, hit headlines with the release of *P.S. I Love You* and, perhaps most simply, as the woman with whom so many readers
have shared more than a decade of their lives. Cecelia's creative power has also been transposed to screen, with audiences
in countless countries falling for movies and TV series based
on her books. Yet – and here's the thing – Cecelia Ahern
would continue to write, even if no one was reading.

I've met, and been inspired by, Cecelia on many occasions.
I've been inspired by her composure, her ability to make a
writer's life look easy. She produces a best-selling book a year –
minimum – and in addition has been knocking out short
stories, novellas, children's books and more with staggering
alacrity. I've watched how this softly spoken, often shy Dub-
liner took on the world with a childhood spark. And I am never
more inspired by Cecelia as when I – twenty-one plus tax! –
face a blank page, knowing it's time to breathe life into it.

On each encounter Cecelia will share reports of a new
book, movie or television project she's added her name to.
This time she's fresh from celebrating the tenth anniversary
of *P.S. I Love You* and is fizzing with excitement at *Love, Rosie*,
the big-screen adaptation of her book, *Where Rainbows End*.
Meanwhile, I can scarcely imagine the day I'll see *this* book,

Spark!, in my hands. I want to learn more about her drive, her will to transform her interior world into a proofed, printed and bound reality. A writer's discipline is the natural spring-board for our conversation.

Cecelia, I was lucky enough to know Maeve Binchy, and she would tell me how she approached writing. It was a job for her: up each day with a mandate to write, say, a few thousand words before lunchtime. Do you share her discipline?
I am very disciplined, yes, and I absolutely view this as my job. I write longhand, from Monday to Friday from 9.30 a.m. to 5.30 p.m., taking Wednesdays off. You can be very creative within those hours, but it's very much work, and it's not going to happen unless you sit down and put pen to paper.

Isn't there a secret, though, beyond hard graft?
No! I do a lot of events with people who want to write, and they're sitting there with their pen and paper think-ing there's some secret that they don't know but authors do . . . and if they could just figure it out, they'd be able to write their novel. And really there is no secret: all you do is you sit down and you write. A lot of the time there is nothing there, so you have to make it happen . . .

You have to light the spark. Do you have a method for 'making it happen'?
I always come up with an idea first and then I decide what kind of character would find themselves in that position . . . and as soon as I hear the voice of the char-acter, I know that it's time for me to start writing. It sounds odd, but I start hearing their voice, and I start hearing how they view the world . . . As I'm walking

down the street I kinda start thinking as them. That's when I know the feeling is strong enough to start writing . . . As soon as I can hear the character and see their world, I can start creating it.

Do the ideas come to you based on your own life experiences or from the people around you?
It's from a mixture of both, really. I'm an observer. I absorb everything around me, which is not really a conscious thing. I know Maeve Binchy used to say she'd go to cafés and listen to people, but I prefer silence. I watch people who are listening rather than those who are talking – because they're the ones who don't know they're being watched! And, of course, I put my own experience and my emotions in there. Everything I write about I have felt at some point.

I think that's the difference between you and the vast majority of people – your daydreams take flight as you apply your personal experience to make them real, almost. Was it always so?
Well, I have books of poems and songs, things that I wrote from the age of eight . . . so I suppose I was disappearing into another world from a very young age. Writing was always a hobby, something I did for myself and wasn't even that bothered about showing anyone else. Because it wasn't about other people reading what I wrote, it was about the enjoyment I got from writing.

Do you ever ask yourself why that is, Cecelia? Why escape into your own world from a young age?
I was obviously much happier there! I still do it now . . . If something bad happens, I just go to that place. I'm also processing what's going on in real life, but in the

same way that someone would switch on the TV, or read a book, dreaming is my outlet. I don't need to read a book – I'll just make something up in my mind!

You do read, of course, and have spoken about how the writings of Maya Angelou influenced you in your teens. It was Maya who said, 'Nothing will work unless you do.' Tell me, how did your hobby become your work? You initially completed a degree in journalism at Dublin's Griffith College.

I did. I suppose I chose to do that course because English was the only thing I really enjoyed in school. With journalism there was an element of creative writing, for film and TV, but overall I found that the writing of fact was not where I wanted to be. I wanted to disappear all the time and think, What if this happened? instead. So I went to do a master's in film production, but I really was finding it too difficult at that stage, so I left and decided to just concentrate on writing . . .

Difficult, how?

I call it my quarter-life crisis! I was actually in kind of a sad place . . . Even though I had my boyfriend and I was very happy with him, I was trying to figure out who I was, and trying to find my place in the world. What happened was that I suffered really badly from panic attacks, which took over my life, and made me step out of my life.

What was the knock-on effect of the panic attacks, do you think?

Well, I started looking at other people and thinking, If this is what's going on in my head, what are other people thinking? I'd hear these figures, like, three in ten people suffer from panic attacks, so I'd be in a room thinking, Who are the three that are thinking like me? But I could never find those other people who seemed to be as unhappy as I was. That totally changed the way I thought. It happened at a young age, and it made me look at life very differently.

Is it fair to say that this tough time sparked action in you?
I suppose so, yes. The panic attacks made me stop enjoying my life, which was terrible, but they also made me go into myself, which is what made me start writing my books. It was my way to express myself.

Looking back, do you consider the writing of P.S. I Love You *a form of self-administered therapy, perhaps?*
Yes – it was hard to write, but it was also amazingly therapeutic. I would sit writing from about ten at night until six in the morning. In a way I was hiding because I didn't want to go out into the world, because I felt it was kind of . . . horrible! So I would sit in at night and get lost in this world, and write about this character who also felt very lost, who had lost her identity, and who was grieving.

Which leads me to a question I've always wanted to ask you, Cecelia. I've lived my life and experienced losing my husband, and I couldn't possibly have imagined beforehand what it would feel like when he was gone. Yet there you were, in your early twenties, writing P.S. I Love You, *a story about a woman losing the love of her life. I can't imagine how you could have thought in that way . . . at a time when most young girls are thinking about romance and getting married . . . all that happy-ever-after stuff. Yet you did have the capacity to think along those lines.*
In my best attempt to answer your question, at that time I had never lost anybody I had loved, but I did feel like I had lost myself. And that's the character I still

write about: someone who has been through something very difficult, has lost a sense of themselves, and
who has to try to figure out who they are again. And
from doing that, with *P.S. I Love You*, I became so much
stronger. By the time I'd finished the novel I had a career, one I really wasn't planning on, and I was on the
path to learning who I was.

I'd like to dwell briefly on that idea of becoming who you are. A tough
question, I know, but was your childhood a happy one?
Oh, yes. I was a generally very happy child – promise! It
was just at nineteen that I had a little blip! Growing up
I did hide behind my big sister, Georgina, a bit, let her
do all the talking, but she tells me that whenever things
got too serious I'd jump out with a quick joke, make
everyone laugh, and then I'd run and hide again.

Your childhood did contain one key point of difference, of course, as your
father was Taoiseach of Ireland – the most powerful political post in the
land – from 1997 until 2008. This meant you've been in the public eye
for as long as you've lived, probably . . .
Yes, it's true in that from a young age I knew the feeling
of walking into the room and people paying attention or
watching you. So me and my sister would always be very
careful about that. But I never really thought about it until
people would say it to me . . . That life felt very normal to
me. I didn't feel like I was missing out on anything.

So who do you take after? Your mum, Miriam, or dad, Bertie? Or are
you the perfect combination of both?
I'm both, really. Me and my mum have a very similar
sense of humour . . . and maybe I got the work ethic
from Dad . . .

Do you think you're moving out from under your dad's shadow? You were kinda dogged with the association when first published. Has that eased as time has gone on?

It definitely has, but I must say that I never really felt like I was in his shadow. I mean, I expected every reaction I got. Of course, at the beginning some people thought it was purely Dad that got me all of these book deals, which obviously wasn't the case, but I think it's changing now. And I think that if I was trying to get into politics, then I would have felt in his shadow, but as a writer I've always felt that I've been able to be me, and do my own thing.

The association would have been felt most keenly on home soil, I imagine. I wonder, when you travel for work, are you still asked about your dad?

They do ask, if it's a bigger interview, and, of course, it's an interesting thing because who my dad is did form and shape me. But generally, no, it's about the books and it's about my career.

I think you've more than demonstrated your ability to stand on your own merits! Novels, short stories, children's books – you've even written a play – and your early love for TV and film production is now being played out beautifully in screen adaptations of your work. There must be a secret – because you're making world domination look very easy!

I know how lucky I am. Everyone says, 'Oh, you're so successful,' but the thing is that for every one thing that has worked there are probably ten things I have failed at . . . so if I write something for television, for instance, there will have been about ten ideas I submitted that haven't quite worked – but one luckily gets there eventually.

I'm always saying it's the failures that teach you, that define you . . .
Well, this is the thing. People think I don't understand
what it's like to have rejection, but it happens to me all
the time! Even if magazines say, 'Do you have a short
story?' and I send it in, they'll say, 'No, that's not what
we're looking for'! And particularly in development for
television: they have something in mind, you send it to
them and then they have no difficulty in telling you,
'Nope!'

Is that a bad thing?
Well, no, it's good, because it keeps you on your toes. I
know that people aren't taking just anything that I'm
writing. It needs to be good!

Finally, Cecelia, you recently marked the tenth anniversary of P.S. I
Love You *with a book signing under the clock of the department
store Clerys on Dublin's O'Connell Street. Why there?*
I had the idea for ages that I wanted to do a signing
there because there are so many romantic stories associated with Clerys' clock – it's a traditional place for
Irish courting couples to meet – so we did it last Valen-
tine's Day. And then I went to lunch with my husband,
which was lovely and romantic, too!

I actually had my first kiss under the clock at Clerys . . .
Did you? You see? I love that everybody has a story about
it – it's such a special place.

In life, there are those who tell themselves they're doing it all. And then there are those who, despite all they do, tell themselves it's not enough. Allow me to introduce one woman who, as difficult as it may be to fathom, falls firmly into the latter category: Pauline McLynn.

The actor, comedian and novelist was born in Sligo, on Ireland's west coast, her family relocating to County Galway when Pauline was six months old. A talented student, she studied history of art and modern English at Trinity College, Dublin. It was at Trinity that she made her first foray into the arts, signing up to the renowned Players, the drama society, 'immediately'. From an administrative role with the group, the self-confessed 'bossy one' soon gravitated to the stage, where her flair caught the eye, and the pen, of director and former theatre critic Gerry Stembridge. His glowing reviews of Pauline's performances led her neatly to a gig with the national radio broadcaster, RTÉ, where she encountered a man familiar to us all: Dermot Morgan, a.k.a. Father Ted.

It was the late 1980s when *Scrap Saturday*, Morgan's iconic radio show that brilliantly satirized Ireland's week in politics, took the nation by storm. It pilloried the great and the good of Irish public life with outrageous abandon, ensuring its immortality. Pauline was selected by Morgan to voice 'all the women of Ireland', thereby marking her out as a rare and hugely versatile actor and comedian, even before we came to know and love her via *Father Ted*.

And so to *Ted*. Here, Pauline's portrayal of Mrs Doyle, the refreshment-obsessed doyenne of Craggy Island's Parochial House, was simply peerless. More than holding her own amid the sitcom's stellar cast was no mean feat. Her inspired take on a nerve-jangled, overbearing and hilariously hapless housekeeper has gone down, kettle ever boiled, in the annals of comedy history.

A role like this is, of course, the stuff that actors dream of; a gig that could ostensibly set one up for life. But here's what's so fascinating about Pauline McLynn: being 'set-up' never has settled well with her. Neither, it seems, has being pigeonholed. 'I love throwing myself around, making people laugh,' she tells me when we meet, 'but I also like making them stop for a moment to think.' The peripatetic Pauline has moved from *Father Ted* to *Angela's Ashes*, to Channel 4's *Shameless* and to a coveted spot in the BBC's *EastEnders*. Her TV and film roles have been punctuated by powerful per-formances on the boards: that's right, Mrs Doyle really can do Beckett. All this, and – did I mention? – Pauline has writ-ten no fewer than eight best-selling novels. She sounds like someone who ought to know she's something special.

When Pauline and I sit down, however, it becomes very clear that her propensity for – or steadfast dedication to, more like! – self-deprecation is anything but an act. She truly believes that nothing she does is ever quite good enough. Her acting success, literary success, even her crafting success (this woman makes and sells amazing tea cosies) do little to quell those constant niggling questions about her ability and worth.

Her internal dialogue, she confides, is heavy on lines like 'Well, you wouldn't be able to do that again, would you?' and 'I don't know how you managed to do that' or even 'You're fooling everyone!' This, I'd venture, chimes with the cogni-tive dissonance so many of us practise – the unlikely art of believing one thing to be true while acting as though the opposite were the case. We tell ourselves we're a bit useless while doing astonishing things. We achieve something remarkable, then wonder how we pulled it off. We do our best, then somehow refuse to accept that our best is enough.

Is this inherent self-disparagement necessarily a faulty vehicle? Must we apply its brakes to maximize our potential? Or, can this floating sense of unfulfilment act not as a power drain but as a powerhouse of propulsion?

Here's an insight to my chat with Pauline . . .

Pauline, you have been many things and many people, once voicing 'all the women in Ireland', in fact! You've certainly never been typecast. Why is that, do you think?

I suppose I'm hard to pigeonhole as an actor, because I do love throwing myself around, making people laugh, but equally making them go, 'Oh', making them think, as well.

It's inevitable I ask you about that other talent, the inimitable Dermot Morgan. Tell me about your relationship with him.

Me and Dermot, we'd done *Scrap Saturday*, and then we'd catch up with one another, usually around Christmas time, and we'd disgrace ourselves around Dublin . . . Dermot gatecrashed my wedding, actually, on New Year's Eve in '96, causing a bit of mayhem. The bride didn't get a look-in with him around!

I rest my case! It was Dermot who taught me how to do the 'apology tour' – you know, the morning after the night before . . . that, if you had any class at all, you'd either replace what you'd drank at someone's house, or give them flowers and an apology. Mostly I remember Dermot as one of those incredibly electric people who was never happy with what he had because he knew there was more to be had.

How so?

When we did *Father Ted*, as much as he loved doing it, we were guns for hire and you could tell that he wanted to be doing something else, something of his own. When the call came that he was dead, I couldn't believe there was to be no more. But I wonder — and I know it's horrible to lose anyone — if that was the way for him to go. In a blaze of glory. Within twelve hours of finishing the last *Father Ted* ever, he was gone. As a statement, that's kind of magnificent when you think about it. But do I still wish he was around? Of course I do.

There's that sense of unfulfilled potential I'm interested in. When I think about you and Dermot, I think there must have been some sort of genetic trait running through you both — that searching to do better always. Looking at your journey from Ted *to* EastEnders, *it has been . . .*

Madness!

Not madness: incredible, actually. And yet I know that you dine out on disparaging yourself, which is extraordinary considering your abilities and achievements. I sometimes think you must be ninety years of age when I look at all you've done. Are you driven, do you think, by that sense of unfulfilled potential?

Do you know what? When you say it like that, I often think I'm telling lies to people. When I say I've written eight novels, I think, Did I? Could I do it again? I'm not sure. I've no idea how it happened. I just go from one thing to the next.

So there's no road map?

Not at all — no plan. I wish there was! And when I get down, which I do — very much so — I get very down because I think nothing's good enough. Mind you, even when I'm up, I don't think anything is good enough either!

I think people will find that hard to believe, but I hear you. I wonder, when you play all these characters – I'm thinking especially of your tough role on Shameless *– does it affect you? Can you leave it behind when the camera stops rolling?*

It's strange you bring *Shameless* up because I had a very strange experience on that show. I got way too involved with all of the series, and some of the actors, and to be honest with you, it kinda broke me. When my time there ended, because it had to, that was the last time I wrote a novel. I got burned out writing, and found myself in a big life crisis. Then, to cap it all off, I got the menopause. Well, lovely. If you're gonna kick a girl, why not do it while she's down?

Did that tough time reinforce you? What has it done for you, in hindsight?

What it has done for me is that it was a big reality check. Now I feel so much for anybody who has any trauma or mental-health issue – let's say depression. When I left *Shameless*, it was like a bereavement, and I feel for any-body who will ever find themselves in that situation in their life, in their career, or whatever. Because it's taken me about three years to get back to being happy again. And that's with help.

When you say a bereavement . . . ?

I think of it as a bereavement for a life you think you might have had. I really do feel for people who are going through any of that.

Life is pretty tough at times, especially if you face several challenges at once. Yet you say you're happy now. How do you protect yourself from the dark clouds coming back?
Well, here's the thing. I don't know how it is for you or anyone else, but I think that when you experience something tough, you're always left a little vulnerable. I think the older you get, the more vulnerable you get, because you've lived, you know. Isn't that it?

Doesn't adversity sometimes make you a bit stronger?
No, I don't think it does. I think it makes you more vulnerable to everything, but you're kind of cuter about how you deal with things, maybe. And I do think the older you get, the more sensitive you get, too.

Pauline, you've given so much laughter to us all, but what makes you laugh? What makes you happy?
Very stupid things make me laugh. Like people falling over – I can make myself laugh by falling over. And misery. I suppose that's why I like *EastEnders* so much. I mean, there's nothing funnier than misery, is there? Nothing funnier than the most unfunny thing in the world!

Michael Carruth

The thing I love most about my work? The people. Time spent in TV, radio and publishing has afforded me a very special privilege: I'm allowed to get under the skin of the most extraordinary people. What they have accomplished in life is interesting, but what I find really fascinating is the psychology that underpins their achievements. Be it the refusal to conform or the will to win, those are the magic ingredients, the dots to join in shaping a blueprint for success.

Boxing is not my strongest subject, but Michael Carruth is a name I know well. Michael – who in 1992 won Olympic gold in Barcelona – was the man who brought a nation to its feet as his hand was raised aloft, victorious. He is the man who, while a relative underdog, won Ireland's first Olympic gold medal since 1956 (and no other Irishman has claimed gold since). The world has come to perceive Ireland as a crucible of boxing excellence, thanks in no small part to the inimitable Katie Taylor, but it was Michael Carruth who put us in the ring.

When we meet, I want to learn more about the magic ingredients – his family, upbringing and talent – that conspired to create a world-beating athlete. By our conversation's conclusion, however, I have come away with an even more intriguing piece of information: in order to succeed, Michael Carruth needed to fail first.

Born in the South Dublin suburb of Drimnagh, Michael was one of Austin and Joan Carruth's ten children, and a triplet to boot. His father, a carpenter, fashioned a three-unit crib for the triplets, meaning little Michael was fighting his corner, quite literally, from day one. 'From the very start we were into boxing, even if we didn't realize it! Dad said there was great competition between us in the crib, and it was great for him to watch.'

It helped that Dad was one of the country's most respected boxing coaches, and it was through the sport that Michael's parents had met. 'My da boxed for St Francis Boxing Club down on Usher's Quay,' he tells me. 'My mother's father was one of the chairpeople of the club and her brothers, my uncles, boxed there. My uncle, Martin Humson, was the first light-middleweight champion of Ireland. So my da was hanging around with the Humson lads when he discovered they had a pretty sister. It went from there.'

With the home support team firmly in place – even if Joan could rarely bear to watch her son compete – honing his craft came next. Here's where Michael had an advantage: while other kids searched to find suitable sparring partners, his ideal opponents came ready-made in the form of his brothers, Martin and William. 'As a triplet, when you get into the ring with one or the other of your brothers, there is no fear there,' he explains. 'So we would absolutely leather each other, and my dad had to pull us out of the ring.'

This was the best kind of competition: the kind where each individual pushes to the last, a healthy rivalry where not only physicality but a winner's mentality ensured the edge. As Michael puts it: 'I suppose the beautiful thing was that we really did help one another. You never wanted to lose face against one of your brothers, so you got that inner toughness and the will to win. That's what drove me on to be as good as I was. I always had that belief in myself that I could win.'

The stars continued to align as, on leaving school, Michael opted to join the army. This was a defining move as, once again, his passion was met with considerable support. 'I won an Irish boxing title within a few weeks of joining the defence forces,' he recalls. 'They saw the potential in me so they kept me in the gym, allowing me to train while holding down my army job at the same time.'

His employers' patronage notwithstanding, Michael's Olympic ambition was such that potential obstacles existed merely to be overcome. 'It was always my dream,' he tells me. 'I remember watching the Olympics when I was eight years old. I had just started with Greenhills Boxing Club at the time, had won my first match. I came back into the corner and the very first thing I said to my dad was, "I'm going to win the Olympics." He looked at me like I was a madman. But he made me promise I'd do it, and so I promised.'

Before Barcelona came the Seoul Olympic Games in 1988. The news landed, courtesy of his father, on a typical Sunday afternoon, that Michael had been selected to compete at sport's highest level. The dream was edging ever closer to reality. The reality of Michael's experience at Seoul was, however, the stuff of nightmares. He made, in his own words, a 'dog's dinner' of the competition, losing in a second-round match that commentators agreed should have been his to win. The reason? A superhuman sportsman had behaved like a very human twenty-one-year-old guy.

'What went wrong in Seoul is that I got caught up in emotion. There was a lot of signing autographs and meeting famous people. I took my eye off the ball and got beaten in my second fight.' It was the classic case of pride coming before a fall, I suggest. Michael tells me that failure was his greatest teacher. 'It was the best experience I've ever got in my life – believe it or not. I just said to myself, "This ain't gonna happen again, and if I can right the wrong of Seoul, I am absolutely going to."'

Four years is a long time to wait, especially in an arena where peak physicality is the premium. Four years of criticism for past failures, too, is endemic in an Olympian's life. Michael had two choices: believe his detractors and bow out, or rebuild his objective, now armed with the wisdom of what not to do. His mother, he confides, was hugely influential in his selection of the latter choice. 'She was there when I lost, when I wouldn't know what to do. She'd give me a cuddle and say, "You'll get him back the next time." After Seoul she said, "It wasn't your time. It will be the next." I was just so disappointed with my failure, but my ma got me back on the bike, as it were, saying little things like, "I know you'll come good." And she was the first one up the steps to congratulate me in Barcelona – she bumped everyone out of the way, including my wife, Paula! She was a great woman, and she always made me believe in myself.'

Cometh the hour, cometh the man: the year was 1992 and Michael Carruth was primed. Meanwhile, his father, Austin, was leaving nothing to chance. 'I called him my tormentor, rather than my mentor,' Michael has said, recounting how his dad would wake him in the middle of the night, dispensing water to allay any risk of dehydration. Before the Olympic final, Austin told his son not to be the aggressor but to 'keep it together' – a line repeated mantra-like from the corner as the Dublin lad of five foot seven took on the might of then world champion, Cuban Juan Hernández, standing tall at six foot three. I ask if Michael can recall how he felt, just as the first-round bell was about to sound. 'I had a sneaky feeling I would win, actually. A gut feeling – we boxers tend to be superstitious and all the omens were looking good to me. I also knew I was in the best condition of my life.'

Nine relentless, bruising minutes later, and that famous

jump flashed into homes across the planet – 'Thank God the ropes were there because I would have done damage to myself otherwise.' The underdog had triumphed, and he scarcely needed a referee's confirmation. 'I knew by Hernández's reaction that I'd won it,' Michael says. 'And it helped that there were around five or six hundred people in the arena for me that day, too . . . We were all waiting for that moment.'

Watching that historic moment raises goose-pimples even now. 'I was remembering that promise I'd made to my father some seventeen years before. I went over to him, hugged him, and he said, "Thanks." I said, "For what?" "For keeping your promise." That made it even more special.'

An intimate exchange was to prove the precursor to a massive public outpouring of pride. 'My dad never was Flash Harry,' Michael reflects. 'After the match he put my gold medal into a dirty sock for safekeeping. I think it was his way of saying, "Just because we have it, it doesn't mean we should walk around like peacocks showing it off."' Ireland, of course, had other ideas. 'We were returning from Barcelona at one a.m. on a Monday morning, and Dublin airport was stuffed full of people, thirty to forty thousand well-wishers. Next, we're driving out of the airport, and there are thousands of people lining each side of the road . . . It was absolutely crazy.'

Amid the euphoria, Michael again looked to his family for stability. 'My wife Paula and the rest of my family were trying to prepare me for what was going on. Because, remember, I went out to Barcelona as a nobody in a sense – and all of a sudden I'm going into this microwave of fame. That's how quick it was.' His wife, his siblings – 'always quick to put me back in my place' – and experience ensured that fame rested easily on Michael's shoulders the second time around. 'I mean, with an Olympic title they can never take it away from you. You'll always be the person asked for an autograph by a kid in the street. But it's very important to have those days where you don't take yourself too seriously. The bottom line was that it was just another fight. I've had ups and downs in my life, and I know that winning a gold medal is not the most important thing there is.'

I ask for his meditations on what matters more than gold. 'Family,' is his immediate response. He talks fondly of his parents: 'They started dating at fourteen years of age and spent fifty-four lovely years together, before my father passed away in 2011 and my ma in 2013. It's been a tough thing for the family, but we'd like to think that they're back together now.' He also mentions a nephew, tragically lost to an accident at the tender age of eight. 'Gary drowned in Blessington Lakes in 1989. That was a terrible blow. His death had actually been a true inspiration for me to achieve in boxing . . . I would push myself even harder for the little fella. Would I have given up my gold medal to have Gary back? In a heartbeat.'

Michael now paces the ropes, as his father before him, putting young boxers through their paces. 'I'm there seven days a week – it's my passion.' I wonder if this Olympic hero ever lets the next generation cut him down to size. 'They do and they don't, Norah.' He smiles. 'I'm the boss . . . but the beautiful thing is that I have so much inside myself that I can give back out. My father gave it all his life, and every boxing coach in the country does the same. My own son, Carl, started boxing only last year. He's doing well, a little south-paw like his dad. He's crafty, but he has a bit to do to catch up!' Michael and Paula are also proud parents to a daughter, Leah, but my suggestion of a Katie-Taylor-in-waiting is swiftly dismissed. 'No, Leah is an aspiring actress. She jokes that when she gets her first Oscar, she's only going to thank her daddy, and not her mammy! That's because her mammy tells her to cop on and get a proper job, but I tell her to chase her dreams.'

Michael Carruth continues to dream, cognizant that every dream may not be realized. A man of few regrets, he concedes that his post-Olympic boxing career might have taken on a different hue. 'All of a sudden, at twenty-five, I had won the greatest prize of them all. People were saying, "Don't go to the next Olympics, because if you don't win, it will take away from the last one, but don't turn professional either." So I'm thinking, You're telling me to give up the thing I love most – apart from family, of course. And I wasn't ready to give up boxing. My only option was to turn professional. I thought, Now's the time to make some money for myself, see if I can set myself up for life . . .' A lack of funding and the inherent volatility of athletic performance combined to make Michael's professional boxing career less stellar than that of his amateur years. The upshot, however, is a man now pursuing a vocation: to provide others with the magic ingredients he had been so fortunate to receive.

We say our goodbyes, Michael leaving me with a very honest, perfectly fundamental account of what international acclaim has meant to him.

'Success like mine is something that changes your life, initially. I mean, "Carruth" was always a name that people got wrong. They'd call us anything from Carruthers to Carrots or whatever . . . and one thing my grandda said, at eighty-nine years old, was, "At least they'll get our name right now." So if I've done anything in my life, people know my name is not Michael Carrot! My name is Michael Carruth.'

'Music is still a mysterious, magical alchemy for me.'

It's a brilliant word, isn't it? Alchemy: a power or process of transforming something common into something special, or, to use its original etymology, an attempt at turning an ordinary metal into gold. Alchemy is a word the articulate Adam Clayton, bassist to the world's greatest rock band, U2, uses when we speak, to describe his enduring belief – his awe, almost – in the transformative power of music. And who better to champion music as a magic elixir? Without music, Adam Clayton's life story could have echoed in an entirely different tone.

That first acoustic guitar, bought in a junk shop for the princely sum of five old Irish pounds, lit the touch-paper that would turn a bedroom strummer into a global, stadium-bursting superstar. Without music, the well providing a life rich in extraordinary experience, success, spiritual satisfaction even, would have run dry. And it is through music that Clayton continues to find refreshment. 'I'm always fascinated by it,' he tells me. 'I'm a little like the goldfish swimming around in the bowl – it always sounds new to me, whichever music is popular at any given time.'

Adam Clayton was born to Brian, an RAF pilot, and Jo, an air stewardess, in Oxfordshire, in 1960; his family relocated briefly to Kenya before making a home in Dublin's coastal town of Malahide when Adam was five years old. Recounting his student experience, he has described himself variously as the 'shy' kid and the 'class clown', a seeming contradiction, yet one thing is certain: academia was not his bag. 'I was a hopeless case,' he tells me, through a wry smile. 'An absolute brat. And I did get asked to leave a couple of schools. I did my Inter and got really very bad grades and I never did my Leaving . . . so I'm not a great example of anything other than perhaps pure determination and awkwardness. I don't recommend it for anyone else!'

The determination element was fuelled, of course, by music, and allied to this an ambition somehow to make his early passion his life's work. Its realization was initially supported by his parents – who gave a fifteen-year-old Adam his first bass guitar – and fated by a friendship with another boy born in England, who now happened to be living down the road. Adam Clayton made firm friends with Dave 'The Edge' Evans, and they answered an ad posted by Larry Mullen at Mount Temple Secondary School. A band was formed (Feedback, later to become U2), and so began a rock story of unbelievable – and unparalleled – scale. Does Adam still pinch himself in disbelief today, I ask, more than four decades, 150 million album sales and twenty-two Grammy Awards later? 'I still scratch my head sometimes and wonder how I got to where I am now,' he responds. 'To have come from North Dublin, with not one piece of education to my name . . . I was just lucky that I ended up in a great band with people who supported me, and that I found music very therapeutic early on.'

I could discuss U2's discography – or ask for a chord of my favourite song – but what interests me is what happens when an untrained group of unknowns becomes globally adored. It's fascinating, especially when you consider it's a question very few individuals on earth can answer. 'I think the very fast rise,' Adam tells me, 'which happened in about 'eighty-seven, 'eighty-eight, when the band was number one with "The Joshua Tree" in America and in something like thirty countries worldwide, was hard to cope with. There's no denying that. And perhaps it took about ten years to adjust to being that kind of – famous is almost the wrong word, certainly being that recognizable to the large majority of young people . . . It was an odd responsibility, let's put it that way.'

Music, the great saviour, led to a great power and hence a great and unusual responsibility. The music that influenced U2 – 'It was very much punk music that represented our generation, spoke to us as seventeen- and eighteen-year-olds' – now fell under their remit, the inspiration of a generation now lying on the shoulders of these four young fellas from Dublin. I ask how Adam and his bandmates approached this mantle: what was their music's mission statement? 'We wanted to push that [punk] further because that music did come very much out of the frustration of the Ireland of the 1970s, the recession, three-day week, very high unemployment. That frustration was an aspect of where we were coming from – because there were no jobs in Ireland at the time – but I think we wanted to move things along on a more spiritual and emotional basis as well.'

Which brings me to the spiritual side of our discussion. As Adam's passion for music was exercised on a world stage, his proclivity to 'escape' from the world – manifested in alcohol abuse – also played out. He has described his relationship with alcohol as something akin to an anaesthetic, one designed to mitigate a low-level depression experienced since his youth. And, as with all false panaceas, a rock-bottom moment tends to light the way to recovery. For Adam, it was his failure to perform at a 1993 sold-out Australian gig, due to overindulgence, that sounded the alarm bell loudly in his ears and those of his bandmates. A successful stint in rehab followed. Of this personal nadir, he has commented, 'That was the end of my world. The only thing I wanted to do was be in a band and perform great songs.'

Now a confirmed and contented ex-drinker, I ask him to discuss his attitude to alcohol today, particularly in the context of the Irish relationship with the stuff. Is depression the root cause of our depressing alcohol-abuse statistics? 'I think depression is generally a symptom of alcohol, rather than a cause,' he says. 'In my case, however, I was kind of aware, but without understanding the language of it, that I was using drinking to escape, quite early on. I always thought, I'll be all right, I'll be able to handle it. But, of course, alcohol feeds back on itself as it is a depressive. It also leads to risky behaviour, which creates more problems.' What has he learned from his experience, and his recovery? 'What I've learned is that two or three drinks for anybody is enough . . .' he considers '. . . enough to create a change in a person's psychology and their physiology – yet that's not how Irish people tend to drink . . . Two or three drinks and they're just getting started. I felt I enjoyed it, had fun with it, but looking back now, I realize that it was not responsible drinking.'

Responsible for himself, responsible to his fans and responsible for a wider message: that's where Adam Clayton stands today, and music can reasonably be thanked for it all. It has provided him with an inducement to overcome personal challenges and, more recently, with a platform to help others battle issues of their own.

I first met Adam at a Walk in My Shoes publicity event, the Irish mental health campaign for which he acts as ambassador. Run by St Patrick's Mental Health Foundation, the aim of Walk in My Shoes is to remove stigmas surrounding mental health and to raise vital funds for vulnerable young adults in crisis. What a coup for St Pat's, to secure the services of a U2 band member. What a powerful thing, too, to have a man of considerable star power admitting vulnerability expressly to promote awareness and acceptance. I ask what drew Adam to the campaign, when requests for his patronage must surely number in their thousands. Could it be linked to his dearly missed mum, who was herself a great fundraiser for the Foundation? 'My mum was drawn to this,' he remembers, 'and she did help fundraise for them, and it was just a strange coincidence that it came back around for me. Then, when I started to look at the statistics of how many people mental-health issues affect, particularly young people – it's one in four, enough to fill about four Croke Parks – I just thought, I really want to be involved in this.'

Adam believes that – for all those not lucky enough to spot an ad posted by Larry Mullen – there are many forms of therapy that can and will make dreams achievable. I think we get to the crux of his motivation when he tells me, 'These young people are full of potential and it's terrible to see wasted talent.' He continues, 'Yet the data suggests that if people get treatment under the age of twenty-four, they can have a full recovery. So this for me is about awareness, it's about letting people know that if they are suffering from any of these mental-health issues they need to seek out help, that it is there for them, and that it will be effective.'

Before we leave one another, I'm keen to learn more about making the creative life work. The early years of U2 saw Adam acting as the band's manager, attempting at least to impose a business structure on musical brilliance. Reflecting on that role, he candidly tells me, 'I had strong ambition for the band, greater ambition than sense. I had this energy that only people between the ages of sixteen and twenty-eight have. Probably looking back now, I don't feel like I'm a natural leader, and I'm not a very good businessperson, but I had the energy to change something back then, and that was what I wanted to do.'

The struggle to make a quintessentially creative existence conform to financial realities is one I've personally witnessed in my business dealings with many a fashion designer, chef or artist. For many, the latter can cow the former into submission; a driving passion dimmed by the quotidian grind. I ask if Adam has ever felt this way, if the waking world has ever trumped his dream relationship with music. 'No,' he replies. 'I find the creative side a much more interesting journey and more interesting conversation to be engaged in. I suppose, going back to our discussion of formal education, the idea that two and two will always be four, no matter what, was and is a disappointment, and slightly dull to me. I think that two and two should sometimes be five, or eight, or whatever . . .'

A bit of a brat he may be. But a hopeless case? Thanks to music, never.

Taking on adversity – and winning – is the theme of many an inspirational life. And to me this holds true for Roma Downey, a woman who has risen from troubled roots to forge a career, and a life, that continues to exceed even her own expectations.

Roma was born against the turbulent backdrop of Derry's Bogside, but is now resident in California, where she sits atop a multi-million-dollar TV and movie business. You may remember her as the beautiful actress portraying Jackie Onassis in the 1991 miniseries *A Woman Named Jackie*, and you'll almost certainly recall her as the leading actress in *Touched by an Angel*, the Emmy-award-winning series starring Roma as real-life angel 'Monica'. What you will be less familiar with is the story of how this Derry girl made an international mark, and how she is now making a triumph of the second chapter in her life. I recently called her at her Malibu home to find out.

We start by discussing her difficult upbringing. 'I grew up in a pretty troubled area,' she tells me. 'We were a city occupied and there were constant riots and explosions.' This was Derry of the 1960s, a place riven by sectarian battle and what she acknowledges as a 'very segregated community', characterized by 'very real fears and very real threats'. She grew up in a 'little row of houses on a hill', studying Irish dancing and piano as a child before taking on her first job as a teenager. 'I worked on a Saturday in a shoe shop in the city centre,' she tells me. An ordinary start, I think, until she sheds light on the quite extraordinary conditions that applied. 'I remember working one Saturday afternoon when we were all told we had ten minutes to get out of the shop. So there we were, wrapped up in our coats, freezing, in the car park, when the shop blew up and it was raining shoes everywhere. That's what I mean by very real fears and very real threats.'

I wonder if she remembers Bloody Sunday, that horrifying day in the Bogside, in January 1972, when the lives of fourteen unarmed civil-rights protesters and bystanders were extinguished and fourteen others were seriously injured by soldiers of the British Army's Parachute Regiment. Roma would have been just eleven years old, yet her response today is immediate. 'Oh, yes, I remember it well,' she says. 'The horror of it, and the darkness that overcame our city and our community. We were a very small community, Norah, so I think everybody was touched personally by any number of the atrocities that happened over the years.' Was she conscious, at the time, of the personal impact of this chaotic environment? 'Well, it was normal for us,' she reflects, 'and it really wasn't until I left for college that I appreciated that most people don't live with a level of constant tension.'

What surely felt less normal, sadly, was that Roma was maturing without a mother's guidance. Maureen Downey, a homemaker and amateur actress, suffered a fatal heart attack at forty-eight, leaving her ten-year-old daughter bereft. In hindsight, Roma has surmised that the Troubles outside her front door were all but eclipsed by the grief experienced on the other side of that door. 'It didn't impinge on me as much as it might have,' she has said, 'because throughout my teens I felt the loss of my mother so acutely.' A decade later her father, Paddy, was also to pass away, leaving Roma no choice but to set about her ambitions unsupported.

She travelled to England's Brighton College of Art, initially pursuing a career in painting before turning her attention to her mother's first love: acting. Her classical training was completed at Drama Studio London, where Roma was named 'Most Promising Student of the Year' on graduation, and was soon thereafter landing roles in respected productions. Next came relocation to the USA, where, she tells me, her income was initially supplemented by a less prominent role: 'My first job in New York was as a hat-check girl in a fancy Upper West Side restaurant,' she smiles, 'but I was doing Shaw and Shakespeare off and on Broadway, and then I got my television break.'

The call came: Roma had been cast to play the iconic Jackie Onassis. This was undoubtedly the big-time, if not quite time to count chickens, as she explains. 'It was a big break. I picked up my bags and moved to Los Angeles. And I remember my publicist calling and saying, "We've got the covers of *TV Guide* and *People* magazine, and it's great." So those covers came out and, of course, who was on the cover but Jackie Onassis herself . . . so I became the actress who played her. It wasn't until *Touched by an Angel* that I was able to create something of my own.'

Touched by an Angel felt right to Roma for several reasons. Here was a chance to play Monica, the show's protagonist, not the 'wife' or 'girlfriend', a trademark of the TV scripts landing so regularly on her lap. The show was also founded on a deeply spiritual theme, chiming harmoniously with the actress's devout Christian faith. Her instinct was to prove correct, of course, as not only did Roma love the series, so too did the world. Millions of enchanted viewers, a ten-year run and an Emmy Award were to follow. And, by a happy twist of fate, the Derry girl was to pick up a very important new relationship along the way.

On-screen, legendary actress Della Reese played *Touch by*

an Angel's Tess, the employer of angel and 'case-worker' Monica. Off-screen, Della and Roma were to develop an amazing bond. 'Della Reese is my mother, you know?' Roma tells me, and she really means it. The pair simply decided to 'adopt' one another, continuing to behave as mother and daughter to this day. They live close to one another, meet regularly, and Della is godmother to Roma's daughter, Reilly Marie. From where did this incredible connection spring? I ask. 'Della also had tragedy in life,' Roma responds. 'And her only daughter passed away while we were working together. I remember she took me in her arms at the time and said, "Baby, God is so amazing because I know he brought me into your life because you needed a mother. I just didn't realize that he brought you into my life because I was going to need a baby girl." Della's family to me, and it is one of the lasting gifts of working on *Touched by an Angel*. What a blessing she has been.'

It's a great example of how the sharing of personal adversity can create an unbreakable bond. But Della Reese's is not the only shoulder Roma Downey can lean on. The actress — and children's author, by the way — is married to Mark Burnett, a TV producer who shares her faith and her ambition. This combination has led to Roma's most incredible achievement yet. She and Mark are executive producers of *The Bible* miniseries, an idea that occurred to them over a cup of tea and became the highest-rating television miniseries of all time. Its 2011 History Channel debut was a staggering hit, and now this dramatic re-enactment of the life of Jesus, featuring Roma as Mother Mary, has amassed an estimated 200 million viewers worldwide. Making it happen — and finding the funds to make it happen — was a passion project for the couple. I ask if the big-budget dream ever felt beyond reach. Was *The Bible* a risk, I wonder, or did she and Mark know that it would just fly?

'I think it was a bit of both,' she replies. 'I don't think you can step out boldly without risk. And I think anybody who's sitting back expecting to have assurance and have everything lined up would never get anything done, would they? There's a certain amount of courage required. But I think we always knew that the stories are big, compelling and moving, so if we could emotionally connect with an audience and get that right, there would be a viewing audience for it. I don't know that we could have dared to dream,' she reflects, 'of what has occurred. As each week unfolded, and the numbers continued to be in the many millions, we were deeply encouraged and we knew that it had touched a core. *The Bible* trended each night on Twitter, which was extraordinary, and we had all kinds of huge stars watching – with Oprah live tweeting! The support was phenomenal and it has all added up to even more people being touched by the story. It's just been fantastic.'

Impressive as *The Bible* is, so, too, I think, is Roma's relationship with her husband. Mark is a former member of the British Army's Parachute Regiment – the guys Roma and her pals would have thrown stones at as youngsters. Today, they not only love one another, they work together, too. On the subject of partners entwined in the personal and the professional – never easy! – Roma confides, 'Yes, we have managed very well, I think! We often joke that other couples can't even do yard work together, but we have managed now for almost five years to be working side by side, together in the trenches. And we're still speaking to each other!'

Before I finish the interview, I want to know what's next for Roma, how she plans to make this second chapter of her

life even more emotionally satisfying. She has recently completed a master's degree in spiritual psychology with the
University of Santa Monica, and is now concentrating on the
next project in her television-production story. 'We have
another series called *A.D.*, which NBC has just purchased,'
she tells me. 'It resets the Bible story from around the time
of the crucifixion – we would all think that that was the ending but we know it was just the beginning. So it will track the
eleven remaining disciples, how their story progressed to
become the start of the early church. It will be a great, exciting drama, and we have also been booked by CBS Network
to bring to the screen a four-hour miniseries called *The Dove-
keepers*, which is based on an Alice Hoffman best-selling
novel of the same name. We hope to bring each of these
projects to the screen in 2015.'

Roma has another project currently in the works, of
course, that of guiding her only daughter, Reilly Marie,
through her transition to adult life. 'She's in her final year in
high school,' Roma tells me. 'I'm hoping that I'm raising a
young woman who's able to go out boldly into the world
with strength and self-confidence, and remembering always
to be kind and gracious, and I'm encouraging her now to
spread her wings. She's going to be heading off to university
in Boston, her life is opening up for her, and it's bittersweet,
isn't it? Anyone who has raised a child knows that you've
raised them to go off independently and yet you want to hold
them close . . . and never let them go!'

Interviewing Roma brought home to me her incredible
energy and drive to succeed. Her beginnings were humble, a
small house in Troubles-torn Derry, and her upbringing
marked by adversity in losing both parents by the age of

twenty, yet she has worked herself to a position of immense influence. When she landed in New York, she was broke and out of work but that didn't dent her determination to succeed. She's an actor, author and producer, and one of the richest people to come out of Ireland. She has retained her appetite for learning and is happily engaged in creating and driving new projects every year. She's a lesson in healthy ambition, self-confidence and the guts to dream bigger than everyone you've ever known. Roma's life is one of vision and aiming high – and she has hit every target.

David Essex

'It's whatever comes along, really, that sparks an interest.'

I met David Essex at the Traveller Pride Awards at Dublin's Rotunda Hospital in June 2014. The awards were designed to promote and protect a sense of esteem within Ireland's travelling, or Pavee, community, and in 2014 David Essex was the guest of honour. No stranger to the spotlight, David has spent more than four decades entertaining the world in a multitude of guises: singer, composer, actor, writer and a breathtaking amount more – which we'll get to later. He was at the awards ceremony because, as you may not know, the Traveller cause is very close to his heart. David's grandfather, Thomas, was a Traveller from County Cork. 'It struck a chord with me,' he tells me, eyes sparkling beneath his flat cap, 'because I like to celebrate my heritage. And I've always had that gypsy, travelling feeling in my heart.'

Post-event, David grants me a personal audience and we conduct an interview for my radio show, *MindFeed*. Here, the sixty-six-year-old Londoner talks to me about his sense of happy restlessness, touching regularly on a need to feel a 'spark' in everything he turns those famous baby blues towards. We discuss his staggering number of incarnations in life, and explore the wandering soul at the root of all. I come away feeling that David's uncompromising attitude offers a fascinating story in itself.

David Essex was born David Albert Cook on 23 July 1947, in Plaistow, east London. His father, Albert, worked on the docks while his mother, Olive ('Dolly'), was a pub cleaner and self-taught pianist. Theirs was not a privileged lifestyle: the trio shared a small house with relatives before securing a council flat in nearby Canning Town when David was two years old. Both parents came from large families, yet David was an only child, his father's tuberculosis a contributing factor. David has described his early childhood – which featured his father's long absences in hospital – as 'a bit rough'. Conversely, however, he has spoken fondly of his 'gregarious' mother's delight in music and dancing, and declared Canning Town a 'fantastic place for a boy to grow up'.

Holidays in Clacton-on-Sea and in County Cork were to provide carefree diversion and a basis for David's credo. 'I used to meet some of my relatives,' he tells me, 'and we would go strawberry and hop picking. Their philosophy was always about natural things. Obviously, as a teenager I thought it would be great to have a sports car, but really, for me, life has always been more about watching the sun come up and the sun go down.'

The sports car might well have materialized, as young David Cook was demonstrating considerable promise on the football pitch. He loved the sport, envisaging for himself a garlanded future as a professional player, his mate Frank Lampard Senior adding ballast to those ambitions. So fond was he of the beautiful game that David deliberately flunked his eleven-plus exam, thus ensuring he could not attend a local grammar school. His motivation? It was a rugby school, and he wanted to play football. Talk about flinty! Don't tell your kids, but his strategy worked: he and Frank were soon signed to the West Ham boys' team. The future was floodlit.

One enchanted evening was to change it all. It was 1961 and David, aged fourteen, set out on an adventure to London's Soho. His destination was the Flamingo Jazz Club and he was, no doubt, exhilarated at what lay ahead. He did not know, however, that in one hour's time the direction of his life would flip. The sounds, the smells, the blues . . . a heady cocktail with one effect: football was out, and music was in.

It was an inauspicious start. David joined a blues band, the Everons, as drummer, and a musical daisy chain across Italian clubs ensued. Percussion was not quite paying the bills, so he found a factory job to fund his passion. Losing faith, he quit the band, determining instead to go it alone. David Essex, singer, was born.

Which brings us to the chapter he doesn't like to dwell on. 'I don't do nostalgia,' he informs me. Trouble is, a generation of screaming, swooning teenage girls – now in their fifties – do. They know that David Essex was the poster boy of the 1970s, the Justin Bieber of his time long before 'Bieber Fever' was coined. David had gone from a struggling singer (whose first ten singles flopped), to a star of the stage (playing Jesus in *Godspell*), to US-chart-topping teen idol. His self-penned album, *Rock On*, was a Grammy-nominated sensation, and stand-out singles, including 'Gonna Make You A Star', 'Stardust' and 'Hold Me Close', formed a soundtrack to the mid-seventies. He was inarguably one of the most successful British male vocalists of the 1970s; even John Lennon announced himself a fan.

I ask David to take me back to that time. Did singing feed his soul? 'Singing is all right,' he responds. 'I've never loved it, to be honest. And you know what? I've never said that before. I have never loved singing. What I have loved is music, and communication.'

This gets me thinking about the difference between success and emotional satisfaction. Traditional career coaches press us to do 'what we're naturally good at', the rationale being that what we're good at will make us happiest. What happens, however, if what we're great at is not something we really want to do? I suspect this was the case with David, his aversion to that wildly successful poster-boy era supporting the idea. It interests me, too, how David's vocation shifted throughout his lifetime – a familiar narrative, I believe, to many of us. His response to shifting sands? He moved with them, and continues to do so. 'For me,' he says, 'to move forward is always important. I don't really like looking back.'

A key shift came in the form of 1973's cult movie *That'll Be the Day* and, crucially, in the man who nourished David's acting ambitions. 'The great influence on me was a manager and mentor I was lucky to have, a man called Derek Bowman,' he explains. 'He was a theatre critic and academic and he introduced me to this whole other world. I was just this East End boy. I'd never been into somewhere posh like the theatre. But Derek took me under his wing, and I saw plays like *Juno and the Paycock*. I thought, Yeah, this is very civilized. I wouldn't mind doing this. So it's all been an accident – a great accident!'

That'll Be the Day featured David as a 'working-class boy in the fifties, really taking music by the scruff of the neck'. His performance alongside Ringo Starr made for box-office gold, and David remains proud of the film to this day. 'I think I wanted to succeed as an actor,' he tells me, 'because Derek believed in me so much. I wanted to succeed on his behalf. Initially I couldn't have cared less. All I'd ever wanted to be was a jazz drummer, really, wearing a black polo-neck, behind the cymbals with a fag hanging out of my mouth. I never wanted to be "famous". As time went on I simply wanted to succeed in whichever project I was doing.'

His mentor might have provided the catalyst, yet a characteristically humble David Essex must thank himself for what has become a thoroughly impressive career on stage and screen. He has starred in big-budget hits, such as *Stardust* and *Silver Dream Racer*, and received critical acclaim for theatre roles in such diverse productions as *Evita*, *Aspects of Love*, *Childe Byron* and *She Stoops to Conquer*. His latest work, meanwhile, includes playing 'Blackberry' in *Traveller*, the movie, and touring UK theatres with a black comedy entitled *The Dishwashers*. 'It was a bit like Pinter, or Beckett,' he reflects. 'Very obtuse, not at all linear, and very, very difficult for the actors. There were only three of us in it and I think I spoke for two hours each performance.'

I did mention there was more: David has written a musical (1985's *Mutiny!*), composed an ice-skate ballet score (1995's *Beauty and the Beast*), played 'The Artilleryman' on Jeff Wayne's *War of the Worlds* album (a consistent bestseller since its 1978 release), penned an autobiography (*A Charmed Life*, published in 2002), starred in several hit TV series (from 1988's *The River* and 2000's *Heartbeat* to his recent turn as *East-Enders'* Eddie Moon), and – deep breath – somehow found time to notch up nineteen UK top-forty singles and sixteen top-forty albums along the way. He has also given generously of his time to a variety of charitable causes, including six years spent as an ambassador to Voluntary Service Overseas (which saw him travel across Africa, conducting music and drama workshops for student teachers). His awards are beyond numerous, chief among them the Order of the British Empire (OBE) presented by Queen Elizabeth II in 1999.

A simple question arises: with such a varied body of work, David, what has made you happiest? 'I think there is something special about theatre,' he replies, 'because there is something about an audience, there with you, entering into this world. That connection is quite special.'

We discuss the contrast between cavernous arena and

small-town theatre, the conversation leading to those manu-factured pop acts causing mass hysteria today. David's take on the likes of One Direction is cautious: 'Fundamentally,' he says, 'the trouble with people that are thrown up quickly, that are manufactured, is that it tends to be a very successful six months. And I think the public at large realize if someone is more substantial, or more truthful, or if someone believes in what they are doing, irrespective of fame and fortune – I think they can feel that.'

Whatever the future for today's pop idols, they would do well to emulate the longevity – not to mention the fluidity – of David Essex. This shape-shifter has more to do, however, so I ask what's next. 'I need to spend more time doing what I want to do and not get too involved in things that I wanted to do initially . . . and then drag on! I have always been very particular about what I do and I have always been my own man.

'For instance,' he continues, 'when "Rock On" was num-ber one in America I never went there. Columbia Records went nuts because to get a number one in America with something like "Rock On" was unusual, but I said, "No, I'm busy." Because I had my little family in the UK . . .'

David's definition of family, too, has changed with the passage of time: he is thrice-married, has four cherished chil-dren, and is a grandfather of three. He has regularly admitted his view that romantic love is 'probably not for ever' – a cor-ollary, perhaps, to that wandering soul within.

Society sanctions stability. Predictability, even. David does not respond well to sanctions, favouring personal integrity over external pressure every time. And while his poster has long been replaced on bedroom walls, David Essex may be a poster child for the power of self-determination. 'A free spirit,' reads the tagline of his movie *Traveller*, 'can never be broken.'

Our time is up. David, however, has not nearly finished. 'I've just been commissioned to write a fiction,' he says, 'which should be interesting, so I've got an idea for that, and I'm going to do seventy-five poems, they'll be illustrated, and that will be out next year. And in the meantime, I'll do whatever comes my way, or whatever I instigate, really . . . I don't have a blueprint . . .'

I want to convince you – no matter your age – that you have many more exhilarating journeys still to embark upon. I also want to convince you that it is never, ever too late to start again. For those of you who need convincing, I have just two words: Pat Falvey.

Pat is something special. Hard to define – because this man has worn many hats in his lifetime – but he is just about the most inspirational guy I know. Now in his sixth decade, he is an explorer, entrepreneur, author, motivational speaker, film-maker and environmentalist. He is the first person in the world to have scaled the seven continents' highest peaks – twice. He led the first Irish team ever to complete the 1,140-kilometre trek to the South Pole, traversing the most desolate of terrain in the process. Pat has experienced life with more than thirty tribes across the world and, through them, has 'discovered fascinating similarities and traits in all of mankind: to challenge, to change, set goals, and to achieve'. It strikes me that the words 'challenge', 'change' and 'achieve' will most likely feature on Pat Falvey's gravestone – not that he's going anywhere anytime soon!

Pat is not only a world-renowned adventurer, he is also the young lad from County Cork who decided to become a millionaire by his twenty-first birthday, and did so. But before you tell me you can scarcely maintain that expensive gym membership, never mind scale Everest with a million euro in your back pocket, there are a couple of pretty important things you need to know about Pat. First, he came from nothing. Second, there was a time in his life when he decided he no longer wanted to live.

Throughout our conversation, I am as stunned by his spectacular highs as I am by his crushing lows. Pat tells me how, following the collapse of his business empire at the age of twenty-nine, he got into his car, put his foot on the accelerator and came instants away from launching himself, and his life, off a pier. Five years later, he had braved Mount Everest's Death Zone and lived to tell the tale. To me, this contrast less ordinary makes for an extraordinary source of inspiration. Because we all love the rags-to-riches, boom-to-bust-to-boom-again stories, don't we? Any scriptwriter worth her salt will tell you that in order to be inspired we must first empathize: the leading character must manifest shades of dark and light, must somehow mirror our flawed, multifaceted selves. At base, we need to feel that if he can overcome, so can we. So here's my question: can we all do as Pat Falvey has done?

The man himself certainly thinks so: 'Believe in yourself, have dreams and goals, be positive, don't quit, and change with changing circumstances. Go for what you want with all of your capacity, strength and tenacity. If you have these attributes, your dreams and goals will become a reality.'

It's good stuff, but I want to drill down a little deeper. I want to know if there are individuals for whom extraordinary achievement is predestined; people programmed to excel, particularly in the face of adversity. I want to know if that indomitable spark flickers more intensely in some, and if so, why.

To dissect the anatomy of an achiever, I look to what psychologists call the biopsychosocial model. Here, the biological, psychological and social factors attendant on a person's existence are analysed, the theory being that every form of human behaviour is predicated on a continuum of interaction between all three. I sharpen my pencil, tackling the biological first.

'I had a great childhood,' Pat tells me, 'and my parents were absolutely fantastic. There was all this positivity around me. At fifteen I was saying, "I'm gonna be a millionaire." And my grandmother was saying, "You can. Go on out there and do it."'

Pat was born in 1957 to Tim and Bina in the north of Cork City. He was sent to live with his beloved grandmother, Mary B. Callaghan, aged six, while maintaining a happy relationship with his parents (child-shifting was common practice in 1960s Ireland!). His father had served as Lord Mayor of Cork – I'm sensing leadership qualities in the blood – but his grandmother's tenacity had the greatest effect on a young Pat. 'She was a tough, no-nonsense lady,' he explains, 'whose husband had left her with six kids, so it was all about hard work.'

It wasn't long before Granny Mary had enlisted her grandson as a cadet. 'She set me up in my first business,' he reminisces, 'when I was seven years of age. She bought me a pram, told me to go around collecting clothes door to door, and I'd get threepence a shift. From there she found out that old people needed turf, so I went out with the pram again, and then I decided to sell firewood. I bought a lawnmower with the profits and started a grass-cutting business. I'd put my earnings into a piggy-bank, and by the time I was ten, I had a thousand pounds.'

Talk about the smartest kid on the block! His early entrepreneurialism seemed a combination of natural instinct and a product of that old Irish saying *Mol an óige agus tiocfaidh sí* (Praise youth and it will flourish). Praise in those days typically came in the form of tough love, I venture.

Pat agrees, sharing this story to illustrate: 'I was a great guy for earning a few pence by getting my photograph taken with visiting Americans . . . this poor Irish child with the pram, you know. On one occasion I remember hearing them say, "These people are far better off poor. If they were like us, they wouldn't be so happy." So I went home and told my grandmother what I'd heard. She gave me a belt across the head and dragged me into the front room, caught me by the back of the neck and lifted me up in front of pictures of the Sacred Heart, of Éamon de Valera, John F. Kennedy and the Pope. She pointed each one out to me and said, "You're as good as any of them and I want you to remember that." She wanted me to understand that we were never meant to be treated as an anthropological museum, having others come in and stare at us, and ever since then, I mean, I've lived with over thirty tribes in the world and that's what I say to people: progress. There's nobody out there who wants to live – as my grandmother would have done – having to go to the toilet between two planks. So her view was that as her grandson I was going to do better for myself, not be living in that anthropological museum.'

And progress Pat did. He left school at fifteen, convinced that wealth was his to claim. Working initially as a bricklayer, within two years he had twenty men at his command, and four years later a million in the bank. Here's where psychological factors present themselves. Was it money that drove him, I ask, or love of business?

'It was anger,' he tells me. 'You see, I had a fantastic father, my greatest mentor, but when I was younger he was caught for a lot of money by a developer and went broke. He had built his business with great pride, but when it went wrong, I thought he was an idiot, a fool. I asked him how he could do such a thing to our family, without ever realizing the pain and anguish he was going through.' His father's reaction? 'Rather than tell me to give up on my business plans and go to college, he said, "Son, you're the biggest dreamer I've ever known so dream, and dream big. Remember that it is in following the dream that success lies." I've lived my life by that.'

Fate can be a cruel mistress, of course, and while flying high on material success – 'I had a big Georgian house of 3,500 square feet when I was twenty-one' – Pat was soon forced to swallow the bitter pill dispensed to his father before him. At twenty-nine he went broke. 'The business crashed slowly,' he tells me. 'It took a couple of years for it to wind down, and I wasn't moving fast enough to stop it. I'd thought I had the Midas touch for as long as I could remember because of my grandmother's belief in me. So when my business went, my self-esteem went, too.' From more money than he had time to spend, Pat found he could no longer afford petrol. Crisis mode ensued. 'My self-esteem hit an all-time low and it turned into depression. I felt I had let my family down, had recreated my father's situation. I had a lovely wife and two lovely kids and was thinking, What the hell have I done? It's all my fault that things are tumbling down around everybody. So I decided, "That's it, time to get out of it." I decided to take my own life.'

A snap decision, he says, found him careening down that pier. Another beat, and he had slammed on the brakes, a flash of his children's faces before him. 'I stopped at high tide on the River Lee,' he says, 'four inches from going in.' A week later, a man named Val asked him to go for a walk up a hill. And that social factor – a simple invitation – was to change Pat Falvey's life for ever. 'At the time it was an irritant to me.' Pat smiles. 'Who the bloody hell does this guy think he is, trying to get me to go hillwalking? I thought. I'm a workaholic, not a walkaholic! But he kept insisting, so I went out for a walk with him and it turned my life around.'

That first hike gave him an unexpected life-saving lesson. 'When I reached the summit, I had transcended from looking at the water flowing down the mountain to being there above it,' he recalls. 'I had accomplished this small target. That made me focus on the fact that, in order to survive, I needed to challenge myself again.' The next challenge was Carrauntoohil, Ireland's highest peak at 1,038 metres (3,406 feet). On reaching its summit, Pat informed his fellow walkers that he would one day climb Everest. They laughed. He believed.

A reignited zest for life saw Pat face challenges head-on as he built up a profitable finance company. Retiring at forty, he has since devoted his time to conquering the extremities of our planet. He has climbed Everest, and then some. He has subjected himself to the most severe conditions imaginable. And he has done so because it makes him feel alive. 'I often try to figure out how I am still alive . . .' he says.

Which circles me back to the idea of a biological impulse. Is Pat's brain geared towards risk? I suspect so when he discusses the Death Zone. 'It's a place above about twenty-six thousand feet,' he explains, 'a height at which the body actually deteriorates and you start losing your mind due to oxygen deprivation, and then you don't recover. I've lost fourteen friends alone in the Death Zone . . . and I probably know of fifty other climbers who have died there.'

So why on earth go? Recent research indicates that neurotransmitters – the chemicals responsible for communication within the brain – may have a key part to play. Dopamine is the neurotransmitter associated with risk-taking: the higher the dopamine level in the brain, the higher a person's gravitation towards risk will be (see Chapter 8).

I look to the preface of Pat's book, *The Summit*, for evidence of his super-high dopamine levels. On scaling mountains, he writes, 'When that impulse has been satisfied and the next challenge has been met, thoughts of returning to the comforts of home are relished, only for the cycle to – inevitably – begin all over again until time or death dictates otherwise.' I get the science, yet this rationale remains brain-bending, especially when considered from the perspective of my comfy couch. It leads me to wonder how the loved one of a dopamine-chaser like Pat might feel.

'Do we know one in four of us is going to die up a mountain?' Pat asks. 'Yes, we do. Are we selfish enough to take that risk and put our families under stress? Yes, we are. Do we believe that we will come back? Yes, we do.'

Pat keeps coming back. The intrepid explorer, the fearless adventurer, he has recently added another title to his résumé: he's become a granddad. I wonder if that biological, risk-oriented urge will skip a generation, if Pat's grandson will feel compelled to climb the highest mountains there are. I wonder, too, if Pat would want that for him.

'Honestly?' he replies. 'No. But would I support him if he decided to do it? The answer is yes. I believe that every person has their own genre in life and that family is there to support it, not restrict it.'

For now, Pat's ambition is anything but restricted. He wants to write a play, he tells me; he is writing a book to be titled *The Psychology of Success*, and his film production company is on the upswing. He will continue to welcome guests to his lodge in the Kerry mountains, pushing them up Carrauntoohil to get a taste of his version of the high life. One remaining ambition is, however, more grounded than you might expect.

'My kids have told me that they are, of course, proud of me,' Pat says, 'but they've also pointed out that I've missed important events, like communions and confirmations. They ask if I realize how much I've lost . . . and I do. So now that I have a grandchild, I can't say I'm going to be brilliant, but I am going to make an effort to become a good grandfather. And I'm excited about that . . .'

Jocelyn Bell Burnell

The 'spark' can be a glint, a glimmer, a vibration within us that ignites a will to achieve and grow. Or it can be something that flickers in the dark matter of our being. For astrophysicist Jocelyn Bell Burnell, this spark, manifested inwardly and outwardly as her scientific brilliance, allowed her to discover her own kind of spark: flashing neutron stars known as 'pulsars'.

In the late 1960s, while working on a PhD project at Cambridge, Jocelyn observed radio frequencies emitted by a pulsing star. Her supervisor initially dismissed the findings as flare stars or other radio-waves, but the young postgraduate student continued her investigations, eventually concluding that the signals were unique. Jocelyn's discovery revolutionized the field of astrophysics by providing the first substantive evidence to Stephen Hawking's theory of black holes, as well as contributing to Einstein's theory of relativity. Her work was to receive the first ever Nobel Prize for Physics in the field of astronomy – but the award was not given to Jocelyn Bell Burnell. Instead her male supervisor and male colleague received the award for what was largely her work. It was a decision that caused outrage among many of her fellow scientists. Incredibly, her 'non-award' did not discourage Jocelyn. She went on to build a tremendous career in astrophysics, and is generally credited with fundamentally challenging what scientists thought about the universe.

Born in 1943, Jocelyn Bell Burnell is a native of Belfast and was immersed in science from an early age. Her father, an architect who worked on the design of the Armagh Planetarium, acted as an early role model and inspiration to her in her flaring interest in the scientific world – more specifically, the outer world of astrophysics. She attended a local grammar school, where gender policy at the time was almost to prevent her star from rising. 'In the first year of secondary school,' she tells me, 'the boys were sent to the science lab and the girls to the domestic science room.' A less determined young woman might have toed the line, but Miss Bell was quick to demonstrate her spark. 'I tried protesting,' she says, 'but the teacher wasn't hearing it. So I enlisted my parents' help, told them that evening what had happened, and they hit the roof! They went to see the head teacher the next day.'

Cross-stitching firmly rejected, the twelve-year-old student promptly found herself, and just two other girls, in the 'boys' club'. An early setback – Jocelyn quite incredibly failed her eleven-plus examination – was soon forgotten as her natural aptitude for science soon saw her topping the class. From there her interest in astrophysics grew as she spent her teens at the Mount School in York, a Quaker boarding school, where her teacher, Mr Tillet, recognized and fostered her talent. 'He was quite an old man, coming out of retirement a second time to teach us,' she recalls. 'But he was just so good at explaining physics. When he realized I was competent, he let me do extra work on my own, at the back of the class, so I got to sit some scholarship exams.' A mentor's belief saw Jocelyn follow the path most natural to her, a path that would eventually lead to a reconceptualization of all that had been held as 'true' in the study of physics.

Next came the University of Glasgow, which I know, having studied nursing in Glasgow many moons ago. It was a place, I suggest, where a woman reading physics was far from the norm. 'In my particular year there weren't any other girls

BRIGHT SPARKS — INSPIRATIONAL PEOPLE

at all.' Jocelyn smiles. 'I was the only one doing honours physics, along with forty-nine men . . .'

Today's study of science does, by and large, promote gender parity. This was the 1960s, however, and the very sight of an attractive, able woman in the physics lecture hall caused significant uproar. 'The tradition then was that whenever a woman walked into the lecture hall everybody whistled and catcalled, stamped and banged the desks,' she recalls. I ask if she felt ostracized. 'Well, I didn't like it,' she responds. 'I discovered that if you blushed, they made more noise, so you had to learn to control the blushing. On one level, I didn't blame my colleagues for doing it because they were only doing what previous generations of students had taught them to do. But I'm still a bit cross with the academic staff, who took no measures to stop it.'

Undiminished, Jocelyn narrowed her sights on the study of radio-astronomy, for which a PhD was required. 'I ended up at Cambridge,' she tells me, 'which wasn't something I had expected to do. I was really rather overawed there, feeling quite provincial, surrounded by all these people who seemed so terribly bright. I wasn't quite sure I was going to make the grade.'

This description calls to mind Malcolm Gladwell's concept of the power of the underdog, as detailed in his illuminating book *David and Goliath*. Here he argues that feeling on the back foot can provide the fuel to outwit and outclass even the most intimidating opponents. The underdog will win, he says, providing the fear of failure can be converted into new strategies to succeed. Jocelyn had identified her strategy: she would simply work harder, longer and more assiduously than anyone else. 'I was quite determined that if they were going to throw me out,' she tells me, 'I would have done my very best before that happened.' Her strategy was not only to secure her place at the college, it was to lay the foundations for something truly spectacular.

And so to the science. At this time, recent theorizations and discoveries in the area of astrophysics were redefining what scientists had believed to be the origins of the universe. Jocelyn began working with her supervisor, Anthony Hewish, who, with the help of Martin Ryle, had built a radio telescope to study quasars. Jocelyn interpreted the radio data, logging unusual or extraordinary information, and observed the pulsations during this analysis. It demanded hard, long hours in the lab, poring over printouts literally miles long. 'I was being very thorough and careful,' she explains. 'And it's because I was being very thorough that I noticed this funny, spurious signal. I could have ignored it, but I wanted to make sure I understood absolutely everything that telescope was picking up.' The discovery of pulsars was, she says, 'an accident, but in one sense it was an accident waiting to happen'.

Further evidence was gathered, and a paper heralding the discovery was drafted for publication in *Nature*, the renowned scientific journal. When it appeared, Hewish's name was listed first and Jocelyn's second. The scientific community lit up, media interest grew apace, and by 1974 the discovery was deemed worthy of a Nobel Prize. Next came the headline that Anthony Hewish and Martin Ryle had been awarded the Nobel Prize for Physics. Jocelyn's name was nowhere to be seen.

I try to imagine how it would feel to be responsible for the twentieth century's most significant astronomical discovery, a Nobel Prize-winning breakthrough, and to be overlooked. But here's what's so inspiring about Jocelyn Bell Burnell: she is almost divinely circumspect on the subject. She has never, as I suspect the majority of us might, bemoaned her exclusion. Moreover, she has never criticized her male colleagues. I wonder if she feels so magnanimous now, forty years on. 'Oh, yes,' she replies. 'It was an important precedent, because it was the first time the Prize was going to astronomers. I was really rather proud that it was our stars that had convinced them there was good physics in astronomy. And I've also discovered that you can do very, very well out of not getting a Nobel Prize!'

It's a trait common to life's success stories, this proclivity to accentuate the positive in any situation. Jocelyn's faith may also have played a part in her outlook: as a ninth-generation Quaker, she follows teachings of forgiveness, acceptance and equanimity. Her Quaker education might also be credited: her alma mater, Mount School, York, follows the maxim, 'A candle loses nothing by lighting another candle.' Interestingly, her religion has also informed her approach to science and her teachings on it. She alludes to the oneness of humanity and the universe, saying that the atomical composition of our bodies — what makes up the human being — is related to the same forces and ingredients that comprise the most distant galaxy. We, like the universe, are organic. In Jocelyn's own words, 'We are made of the stuff of stars.' Such a quasi-ethereal understanding has inspired her passion for physics and for the world.

Like stars, however, no human is exempt from the pressures of external forces. For Jocelyn, I'm inclined to imagine her discovery created its own unique pressure: how ever can you best an early incidence of genius? Again, her response comes in coolly circumspect tones. 'The problem is living up to that,' she says. 'And that's actually impossible, as I fairly quickly realized. The luck to make that kind of discovery is something most people never have. And when you do, you have to realize that you're not going to have that luck again. That's just part of life.'

Jocelyn Bell Burnell has lived a life less ordinary. Her pioneering spirit saw her not only follow a path less travelled but place a landmark upon it. While not in receipt of a Nobel Prize, she has, she tells me, 'won just about every other prize that moves!' These accolades have included more than ten significant honours, a CBE and DBE among them, and at least twenty honorary doctorates. She was the first female president of the Institute of Physics, served as president of the Royal Astronomical Society, and in 2014 became the first woman ever appointed president of the Royal Society of Edinburgh. Perhaps most saliently, she is the woman credited with shining a light for other young women to follow, such is her dedication to changing how females in science are perceived. 'What we've got to do is change how society thinks about what's suitable for young women,' she says. 'This varies enormously from country to country . . . so we can see that the problem is to do with the culture in a particular country and nothing to do with women's brains or abilities. We've got to somehow convince people that science and engineering are perfectly acceptable occupations for women – quite appropriate in fact.'

Jocelyn took adversity and thrived on it, took a knock and turned it into a motivational driver in the creation of a dazzling career. She's now in her seventies, and I ask if there's anything left to do, any burning ambition untapped. 'I'm not sure there is,' she replies. 'There are places I want to visit, holidays I want to take . . . but in terms of my professional career, I've had a ball, I really have.'

As she prepares to return to her day job, I have just one

parting shot. If you were writing a letter to your younger self, Jocelyn, back in Cambridge, how would it read? Her response is an exercise in rational thinking.

'I'd say that it was good that I knew from quite an early age what I wanted to do. Knowing where you want to go is enormously helpful when you meet obstacles. And obstacles aren't entirely bad things, either, because they help you sort your priorities. Do I really want to do this? Yes, I do. Therefore I'm going to stick at whatever the current phase is, whatever the issue is, so that I get to do what I want to do. It's as simple as that.'

Fionnula Flanagan

'I like your girl, Wheeler. I get the feeling she's female. You know what the difference between female and feminine is? Huh? Well, here's a hint: a feminine woman never laughs out loud and always shaves her armpits . . . I've only met about a half-dozen females in my life, and I think you've got one there.'

You might recognize this quotation from Richard Yates's *Revolutionary Road*. If you don't, suffice to say it's one man's take on another's wife, and intended as high praise indeed. And – while ignorant of her shaving habits! – this 'all female' description comes to mind when I consider my next heroine, Fionnula Flanagan.

Image-search her name and this is what you'll find: a striking, stylish woman with a witty spark in her eyes; a woman on a red carpet, fingers aloft in a peace sign, collar up in cool elegance, pearl-coloured hair teased to the right side of rock'n'roll. You'll find this Irishwoman in Hollywood, walking with kings, or in the wilds of Connemara, a firm grip on the common touch. You'll find a seventy-three-year-old superstar, whose inner fire has illuminated the world.

Born Fionnghuala Manon Flanagan in 1941, she is a renowned actress who has portrayed all the females you could conceive. Highlights of her fifty-year career include roles in such films as *The Others*, *Transamerica*, *Divine Secrets of the Ya-Ya Sisterhood*, *Waking Ned Devine* and *The Guard*. Name a major TV series, meanwhile, and there's a good chance she's done it: from *Cagney & Lacey*, *Murder, She Wrote* and *Columbo* to, in more recent years, *Lost*, *Nip/Tuck* and *Brotherhood*. She's won an Emmy Award, has been nominated for a

278

Tony, and this classically trained thespian has even travelled to a galaxy far, far away, featuring in not one but three series of *Star Trek*!

Her versatility is what marks her out, as does, I suspect, her tendency to shatter the status quo. It is in this latter trait that necessity has been the mother of invention, as she explains: 'I'm a character actress. Always have been. And Hollywood has never known what to do with character actors. Look at the career of Sean Penn, a friend of mine. When he was younger they tried to push him into being a leading man. He is a fine, wonderful character actor, not someone who fits into a leading-man mould. So I had that strong sense of myself. I knew I was never going to be a slip of a thing playing the juvenile lead. I also knew I needed to be strong, because when I first went to Hollywood there was not so much room for foreign actresses, and I will always be regarded as a foreign actress.'

To understand her grit we need to rewind. Before Beverly Hills, and before becoming a 'foreign actress', Fionnula enjoyed a happy upbringing in Dublin. The eldest of five, her parents Terry and Rosanna were avid readers with a passion for language. And while English was spoken at home, the couple made the unusual decision to send their children to all-Irish-speaking schools. 'My mother had some Irish because she had worked in the civil service,' Fionnula recalls, 'while all my father could say was *tá*, the Irish word for "yes", which used to amuse us all very much.' What prompted their choice? 'They both believed passionately that you should have your native language. They believed in the principle of *Tír gan teanga, tír gan anam* – a nation without a language is a nation without a soul.'

Bilingual children have been proven to perform better

academically than their monolingual counterparts, to display a greater dexterity for language and learning throughout their lives – a clue, perhaps, to Fionnula's mastery of the spoken word. Statistics aside, she tells me her bilingualism 'has given me a kind of solidity about where I come from and where I belong that others don't have. I am so grateful for that because it has enriched me. Lots of Israelis I speak to, who never learned Hebrew . . . well, there's a difference, you know, if you own your own language, whether you use it on a daily basis or not.'

While the young Fionnula could speak two languages, I'm surprised to learn she found speaking up in either of them a challenge. 'I was terribly shy,' she says. 'I remember my father bought me a watch for my tenth birthday and I was so appallingly shy that I didn't wear it. I was afraid someone would ask me the time, and I would have to speak!' A shy actress? Before I can interject with flying pigs, she continues, 'I think all actors are shy deep down. I really do. You can be a private person but it doesn't mean you're not confident about what you do. I think there is a reserve within most actors, because it is our job to observe. It is what we spend a lot of time doing, trying to learn how to recreate what we see.'

Fionnula's quieter years were put to good use, it seems, as once she found her voice there was no holding her back. She played in the acting big league from the outset: she trained first at Dublin's Abbey Theatre, then honed her craft at London's Old Vic. Next came a move to the USA, where she has now lived for more than four decades. California – and all the glitzy adjectives that go with it – is her address, yet good old Dublin will always be home.

I think I know the feeling, having lived in London for twenty years. My late husband would laugh when I talked about 'going home for the weekend'. 'But London is your home!' he'd say. I might agree with him – momentarily – but once I was through the doors of Dublin airport, the damp, comforting smell of the air alone made a liar of me. Fionnula smiles in recognition, saying, 'I've lived in California for forty years and I still say I'm "going home for two weeks"!' She talks about a magnetism that will always draw her back. 'I mean, Ireland is the well,' she says. 'I remember coming home at Christmas time some years ago and there was a wonderful sign at the airport that simply said, "Welcome Home for Christmas". I thought that was so moving and it certainly touched me very much.'

Fionnula comes home often – to support the film industry, accept an award, or to carry out her duties on the board of the Picture Palace Galway. Back in her adopted home, meanwhile, parties thrown for California's Irish immigrant community at 'Fionnula's house' are famous. There she hosts with the man she married in 1972, Irishman Dr Garrett O'Connor, internationally renowned psychiatrist and former CEO of the Betty Ford Institute. Fionnula's roots are never more evident, however, than when you steer her towards the subject of James Joyce.

'I went to school in Eccles Street,' she tells me, 'and as far as I was concerned that was where [Joyce's] the Blooms had lived. And at home, my father liked to pontificate about the many things he'd read . . . from George Bernard Shaw and James Joyce right down to the *Beano* comic. Mid-conversation, he'd jump in with things like "And Joyce said . . ." or "Shaw said . . ." So, as a kid, I thought that Joyce and Shaw were people my parents knew! I never questioned that they didn't!'

This early familiarity with the great Irish scribes was to lead to something extraordinary. Finding herself pigeonholed in 1980s Hollywood, Fionnula looked inwards for inspiration. 'I was fed up with the limitation of episodic television,' she has said. 'And that was when I sat down and researched *Joyce's Women*. It was a journey. I told myself that I didn't care if it didn't work or I went broke. It was a hard row to hoe, since I was so unknown.'

The result: a one-woman show adapted, produced and performed by Fionnula Flanagan. Women saw her play six females, each influenced by Joyce, a *tour de force* that went on to become a multi-award-winning film. The pay-off? 'It got my phone calls answered,' she quips, 'and it did garner me a lot of respect in Hollywood . . . but you can die of terminal respect, you know!'

Like so many working in the creative industries, Fionnula Flanagan has spoken of the fear that each gig could be her last. With *Joyce's Women* under her belt, however, she could begin to believe the calls would come, and she could afford to be more selective as to the roles she would accept. In 1996 a call came through from Irish director Jim Sheridan. He and Terry George had written a script based on the 1981 hunger strikes in Northern Ireland, and they wanted her on board. Now, Fionnula has played many mothers (John Cusack and Molly Ringwald are just two actors who have been 'mothered' by her on screen), but this movie was to produce her most memorable matriarch yet.

Some Mother's Son starred Fionnula Flanagan and Helen Mirren as Annie Higgins and Kathleen Quigley, mothers of two hunger strikers. 'This is one of my favourite pieces of work,' Fionnula tells me, 'because it is a picture about something that mattered. It is about a watershed in our history. We are still today feeling the fallout, in Northern Ireland, from those dreadful days. I think what Jim and Terry did in writing it was to address something that nobody else had. Several scripts on the hunger strikes had been sent to me, but they were all told from inside the prison . . . The real story of how it tore the community apart was set among the families. The brilliance, you see, was in focusing on the mothers.'

Not only is *Some Mother's Son* a powerful piece of film, it's also key to understanding what Fionnula Flanagan did next. First of all, she stopped dyeing her hair. 'I wanted to find out who I was underneath all that red dye,' she explains. 'I had it cut short and went around for a few months with pinky-orange hair. The white colour I have now grew out. People said to me, "It makes you look old, you'll never work." Well, I haven't stopped working!'

Something deeper changed, too, as this proud Irishwoman became increasingly politicized. She and Garrett opened their Los Angeles home to Gerry Adams, the leader of the republican Sinn Féin party and a controversial figure to say the least. 'We threw open our doors to Sinn Féin when they initiated the Peace Process,' she states. 'That was why Gerry Adams came to America, to spread the word and get support for it.'

If you are not from Ireland, this may not sound like a big deal. If you are Irish, however, you'll know that an actress having the leader of Sinn Féin stay over . . . well, it's certainly a divisive move. So, too, was her vocal backing of Martin McGuinness, another key Sinn Féin figure, in the 2011 Irish presidential campaign. But if one thing is true of Fionnula Flanagan, she is not faint of heart, preferring instead to push the limits of possibility for what she believes in. She supported what was to be an unsuccessful campaign, and did so without regret.

Fionnula has fire in her belly, and to fuel it she devours

politics and the arts, soaking up everything – and everyone – around her. Her stirring characterizations continue, she has become a scriptwriter on the side and is now a doting great-grandmother, too. She is an energetic, engaged woman with a few axes yet to grind, chief among them what she views as the patriarchy of the Irish creative arts. While pleased to see names like Joyce, Beckett or Fassbender up in lights, she queries why names like Edna O'Brien remain relatively obscure. 'It will take time,' she has said of the shift, 'and it is changing slowly. Part of it, I believe, is training women to take ownership of their talent.'

At seventy-three, Fionnula Flanagan has a remarkable zest for life. She has many things yet to learn, stories to tell, and words to breathe new meaning into. One word this fearless female will never understand, however?

That's easy. 'Retirement'.

Conclusion

It is difficult to conclude a book such as this. It is a hybrid, composed of so many strands of my life, of me, that I'm not sure how to bind them all together and present a final scene. I would like to end by presenting you with a nugget of thought-provoking wisdom to take away and, more than that, by sounding a call to arms that will inspire you to follow through on the audit and account section and perform a brave and honest assessment of your own life and self. But what form of words could achieve all that? Perhaps the best way to finish, then, is to pose some questions. In our answers, we may discover we have found what we were looking for.

What have I learned from writing this book?

An awful lot, is the short answer.

I approached this book with a sense that I had to do it, but also with trepidation. I was plagued by so many questions and doubts: how much should I tell? What should I keep hidden? Why should I put myself forward as someone with some answers? In the end, I ignored the doubting voices in my head and opted for doing it my way, through honesty and confrontation. It was horribly difficult to write about Richard – his life and his death. I cried over the keyboard as I wrenched out those words and often finished my day exhausted, with only a few hundred words to show for it. It was a deeply emotional experience and at times I hated it, but I'm glad now that I saw it through. I'm glad because I believe it might help others who are feeling the same emotions, people who are sinking under the weight of grief and raw bereavement, and are desperately casting about for any kind of lifeline. My greatest hope for this book is that it acts as a lifeline for someone to catch on to.

I have learned that that hope can only be fulfilled through honesty. That is why I have been as honest as possible, never flinching from remembering or revealing. It wasn't always pleasant, but I think it has been worthwhile.

This is the first book I've written, and before I started, I didn't know if I could do it. But I tried and – whether it's well received or not – I succeeded in completing it. That means a huge amount to me because of a couple of other things I've learned: it really is true that you're never too old to learn a new trick; and you should always set the bar a bit higher than what you believe you can achieve. This is a key lesson I'm going to take from the experience of writing *Spark!*. When I set the bar at a comfortable height, it doesn't involve any reach or stretching, threat or fear of failure. I know not everyone will agree with me, but I'm certain that that is no way to live. I want to push that bar above my comfort zone, then fling myself at it, because as I stretch and reach, I also learn and grow and master. This is a cornerstone of vital living and I'm going to keep doing it, in my professional and personal life. My role model in this is my wonderful mother – if she can be proficient on iPad, it shows me that there is so much more I can do that I might have once thought impossible. It's a comforting and inspiring thought!

This book is the culmination of a long and strange journey. Unknown to me, I started the first page on that day when Richard complained of backache, three years ago.

286

Since then, my life has been destroyed, bleak and, finally, reignited by the spark of my own desire to live and not give up. Grief has been described as a time of 'magical thinking', and I've learned that 'magical' can be negative and positive. There is the 'magical' of disillusion, of despair – the feelings that magic away your ability to live. But there is also the painful alchemy of death turning into new life. Richard died and I was bereft of everything I felt was necessary to live, but slowly, slowly, a form of life switched on again. The moment when the spark was reignited was born out of a simple question: 'Are you done yet?' I didn't know it at the time, but asking and then trying to answer it was a pulse – weak at the start, but it kept beating away in my brain until I couldn't ignore it. From that weak pulse came the will to live again. It had to be in a wholly new way, it had to be reimagined from scratch, but I learned that I was able to do what had seemed entirely impossible. I had to let go of the life I wanted to lead, then create a new version that I could live. It wasn't easy, but then, as they say, things worth doing rarely are. I learned that it's really hard, but necessary – and worth it.

What might you have learned from reading *Spark!*?

I can't tell what readers will have thought or hoped they would get from reading this book, but I hope that the key messages sounded true and struck a chord with you. One of the most important aspects of this book for me was the inclusion of the ten profiles: a brief insight into the very different lives of ten individuals who have faced down adversity and designed their own ways of enjoying their life's chapters with vitality and passion. I admire those ten people hugely, and my aim in sharing those interviews with you was that you would be inspired by their stories. I hope you have learned that there are all sorts of paths and all sorts of ways of travelling down them.

I think for you, the reader, the key chapter in the book is Auditing and Accounting (Chapter 5), which interrogated you about your life decisions and how you came to reach your current position in life. This was always the crux of *Spark!*: to ask the reader to perform a very honest self-analysis and find out if things were right within, if there were stones left unturned or journeys not undertaken and regretted. The underlying question, of course, is: are you living vitally? I hope you have learned not to fear the answer to that question because you have realized that you hold the considerable power to assign meaning to your own life and life choices. I'm aware that the audit sounds simplistic to some, but it was important to me to share it because I have found that when I perform it, whether with individuals or groups, it always surprises them by proving to be a powerful motivator and tool for their journeys, professional and personal. I think it's essential to find out why you are who you are, to examine the myriad factors that have contributed to the unique person that is you.

The word 'empowering' has become woefully overused, but I'm afraid I'm going to invoke it anyway, because it does bring a sense of control and power when you figure out the layers of your own make-up. It allows you to hold your own self up to the light and see yourself for what you really are – and my hope is that what you have seen has spurred you on to be an ever better version of yourself. It's within all of us to strive for more, to pursue, to challenge ourselves and to grow throughout every year of our lives, and that is my hope for you. I hope you have learned that vital living is desirable and achievable.

CONCLUSION

On the question of achieving it, the other very important thing I hope you have learned from reading this book is the power of strategy. This is a philosophy very close to my heart because it has served me extremely well in life and I believe that it can do the same for others. As humans we are hardwired to look ahead, to anticipate and plan – think of Neanderthal man again, and the fact that his survival depended on his ability to do this. However, as we get older and pass through certain milestones – forty being a major one – we can get a little lazy, our energy can flag, our sense of anticipation can feel jaded and we end up in stasis. The routine is so ingrained, we don't even see it any more; we accept it as our 'life'. The greatest obstacle to vital living becomes our reluctance to step away from our comfort zone, our reluctance to embrace fear, to test ourselves and fail. When we lose this, we relinquish a hell of a lot, and it shows. So my hope is that you have learned from *Spark!* the necessity and benefits of planning, looking ahead with relish and setting new goals continually, to keep body and brain engaged, vital and thriving.

What do I hope you will conclude from all this?

That's a hard one because obviously it's not possible to account for all the permutations of thought that this book will create in each individual who reads it. However, if I could boil it down to just one thing, I think it would be this: that through reading about how I dealt with adversity, adapted and rearranged in the face of it, you will gain strength in the face of your adversity and, crucially, that you will grant yourself full permission to live again. If you have bowed down under the weight of an adverse experience, there is no shame in that. All of us who have experienced something of that nature can understand that completely. But after some time has passed, it is essential that you fight to get off your knees to your feet and stand tall again. I know how difficult that is. In my situation, losing a beloved husband, I felt for a long time that I wasn't allowed to laugh, that it was unseemly. I felt I shouldn't enjoy music or theatre or books or friends. I felt I should never flirt again, or fall in love. I felt, to be honest, that I ought to live a sort of shadow life, half a person – because I was half a person without Richard. But, thanks to my own inner strength and to the sense of life I had to foster for my son, I found the will to stand up again. And I am happy in myself that Richard would have encouraged me from the sidelines all the way.

Not everyone is so lucky, or so robust. I have met the shadow people I mentioned earlier in the book – those who do not want to stand up again because they feel they shouldn't, or can't. Whatever the initial impetus, I believe it gets lost over time and then an unthinking acceptance creeps in, takes root and ends up strangling every other emotion and possible motivation. For these people, the shadows become 'life', and they forget there's another way to live. If you are living like this, shut off, shut down, then I sincerely hope reading *Spark!* might have generated new thoughts in your head and heart. I hope it has reignited that other you, the one you abandoned, or were separated from. And that from that realization, I hope you get that pulse – no matter how weak – just as I did. And from that, I hope you ask yourself honestly, 'Am I done yet?' And from that, I hope you answer, 'No.' I hope you shout it from the rooftops and that it shifts those obstacles inside you and shatters them. I know it's hard, I know sometimes it's too hard even to contemplate, but

I really hope you conclude that you can do it and that it's worth the doing.

It's time to complete the circle, so let me bring you back to James C. Rettie and his marvellous essay about the history of the Earth. We are part of the history of the Earth, you and I. Here we are, using up resources and contributing . . . what? Think about it: so far my life on this planet, the microsecond that is my years, has amounted to this. I have consumed nearly two million litres of air, almost half of that as pure oxygen. I have eaten 2,400 kilos of red meat, 1,300 of poultry, 4,000 of vegetables and fruit. I have managed to drink 35,000 litres of water, and the less said about the wine the better. And so far, what do I have to show for the consumption of all that food, water and air? My body, like yours, recycles tens of billions of cells on a daily basis, but overall there is less of me – remarkable given all of the fuel I have expended on living my life so far.

Laughter lines is a nice way to describe them, but the science behind those tell-tale wrinkles tells me that my cells are ageing and no amount of expensive face cream will reverse the process. I am, as Heidegger so succinctly put it, a 'being towards death'. I am dying a little bit every day. That's just a medico-scientific fact. The antidote? To live a huge amount every day. That's my aim, that's my contribution.

James C. Rettie was preoccupied with humanity's clock. The bottom line of *Spark!* has been to get you to think about your personal clock. I want you to hear it ticking, and I want that sound to ignite a new passion in you, a new drive, a new thought, a new goal. It's New Year's Eve, five seconds to midnight, you have just arrived on Earth . . . what are you going to do about it?

Reading List

If I have ignited your interest in the course of the book, you may want to do some follow-up reading of your own around some of the issues discussed. To that end, I have compiled a list of the resources I used when writing it, which provide a good starting-point.

Adversity

Landro, Laura, 'Study finds adversity does make us stronger', Dow Jones Reprints, 18 October 2010, http://www.buffalo. edu/content/dam/www/news/imported/pdf/October10/ WallStJournSeeryMentalResilience.pdf

Being human

Suddendorf, Thomas, *The Gap: The Science of What Separates Us from Other Animals*, http://www.huffingtonpost.com/thomas-suddendorf/what-makes-us-human_b_4414357.html and http:// edition.cnn.com/2013/11/21/health/animals-humans-gap/ and http://www.newscientist.com/article/mg22129531.100-what-separates-us-from-other-animals.html#.U1e6kfldWSo

Brain health

Bower, Bruce, '"Love hormone" arouses suspicion, too', http://www.wired.com/wiredscience/2011/01/oxytocin-suspicion-trust/

CNRS (Délégation Paris Michel-Ange), 'Autism: oxytocin improves social behaviour of patients, study finds', http://www.sciencedaily.com/releases/2010/02/100216221350.htm

Kain, Debra, 'Could "love hormone" help treat depression?', http://www.ucsdnews.ucsd.edu

Merzenich, Michael, http://www.ted.com/talks/michael_merzenich_on_the_elastic_brain.html

Dopamine and serotonin: the neurotransmitters

Asociación RUVID, 'Dopamine regulates the motivation to act', 10 January 2013, http://www.sciencedaily.com/releases/2013/01/130110094415.htm

Bardot, J. B., 'Supercharge your brain with foods that stimulate dopamine production', http://www.naturalnews.com/040537_brain_foods_dopamine_production.html

Berridge, Kent C., and Terry E. Robinson, 'What is the role of dopamine in reward: hedonic impact, reward learning, or incentive salience?', *Brain Research Reviews*, 28, 1998, 309–69

Buckley, Christine, 'Dopamine not about pleasure anymore', *UConn Today*, 30 November 2012, http://today.uconn.edu/blog/2012/11/uconn-researcher-dopamine-not-about-pleasure-anymore/

Carver, Joseph M., PhD, 'The "Chemical Imbalance in Mental Health Problems"', http://www.drjoecarver.com/clients/49355/File/Chemical%20Imbalance.html; and http://www.kci.org/meth_info/lori/Dopamine_Methamphetamines_and_You.htm

Fisher, Helen, 'Biology: your brain in love', http://www.time.com/time/magazine/article/0,9171,993160-3,00.html#ixzz1Cq LUN8ii

Friedman, Richard A., MD, 'Lasting pleasures, robbed by drug abuse', http://www.nytimes.com/2010/08/31/health/views/31mind.html

Graziano Breuning, Loretta, PhD, 'Your neurochemical self', http://www.psychologytoday.com/blog/your-neurochemical-self/201212/five-ways-boost-your-natural-happy-chemicals

Gwin, Peter, 'The mystery of risk', *National Geographic*, June 2013, http://ngm.nationalgeographic.com/2013/06/125-risk-takers/gwin-text

Lang, Susan S., 'Dopamine linked to a personality trait and happiness', *Cornell Chronicle*, 24 October 1996, http://www.news.cornell.edu/stories/1996/10/dopamine-linked-personality-trait-and-happiness

Le Merrer, J., J. A. Becker, K. Befort and B. L. Kieffer, 'Reward processing by the opioid system in the brain', http://www.ncbi.nlm.nih.gov/pubmed/19789384

Lerner, Talia, 'Are you there God? It's me, Dopamine Neuron', *Stanford Neuroblog*, 30 September 2013, http://neuroblog.stanford.edu/?p=4765

Mandal, Ananya, MD, 'Dopamine functions', http://www.news-medical.net/health/Dopamine-Functions.aspx

Murakami, H., K. Bessinger, J. Hellmann and S. Murakami, 'Manipulation of serotonin signal suppresses early phase of behavioral aging in Caenorhabditis elegans', *Neurobiology of Aging*, July 2008

Nordqvist, Christian, 'What is serotonin? What does serotonin do?' http://www.medicalnewstoday.com/articles/232248.php

Paddock., Catharine, http://www.medicalnewstoday.com/articles/120091.php

Peacock, Jeromy, 'The role of dopamine and serotonin on motivation: implications for academic advising', http://jeromy

peacock.com/academic-writing/the-role-of-dopamine-and-serotonin-on-motivation-implications-for-academic-advising/

Rogers, R. (2011), 'The roles of dopamine and serotonin in decision-making: Evidence from pharmacological experiments in humans', *Neuropsychopharmacology*, 36(1), DOI 114–32, doi:10.1038/npp. 2010.165

Salamone, John D. and Mercè Correa, 'The mysterious motivational functions of mesolimbic dopamine', DOI: http://dx.doi.org/ 10.1016/j.neuron.2012.10.021

Salisbury, David, 'Dopamine impacts your willingness to work', http://news.vanderbilt.edu/2012/05/dopamine-impacts-your-willingness-to-work/

Suo, Satoshi, J. G. Culotti and H. H. M Van Tol, 'Dopamine suppresses octopamine signaling in C. elegans: possible involvement of dopamine in the regulation of lifespan', *Aging*, 1 (10), 2009, 870–74

Treadaway, Michael T. *et al*, 'Dopamine mechanisms of individual differences in human effort-based decision-making', *Journal of Neuroscience*, 32 (18), May 2012, 6170–76, http://www.jneurosci. org/content/32/18/6170.short

Wacker Foundation, the, 'Thrill-seekers may get bigger dopamine "hit" when taking chances', http://www.crimetimes.org/09b/ w09bp2.htm

Weinschenk, Susan, 'Why we're all addicted to texts, Twitter and Google', http://www.psychologytoday.com/blog/brain-wise/ 201209/why-were-all-addicted-texts-twitter-and-google

Wylde, Bryce, 'The dopamine diet', DoctorOz.com, 5 October 2013, http://www.doctoroz.com/videos/dopamine-diet

Zald, D. H. *et al.*, 'Midbrain dopamine receptor availability is inversely associated with novelty-seeking traits in humans', *Journal of Neuroscience*, 28 (53), December 2008, 14372–8

Emotional health

Charles, Eric P., and Michael D. Bybee, 'A behaviorist account of emotions and feelings: making sense of James D. Laird's: *Feelings and the Perception of Self*', *Behaviour and Philosophy*, 29, 2011, 1–16

Kraft, Tara, and Sarah Pressman, 'Grin and bear it: the influence of manipulated facial expression on the stress response', http://www.psychologicalscience.org/index.php/news/releases/smiling-facilitates-stress-recovery.html

Laird, J. D., 'Self-attribution of emotion: the effects of expressive behaviour on the quality of emotional experience', *Journal of Personality and Social Psychology*, 29(4), April 1974, 475–86

Mayo Clinic Staff, http://www.mayoclinic.com/health/antidepressants/HQ01069

Soussignan, Robert, 'Duchenne smile, emotional experience, and autonomic reactivity: a test of the facial feedback hypothesis', *Emotion*, no. 2, March 2002, 52–74

Exercise

Colcombe, Stanley, and Arthur F. Kramer, 'Fitness Effects on the Cognitive Function of Older Adults: A Meta-Analytic Study', *Psychological Science*, no. 2, March 2013, 125–30

Elward, K. and E. B Larson, 'Benefits of exercise for older adults. A review of existing evidence and current recommendations for the general population', *Clinics in Geriatric Medicine*, 8(1), February 1992, 35–50

Fear and overcoming fear

Brain@McGill, the, 'The brain from top to bottom', https://www.mcgill.ca/brain/resources/brain-top-bottom

Chillot, Rick, 'What are you afraid of?: 8 secrets that make fear disappear', *Prevention*, 50(5), May 1998, 98 (7)

Cowley, Geoffrey, *et al.*, 'Our bodies, our fears', *Newsweek International*, 3 March 2003, 40

Dadis, Glyn, Review of 'Fear: a cultural history', http://www.theage.com.au/news/Reviews/Fear-a-culturalhistory/2005/05/06/1115092634475.html?oneclick=true

DuPont, Caroline M., Robert L. Dupont and Elizabeth DuPont Spencer, 'The anxious brain: the anxiety cure: an eight-step program for getting well', in *The Anxiety Cure*, Wiley, 1998

Gersley, Erin, 'Phobias: causes and treatments', http://allpsych.com/journal/phobias.html

Layton, Julia, 'How fear works', HowStuffWorks, http://www.1access.net/~charlie@1access.net/hswfear.html

Robinson, Victoria, 'What gives you goosebumps?' *Science World*, 18 October 1996, 53, no. 4, 18 (2)

Schmidt, Brad, PhD, and Jeffrey Winters, 'Anxiety after 9/11', http://www.psychologytoday.com/articles/200201/anxiety-after-911

Travis, John, 'Fear not: scientists are learning how people can unlearn fear', http://www.sciencenews.org/articles/20040117/bob9.asp

Food and diet

Boyle, Matthew, 'You will eat your peas now as big food binges on protein', http://www.bloomberg.com/news/2014-04-23/you-will-eat-your-peas-now-as-big-food-binges-on-protein.html

Delahunt, Peter, 'Junk food and addiction – how cheesecake and bacon are like heroin and cocaine', http://blog.positscience.com/2010/04/26/junk-food-and-addiction-how-cheesecake-and-bacon-are-like-heroin-and-cocaine/

Ferriss, Timothy, *The 4-Hour Body: An Uncommon Guide to Rapid Fat-Loss, Incredible Sex, and Becoming Superhuman*, Crown Publishing, 2010, http://en.wikipedia.org/wiki/special:Booksources/978-0-307-46363-0

Hand, Becky, 'The benefits of eating together': http://www.sparkpeople.com/resource/nutrition_articles.asp?id=439

Thompson, Derek, 'How "healthy" food and labels trick our brain into unhealthy eating', http://qz.com/202159/how-healthy-food-and-labels-trick-our-brain-into-unhealthy-eating/

WebMD, 'Super foods for optimal health', http://www.webmd.com/a-to-z-guides/antioxidants-your-immune-system-super-foods-optimal-health

Joy of music

Guardian, 'Music gives people a voice when words fail them at the end of their lives', http://www.theguardian.com/science/2013/nov/05/music-therapy-palliative-care

Posit Science, 'Your brain in love: part 5 – no room for romance? try music instead . . . but not junk food', http://www.brainhq.com/brain-resources/brain-facts-myths/brain-in-love

Townsend, Angela, 'Study findings give added proof to music therapy benefits for pediatric, adolescent cancer patients', http://www.cleveland.com/healthfit/index.ssf/2014/01/study_findings_give_added_proo.html

Meditation

Szalavitz, Maia, 'Aaron Alexis and the dark side of meditation', *Time*, September 2013, http://healthland.time.com/2013/09/17/aaron-alexis-and-the-dark-side-of-meditation/

Relationships and love

Fisher, Helen, TED Talk, http://www.positscience.com/pop-up/video/video-helen-fisher.html

Hendrick, Bill, 'Still madly in love? Brain scans can explain', *WebMD Health News*, 14 January 2011, http://www.webmd.com/sex-relationships/news/20110114/still-madly-in-love-brain-scans-can-explain

Heussner, Ki Mae, 'Addicted to love? It's not you, it's your brain', *ABC News*, 8 July 2010, http://abcnews.go.com/Technology/addicted-love-brain/story?id=11110866

Livermore, Beth, 'The lessons of love', *Psychology Today*, http://cms.psychologytoday.com/articles/pto-19930301-000028.html

Parker-Pope, Tara, 'Reinventing date night for long-married couples', http://www.nytimes.com/2008/02/12/health/12well.html?em

Posit Science, http://www.brainhq.com/brain-resources/brain-facts-myths/brain-in-love

Szalavitz, Maia, *Born for Love: Why Empathy Is Essential – and Endangered.* (William Morrow Paperbacks, 2011)

Wayne State University, Office of the Vice President for Research, 'Enhance romance by going out with other couples', http://www.sciencedaily.com/releases/2011/02/110210153012.htm

Retirement

Department of Jobs, Enterprise and Innovation (Ireland), 'Action Plan for Jobs 2014', http://www.djei.ie/publications/2014 APJ.pdf

Lyon Levine, Martin, 'Age discrimination and the mandatory retirement controversy'; Holden, Karen C., and W. Lee Hansen, 'The end of mandatory retirement: effects on higher education', in Ralph S. Brown, *Academe* 75 (1989), 60–62

Hashimoto, Kenji, 'Agri-business for elderly people through the Internet: the example of the Irodori leaf business', Netcom, 26, 2012, 235–50

Nilsson, K., A. R. Hydbom and L. Rylander, 'Factors influencing the decision to extend working life or retire', *Scandinavian Journal of Work, Environment & Health*, 2011, 473–80

Yamada Village E-Project, Japan, http://siteresources.worldbank.org/INTEMPOWERMENT/Resources/14874_YamadaJapan-web.pdf

Seasonal Affective Disorder

Eagles, John M., 'Seasonal affective disorder', *British Journal of Psychiatry*, 182, 2003, 174–6

Henley, Jon, 'Rjukan sun: the Norwegian town that does it with mirrors', *Guardian*, 6 November 2013, http://www.theguardian.com/world/2013/nov/06/rjukan-sun-norway-town-mirrors

Kryger, Meir H., 'Sleep and be well, mysteries of the slumbering psyche', *Psychology Today*, http://www.psychologytoday.com/blog/sleep-and-be-well

Acknowledgements

I was in danger of having the cleanest cupboards in Ireland but for the encouragement and support of a team of people who helped me to get started on *Spark!* and stuck the course to cheer me on to completion. So thank you to all of you (and you know who you are) who listened patiently as I listed the myriad of reasons as to why I was not at my desk writing – chief among them the tragic state of the cutlery drawer, which necessitated a regular clear-out during those all too frequent bouts of procrastination.

The avoidance was for a very good reason, however. I earned my living as a writer for much of my life and I'm used to working to a deadline and churning out those words on screen. But to write this book I had to relive parts of my life that I had scarcely allowed myself to think about. There were mornings when I didn't have the courage to face the rawness of being back in the darkest moments. There were days when I was so lost in that world that I didn't want to leave it behind. But I also knew that there was no avoiding that pilgrimage back in time. It was the catalyst for seismic changes in my life and I knew it was important to share it – no matter how hard that was. Without it I know that the story would only be half told.

There are people who helped me to reignite my life and gave me the strength to tell my story. I am most grateful for my family and friends – particularly for my mother Mags, my role model and inspiration in life, and for sharing her story in

Spark! Special thanks to my sisters Catherine and Carissa, my brothers Leo and Ciaran and the two great women who married them, Máire Ní Bhroithe and Marie Casey. And to all my nieces and nephews who give me hope for the next generation of Caseys, and they will forgive me for mentioning by name Derek, Ciara, Shauna and Gavin – the remarkable children of my sister Betty (RIP). My thanks also to Richard's mother, Adria Lammiman, who raised such a wonderful man, and his brother Simon Hannaford. Thanks to the Reverend Alan Hilliard for his wise counsel and great friendship.

Behind every successful woman there is an army of successful women and I have had amazing girlfriends who minded me after Richard died and since (in alphabetical order): Anne O'Donoghue, Audrey Cunningham, Bláthnaid Ní Chofaigh, Carmel Breheny, Carolyn Odgers, Charlotte Bradshaw, Claire Ronan, Emma Coppola, Flo McSweeney, Frederique Thoummany, Gabriel Burke, Jean Ann Taylor, Karen Hickey Dwyer, Kari Rocca, Lorraine Keane, Mairead Sorenson, Margaret Kiong, Margaret Nelson, Mary Harney, Michelle Spillane, Noelle Campbell Sharpe, Sallyanne Clarke, Susan Davis, Val Quin http://www.irishmirror.ie/showbiz/irish-showbiz/blathnaid-ni-chofaigh-reveals-sex-3198743. Thanks to my London-based Women's Irish Network: Mary Clancy, Cecilia Gallagher, Hazel Hutchinson Ros Hubbard, Rosaleen Blair, Avril MacRory, Fiona Calnan, Maire Brankin.

I have to make mention of the Curry Club – the inspiration of Richard and his good friend Andrew Heynes. In his final months the Curry Club, along with some very close friends, minded him, made him laugh and kept him company – John Cunningham, Paul Donovan, Tim Jarvis, Kenny Robertson, Gary Morton, Marcus Hewson, Sebastian Hamilton, Julian Davis, Jim Aveling, Stephen Aiken and Julian King. And thanks also to my manfriends: Darryl Downey, Vinog Faughnan, Dylan Bradshaw, Barry McCall, Peter Devlin, Barry Murphy, Derry Clarke, Loughlin Murhpy, Dylan McGrath, Ray Power, Declan Keane, Fergus O'Hagan, Conor Ronan, Donall Curtin, Gerry Treacy, Brian Geoghegan and Peter Woo.

My fellow Dragons who were incredible when Richard was ill and during the filming in the Den just a few months later: Gavin Duffy, Bobby Kerr, Niall O'Farrell, Sean Gallagher and Sean O'Sullivan.

When lots of well-meaning friends offer to do anything to help during and in the aftermath of personal tragedy there is often very little you can ask them to do. However, my colleagues at Harmonia gave us a very special gift – they looked after the business when we were unable to – so my thanks to the Harmonia family, too many to mention but particularly Frances Neeson, Michael Fitzpatrick, Rachel Supple, David Gibbons, Jessie Collins, Aine Toner, Jennifer Stevens, Ross Golden Bannon, Raymond Blake, Alex Fitzgerald, Zab Malik, Brian Foley.

Heartfelt thanks to Dara's school, St Conleth's College, and his friends for looking out for him, and for all of the doctors and nurses who cared for Richard, especially the team at Our Lady's Hospice in Blackrock.

Thanks too for the sensitivity of those in the media who helped me kick-start a conversation about death and bereavement, especially Nuala Cunningham and Ciaran O'Connor (*New Decade*), Gay Byrne and Roger Childs (*The Meaning of Life*), Ryan Tubridy, Larry Masterson (*The Late Late Show*), Brendan O'Connor, Carol Louthe (*The Saturday Night Show*), Barry Egan, Marian Finucane, Matt Cooper, Anton Savage and all the others who shared my story.

To my colleagues in the world of television and radio,

thanks for taking a chance on me and for your support as I re-entered the world of presenting and broadcasting, especially Larry Bass, Eugenia Cooney (ShinAwiL), Adrian Lynch, Debbie Thornton (and all at Animo), Ruth Roden, Eoin Kavanagh (Toto), Linda Cullen, Hilary O'Donovan (and the team at Coco), Garrett Harte, Chris Donoghue (and all the *Breakfast* team), Aoife Breen and Aoife Gillivan (Newstalk), Colm Crowley, Janet Frawley (and the team at RTÉ Cork), Glen Killane, Bill Malone, Eddie Doyle, Roger Childs, Grainne McAleer, Geraldine O'Leary, Rayna Connery at RTÉ.

Then there is the front-line team who shaped and nurtured *Spark!* and brought it to fruition. My thanks to my good friend and agent, the very wise Sheila Crowley. To managing director Michael McLoughlin and editorial director Patricia Deevy at Penguin Ireland (especially for your patience). To Rachel Pierce for her great input into structure, language and content, and to Hazel Orme for her work in shaping and editing the book.

I'm so glad to have my former editorial colleague Elaine Prendeville back working with me and for her help in transforming my *MindFeed* radio interviews into great profiles. Thanks also to Newstalk for giving permission for the transcripts from those *MindFeed* interviews to be used and to my interviewees: Joanne O'Riordan, Cecelia Ahern, Pauline McLynn, Michael Carruth, Adam Clayton, Roma Downey, David Essex, Pat Falvey, Jocelyn Bell Burnell, Fionnula Flanagan.

My final thanks are to two special people, my boy Dara and the man who helped us to love life again, Peter Allen.